The Future of the U.S. Domestic Air Freight Industry

The Future of the U.S. Domestic Air Freight Industry

An Analysis of Management Strategies

Lewis M. Schneider

DIVISION OF RESEARCH
GRADUATE SCHOOL OF BUSINESS ADMINISTRATION
HARVARD UNIVERSITY

BOSTON • 1973

387.7
S 359

Library of Congress Catalog Card No. 72-94363

ISBN 0-87584-106-6

Faculty research at the Harvard Business School is undertaken with the expectation of publication. In such publication the Faculty member responsible for the research project is also responsible for statements of fact, opinions, and conclusions expressed. Neither the Harvard Business School, its Faculty as a whole, nor the President and Fellows of Harvard College reach conclusions or make recommendations as results of Faculty research.

PRINTED IN THE UNITED STATES OF AMERICA

Preface

THERE IS LITTLE QUESTION that air freight represents one of the most visible and dramatic segments of the nation's transportation industry. Growth has been vigorous—year-to-year increases in traffic of 20% are not uncommon. Technological innovation has been rapid. In the space of about one decade air freighters moved from the high-cost piston engine stage, through turboprops and 707-DC-8s to the 747 jumbo. Yet, profits in the freighter segment of the business have been conspicuous by their absence.

Is air freight doomed to follow the path of the railroad industry, that is, performing an important service yet generating a minimal return on investment as capital productivity plummets? To what extent is the future destiny of the industry within the control of management variables? If the management variables are important, in what directions might the industry move to meet the demand for high-speed freight transportation yet at the same time generate adequate profits? It is hoped that this study will provide some answers to these crucial questions.

It would be impossible to list every person who contributed their time and insights to this study. I should, however, like to single out Professor Paul W. Cherington, James J. Hill Professor of Transportation, Harvard Business School, for reviewing the manuscript; John Drake, Research Assistant at Harvard Business School for developing the ANALYZER program; W. Fletcher Lutz, Bureau of Accounts and Statistics, Civil Aeronautics Board; Mr. George James, Senior Vice President, Air Transport Association of America; Messrs. Richard Lambert, Joe Kingsley, and Thomas Gallagher of American Airlines; Messrs. Robert Mangold and Jack Bland of United Airlines; Messrs. Mark Requa, Ed Smick, and John Heilner of Trans World Airlines; Messrs. Donald Chickering and Robert Cashman of Flying Tiger Lines; Mr. Lloyd Aschenbeck of McDonnell Douglas; the late Dr. E. W. Eckard of Lockheed-Georgia; Mr. H. W. Montgomery of the Boeing Company; Mr. Remson Henry, Vice President, Lester B. Knight & Associates; and Mr. David Booher, The Boston Corporation. Inasmuch as some of the ideas presented in the manuscript proved to be quite controversial, the fact that the above individuals helped me should in no way be construed to mean that they agreed necessarily with all of the analyses and conclusions.

The research, carried out under the supervision of the Division of Research, was supported by funds allocated from The 1907 Foundation. On my behalf, as well as for the Harvard Business School, I should like to express our appreciation for this contribution.

I should also like to thank Miss Hedwig Pocius, Miss Deirdre Elliott, and Miss Linda Brown for typing the manuscript; Miss Sylvia Gilman for preparing the exhibits; and Miss Hilma Holton for guiding the manuscript through to publication.

Finally, my wife Josie and my children Lisa, Nancy, and Jacqueline, deserve special praise for providing the equally necessary moral support for this study. Naturally, any errors of omission or commission are mine alone.

Lewis M. Schneider

Waban, Massachusetts
July 1972

Table of Contents

List of Tables

ix

List of Exhibits

Chapter 1

Introduction

THE U.S. AIR FREIGHT PROBLEM

THE WORLD OF AIR FREIGHT IS ONE OF CURIOUS CONTRASTS—a mixture of incurable optimism in the face of highly variable profits and an almost negligible return on investment.

The optimism stems from two factors: dramatic increases in traffic, and the development of ever-larger jet aircraft which feature declining operating costs per available ton-mile.

Two sets of statistics chosen from the overwhelming mass of data emanating from the industry illustrate these trends. U.S. air freight, the largest component of air cargo,[1] increased at an annual rate of almost 15% between 1959 and 1969. On the other hand, total operating expenses per available ton mile of domestic scheduled all-cargo service fell by 50% between 1963 and 1968.[2]

Although traffic forecasts in the past had erred significantly on both the high and low sides, most analysts in the 1960s agreed that the growth potential for the air freight industry was excellent (see Exhibit 1.1).[3] For example, three forecasts of U.S. domestic scheduled air freight traffic growth per annum were: Lockheed, 22%, 1965–1980 (forecast made in 1966); McDonnell Douglas, 21%, 1970–1980 (made in 1969); and a research committee of the Air Transport Association of America, 19%, 1970–1980 (made in 1969).[4]

---

[1] As will be discussed in more detail in Chapter 2, air cargo includes air freight, air express, air mail, and excess baggage. This study will be confined to air freight.

[2] Depending on which years and service classification are used, the growth statistics become even more impressive. Between 1964 and 1968, scheduled air freight traffic carried by the combination carriers increased at an annual rate of almost 22%. Operating expense data are from Civil Aeronautics Board, *Trends in All-Cargo Service* (Washington, 1970), p. 10. See Table 2.5.

[3] This exhibit provides a history of U.S. domestic air freight forecasts.

[4] These forecasts can be found in:

Lockheed-Georgia Company, *Marketing Planning Report CMRS 59* (Commercial Marketing Research Department, 1966), p. 8.

McDonnell Douglas Corp., *Advanced Cargo Systems Report C1-801-1610-1* (Long Beach,

EXHIBIT 1.1

COMPARISON OF SELECTED FORECASTS—U.S. DOMESTIC AIR FREIGHT AND EXPRESS

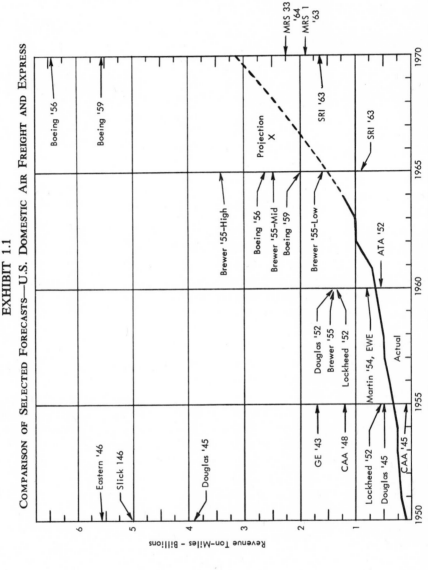

SOURCE: Lockheed-Georgia Company, *Air Cargo Growth Study*, prepared by E. W. Eckard, Marketing Research Department, MRS-49, December 1965, p. 49.

These projections reflected the booming airline traffic of the 1960s. The annual rates of growth of passenger and cargo revenue ton miles for the total certificated and supplemental air carriers during 1965–1967 were 23.8%, 27.2%, and 26.0% respectively. In two of the three years traffic outstripped capacity increases, and interest in a new generation of large capacity aircraft soared. There was one dark spot on the horizon, though; industry return on adjusted investment, including investment tax credits, peaked at 14% in 1965 and fell to 9.85% by 1967.[5] But, optimism reigned supreme.

Lockheed won the competition in 1965 to produce a huge cargo plane (the C5) for the military, and Boeing decided to enter the commercial field with its version of a jumbo jet (the 747). By April 1966, the first orders for the Boeing 747 passenger version had been captured, and attention was turned to a freighter version of the 747. Lockheed, meanwhile, began to think in terms of a civilian version of its C5, to be called the L-500.

In 1968, the president of Lockheed-Georgia estimated that there would be sufficient air cargo growth to warrant a fleet of 250 L-500 freighters by 1980, a commitment of over $5 billion in 1968 dollars. Boeing estimated air freight traffic growth rates of 25½% annually between 1971 and 1975, with 100 747 freighters sold by 1975.[6]

But, by the close of 1969, this optimism was tempered with second thoughts. Although scheduled U.S. international air freight traffic in 1969 increased 22% over 1968, domestic scheduled air freight traffic grew only 12% and the freight traffic for the total scheduled industry increased but 15.7%.[7] In other industries, this performance would be considered excellent, but in an industry which had been anticipating much greater increases in capacity, the reduced traffic growth was viewed with alarm.

The slowdown in national economic activity in 1970 intensified the air freight traffic dilemma. Scheduled international freight declined 5.5%, domestic scheduled freight increased 12.8% and the increase for the total scheduled industry fell to 5%.[8]

The reduction in traffic growth was accompanied by a change in the character of aircraft operating costs. Until the advent of the jet freighters in 1963, air cargo carried in piston engine all-cargo planes was usually unprofitable.[9] The 707 and

1969), pp. 46, 59. Data include mail and express, but mail and express growth rates are projected at substantially less than 21%.

Air Transport Association of America, *Industry Report A.T.A. Airline Airport Demand Forecasts* (Washington, 1969), p. 20.

[5] CAB, *Handbook of Airline Statistics, 1969 Edition* (Washington, 1970), p. 371.

[6] The L-500 forecast can be found in "The Air Cargo Airplane," *Handling and Shipping* (July 1968), p. 50. The Boeing forecast of 100 747s is in "Four Carriers Drop Plans to Buy 747F and 747Cs," *Aviation Week and Space Technology* (March 11, 1968), p. 30, and the 25½% growth rate projection in "The Air Cargo Airplane," *op. cit.*, p. 54.

[7] See Tables 2.4, 2.5, and 2.7.

[8] Calculated from data contained in Air Transport Association of America, *Air Transport 1971* (Washington, 1971), pp. 26, 30.

[9] See Stanley H. Brewer and Don T. DeCoster, *The Nature of Air Cargo Costs* (Seattle, University of Washington Graduate School of Business Administration, 1967), pp. 8–9.

DC-8 jet freighters reduced aircraft ton-mile costs to a level sufficient to produce operating profits, though return on investment was relatively low. But, by 1969, inflationary pressures resulted in increased operating costs per available ton-mile. This reversal of the declining operating cost per available ton-mile curve, combined with a plunge in load factors stemming from the reduced traffic growth, erased freighter profitability.

For the twelve months ending December 31, 1970, the domestic carriers lost $45.2 million (before taxes) operating freighter planes, and for the twelve-month period ending June 30, 1971, the operating loss (before taxes) climbed to $54.8 million.[10]

At the same time, the airline industry encountered the same severe problems of overcapacity and rising costs in its passenger operations. In 1970, the total industry reported a substantial net loss, the first since 1961.

Thus, as the air freight industry entered the 1970s, the purchase of the jumbo jet Boeing 747 or Lockheed L-500 freighters was out of the question. Indeed, several orders for freighter versions of the 747 were cancelled in favor of passenger equipment.[11] Lockheed despite intensive marketing efforts had been unable to obtain sufficient orders to warrant commercial production of the L-500. McDonnell Douglas had been promoting its "uncompromised" cargo planes—the C4 and C6s —but it, too, had found no purchasers.

OBJECTIVES OF THIS STUDY

There is a considerable body of literature on the air freight industry that falls into three basic categories: (1) studies of the industry structure with major emphasis on the regulatory and promotional policies of the government,[12] (2) marketing oriented studies of the demand for air freight transportation,[13] and (3) a vast amount of material describing the technology of flight and ground equipment.

[10] Sources: CAB Form 242 and Form 41 reports as shown in a study released November 12, 1971, by the Cost and Statistical Analysis Section; Accounting, Cost and Statistics Division; Bureau of Accounts and Statistics, Civil Aeronautics Board.

[11] Compare Footnote 6.

[12] See, for example, D. H. Reeher, *The Domestic Air Freight Industry and Introduction of Large Subsonic Transports* (Falls Church, CFSTI AD 658397); the monographs by Stanley Brewer listed in the bibliography; Harold H. Wein, *Domestic Air Cargo: Its Prospects* (East Lansing, Michigan State, 1962); Kit G. Narodick, "The Domestic Air Cargo Industry" (unpublished thesis, Columbia University, 1967); Henry Orion, "Domestic Air Cargo, 1945–1965: A Study of Competition in a Regulated Industry" (unpublished thesis, Columbia University, 1967); and Philip Braudt Schary, "Competition in the Domestic Air Cargo Industry" (unpublished thesis, University of California at Los Angeles).

[13] For example, see Stanford Research Institute, *How to Identify Potential Uses of Air Freight*, A Report prepared for Emery Air Freight Corporation (S. Pasadena, SRI, 1963); the DISCOM Model of McDonnell Douglas cited in *Advanced Cargo Systems Report*; and David P. Herron, "Buying Time and Saving Money with Air Freight," *Transportation and Distribution Management* (December 1968), pp. 25–29; and Air Cargo Analysis Unit, Commercial Airplane Group, *Boeing Air Cargo Market Analysis Activities* A9-4710 (Renton, May 1970).

On the other hand, there is relatively little material which focuses primarily on the role of management in this industry, and a major objective of this study is to fill that gap. This will be accomplished by analyzing management strategy in the domestic air freight industry during the years 1965–1969 to determine: (1) the degree to which different strategies were employed by the airlines during this period of exceptional growth, and (2) the success or failure of these strategies. The underlying hypothesis is that the airline managers had significant discretionary power during this period within an external environment of economic, social, technological, and political pressures. What we want to determine is how these officials used their power and with what results.

The second objective of this study is to look forward and analyze the opportunities and problem areas facing this industry in the 1970s and 1980s. Major emphasis will be placed on economic and technological trends, but consideration will be given to social and political factors as well. By looking ahead to the next decade with a clear understanding of the events of the 1960s, we should obtain better insights as to the ultimate fate of this industry.

METHODOLOGY AND ORGANIZATION

Sources of Information

This study relies on three basic sources of information: (1) field trips and interviews with airline officials, manufacturers, consultants, representatives of trade associations, government officials, and academicians; (2) a search of the literature with particular reliance on statistical data published by the Civil Aeronautics Board and the schedules of freighter planes published in the Official Airline Guide; and (3) a seminar held at the Harvard Business School in the Fall of 1968, which spotlighted a variety of research questions, and produced several student research reports on air cargo.

At one stage of the research, it was hoped that a series of detailed case studies could serve as the primary basis for generalizations on management strategy in the industry. A pilot case study was developed and is included as Appendix A. Unfortunately a combination of budget constraints and difficulty in obtaining permission to undertake case research in sensitive areas made it impossible to write the contemplated series of cases.

As a result, the conclusions concerning management strategy are derived from the insights gained from interviews and the analysis of published statistical data.

Analytical Techniques

As detailed more fully in appropriate sections of this study, the analysis of management strategy involved several analytical techniques: (1) regression analysis of combined time series and cross-section data; (2) rank order analysis; (3) the determination of important elasticities, for example, the percentage change in various expense categories as a function of changes in traffic; and (4) the development of a computerized method of analyzing freighter schedules. The latter project called ANALYZER produced very interesting insights as to the results of different competitive strategies. It is hoped that further refinements in the ANALYZER program can be carried out in the future.

Outline of the Study

The following chapter gives an overview of the U.S. domestic air cargo industry in terms of industry structure, the demand for air freight service and developments in technology.

The analysis of the industry's complex structure will serve not only to introduce the variety of public and private institutions and interest groups affected by air freight, but also explain why this study focuses primarily on the scheduled freighter operations of the certificated carriers.

The treatment of the demand for air freight service summarizes the results of several statistical studies, then moves on to discuss a relatively simple conceptual framework for defining and implementing an air freight marketing strategy.

Much of the air freight literature concentrates on the technology of aircraft and ground support systems. Yet, often the published material emphasizes only the benefits of technological innovation, not the risks. The objective of the review of technology is to present a more balanced picture of its opportunities and pitfalls.

Chapter 3 takes a detailed look at management strategy in the recent past, during the period of air freight's almost explosive growth. After considering the question of the appropriate measures of management strategy, the chapter introduces the study carriers: American, United, Trans World and Flying Tiger.

The components of management strategy, i.e., the inputs, include: commitment to air freight—percentage of cargo carried on freighters and expansion of freighter capacity; type of freighter equipment; routes and service including breadth and depth scheduling strategies; pricing; other marketing policies; and traffic servicing and terminals.

The outputs of management strategy analyzed in this chapter are: competitive position and traffic, operating efficiency, and financial performance.

Chapter 4 examines the outlook for domestic air freight in the future, including traffic growth, comparative line haul and terminal costs versus surface transportation, capital productivity under different pricing policies, and the potentials and risks of investing in the next generation of freighters.

Chapter 5 summarizes the findings of the research, calls for additional studies, and closes with specific recommendations to the carriers and governmental agencies.

IMPORTANCE OF THIS STUDY

Timeliness

The airlines are currently emerging from one of their chronic periods of over-capacity and financial disaster. In their passenger service they are hoping that the new generation of wide body aircraft will lower costs or at least keep the operating cost increases at reasonable levels, while the improved economy generates enough air travel to produce profitable load factors.

The new wide body jets have increased substantially the amount of belly cargo capacity, and the combination carriers have proposed low incentive rates in order to utilize this capacity. What we may see is a repetition of the early 1960s when the airlines slashed freight rates to fill the bellies of the new 707, DC-8 generation of passenger aircraft.

In the 1960s, the next step was to invest heavily in jet freighters in the hope that overall freight costs per ton and per ton-mile, as well as freight rates, would decline. Freight traffic would be stimulated further and the freighters would provide the capacity to handle this traffic. We shall see the results of this strategy in Chapter 3.

As the airlines' financial position improves in the 1970s, they might well be tempted to make the investment in the next generation of freighters. It is hoped that this study will be useful to management as it considers this investment.

Analysis and Recommendations

The conclusions and recommendations of this study will be of interest to airline managers as they formulate their equipment, scheduling, and pricing strategies for the 1970s and 1980s. But, other interest groups—regulatory agencies, the financial community, shippers, suppliers, surface carriers—should also find the results of the research useful. For the recommendations go beyond questions of technology or pricing to consider the issue of the structure of this industry. Indeed, the structural considerations might well transcend the others.

The optimists have always believed that traffic growth would one day solve all the problems of the industry. Under certain structural conditions, this might well be true. On the other hand, one discovers quickly that growth in the past has not produced a financially viable air freight industry. Will history continue to repeat itself? The search for the answer to this question provided the impetus for this research.

Chapter 2

An Overview of the Air Cargo Industry

The Structure of the Industry

IN A NARROW SENSE, THE UNITED STATES AIR CARGO INDUSTRY includes air carriers providing scheduled and nonscheduled (charter) transportation of freight, express, and mail. Before considering the industry in its broader dimensions, it is important to understand the differences between the categories of air carriers. Inasmuch as this study focused on management's air freight strategy during the last half of the 1960s, the year 1968 was used as the reference point for comparing the carriers. (See Table 2.1.)

The Importance of Air Cargo

Scheduled air cargo traffic in 1968 produced almost $2 billion for the ICAO "free world" carriers, 15% of their total passenger and cargo revenue. Thus, despite the substantial growth of air cargo during the 1960s, it was still a secondary, though significant, part of the total airline business. It is not surprising why much of the attention of airline management was directed toward passenger operations.

U.S. scheduled air cargo traffic was 59% of the ICAO scheduled total. Air cargo revenue was a relatively small proportion of airline industry revenue, but it was not insignificant. As indicated in Table 2.1, the U.S. air carriers grossed over $1 billion from cargo in 1968. In that same year, the U.S. railroads took in $10.85 billion in operating revenue, yet produced over 130 times as many revenue ton-miles.[1]

---

[1] Transportation Association of America, *Transportation Facts and Trends, Eighth Edition* (Washington, 1971). In 1969, domestic air freight revenues as tabulated by the TAA were .8% of the total domestic freight transportation bill including private carriage. Air freight revenue was 2.4% of the total freight revenue produced by ICC and CAB regulated carriers in domestic operation.

8

TABLE 2.1

Analysis of Air Cargo Traffic and Revenue

Free World and U.S. Airlines

1968

(Data in Billions)

	Scheduled and Nonscheduled Air Freight		Scheduled Air Priority and Nonpriority Mail		Scheduled Air Express		Total Air Cargo		Total Passenger and Cargo		Air Cargo Percent of Total		Air Freight Percent of Total	
	Ton-Mile	Rev. $	Ton-Mile	Rev. $	Ton-Mile	Rev. $	Ton-Mile	Rev. $	Ton-Mile	Rev. $	Ton-Mile	Oper. Rev.	Ton-Mile	Oper. Rev.
Free World (ICAO)[a]	5.333[a,b]	1.305[a]	1.651	.562	.105	.038	7.089	1.905	25.650	12.754	27.6	14.9	20.8	10.2
U.S. Air Total	4.262	.816	1.257[c]	.276	.105	.038	5.625	1.129	19.499	8.090	28.8	14.0	21.9	10.1
U.S. Air Scheduled:	2.805	.547	1.257	.276	.105	.038	4.167	.861	15.249	7.131[d]	27.3	12.1	18.4	7.7
Domestic	1.671	.334	.567	.139	.104	.038	2.342	.511	10.726	5.468	21.8	9.3	15.6	6.1
International	1.134	.213	.690	.137	.001	NEG	1.824	.350	4.525	1.663	40.3	21.1	25.1	12.8
U.S. Air Non-scheduled (Including Supplements)[c]	1.458	.269	[c]	—	—	—	1.458	.269	4.249	.960[e]	34.3	28.0	34.3	28.0
Domestic	.553	NA	—	—	—	—	.551	NA	1.126	NA	48.9	—	48.9	—
International	.905	NA	[c]	[c]	—	—	.905	NA	3.123	NA	29.0	—	29.0	—

[a] Scheduled flights only.

[b] Normally ICAO reports freight and express together. In this table, U.S. express has been separated out.

[c] In addition, 242 million RTMs of mail moved in international nonscheduled service. Revenue for this traffic is not identified clearly in routine CAB publications. Foreign mail (10.7 million RTMs in 1968) is also excluded in this tabulation.

[d] Total Operating Revenue less "Other" (includes Charter). This includes Passenger, Mail, Express, and Scheduled Freight Revenue.

[e] "Other Revenue" of Certificated Carriers plus total Supplemental Revenue.

SOURCES: CAB, *Handbook of Airline Statistics*, 1969 Edition; International Air Transport Association, *World Air Transport Statistics*.

The Components of Air Cargo

Table 2.2 examines the U.S. air cargo traffic and revenue in 1968 more closely, again using the classification scheme of the CAB. If we look at the columns we can determine the relative importance of each type of traffic in the air cargo total.

Approximately 75% of both cargo traffic and cargo revenue resulted from scheduled flights. Scheduled freight represented about two-thirds of the total freight ton-miles and revenue.

The charter statistics are also of interest, notwithstanding a problem of matching the geographic domicile of the carrier and the routes served by its charter aircraft.[2] A major issue confronting the industry is the future balance between scheduled and nonscheduled service. The scheduled carriers claim that nonscheduled operations "skim the cream off the top" and divert lucrative high-load factor traffic. The supporters of charter operations claim that the lower charter rates and specialized service stimulate new demand, rather than divert existing traffic.

This argument during the 1960s was somewhat moot, for much of the charter traffic in fact represented military procurement. The statistics are somewhat confusing, for the military also shipped cargo and personnel on scheduled flights, and the payments for scheduled services were lumped into a "total buy" figure. Nevertheless, a tabulation such as that shown in Table 2.3 indicates that military traffic was of critical importance to the two major all-cargo carriers, Flying Tiger and Seaboard. In addition, as shown in Table 2.2, 93% of the supplemental airlines' cargo revenue ton-mile and 73% of their freight were derived from Department of Defense charters.

Table 2.2 also spotlights the relative importance of priority and nonpriority scheduled mail in the cargo industry. Together, the two classes of mail accounted for 22% of the cargo ton-miles and 25% of the cargo revenue. Most forecasts assume that the rate of mail traffic growth will lag behind air freight and that air mail's share of total cargo traffic will decline substantially as the industry grows.[3]

If we look across each row instead of down the columns, we can determine the relative roles of the different types of carriers. For example, the combination pas-

---

[2] The CAB classifies certificated carriers under the headings of "domestic" and "international" based on their certificated routes. Flying Tiger Lines, one of the major certificated all-cargo carriers, did not obtain international certificated routes until 1969. At the same time, it performed a substantial amount of military charter service over international routes during the 1960s, which was reported as "domestic" nonscheduled traffic.

[3] In 1959 mail's share of the cargo revenue ton-miles was but 17.6%. The increased importance of mail reflected the requirements of the Vietnam war to a major extent. For example, in 1968 Pan American's Pacific Operations generated 414 million revenue ton-miles of scheduled priority and nonpriority mail, and 33% of the entire U.S. domestic plus international scheduled mail traffic; whereas in 1959 Pan American's Pacific Operations' share of U.S. mail traffic was only 8%. The Air Transport Association in 1969 predicted air mail growth rates of 5% per year during the period 1975–1985, whereas air freight was expected to grow in excess of 17% per year. See Air Transport Association of America, *A.T.A. Airline Airport Demand Forecasts Industry Report* (Washington, by the Association, 1969), p. 20.

TABLE 2.2
Analysis of Air Cargo Traffic and Revenue
U.S. Airlines
1968
(Data in Millions)

	Scheduled Air Freight		Nonscheduled Air Freight		Air Express		Priority Mail Scheduled		Nonpriority Mail Scheduled		Total Airline Cargo		Percent	
	Ton-Mile	Rev. $	Ton-Mile	Rev. $	Ton-Mile	Rev. $	Ton-Mile	Rev. $	Ton-Mile	Rev. $	Ton-Mile	Rev. $	Ton-Mile	Rev. $
U.S. Domestic Passenger-Cargo Carriers	1,477	306	65	11	104	38	301	92	266	47	2,213	494	39	44
U.S. Domestic All-Cargo Carriers	194	28	183	29	NEG	NEG	NEG	—	NEG	NEG	377	57	7	5
U.S. International Passenger-Cargo Carriers	926	185	478	95	NEG	NEG	273	75	396	58	2,073	413	37	37
U.S. International All-Cargo Carriers	208	28	238	37	NEG	NEG	8	2	13	2	467	69	8	6
U.S. Supplemental Military Civilian	NONE	NONE	432 62	71 26	NONE	NONE	NONE	—	NONE	—	433 62	71 26	8 1	6 2
TOTAL U.S.	2,805	547	1,458	269	105	38	582	169	675	107	5,625	1,130		
Percent Ton-Mile Revenue	50	48	26	24	2	3	10	15	12	10			100	100

NOTE: Carried on Nonscheduled flights and foreign mail excluded from tabulation of air cargo.
NEG = Negligible.

SOURCE: CAB, *Handbook of Airline Statistics*, 1969 Edition, pp. 105, 193, 199, and 288.

TABLE 2.3
Impact of Military Procurement
Flying Tiger and Seaboard World Airlines
1962–1968
(*Data in Millions*)

	Military Passenger and Cargo Revenue[a]		Total Passenger and Cargo Charter Revenue	Total Operating Revenue	Military as Percent of	
	Fiscal Year	Calendar Year			Total Charter Revenue	Total Operating Revenue
1962 FTL	$30.7	$31.4	$41.8	$52.3	75%	60%
SW	10.5	12.2	7.5	23.1	163%	53%
1963 FTL	32.1	28.3	31.3	42.2	90%	67%
SW	13.8	14.0	11.5	27.3	122%	51%
1964 FTL	24.5	27.2	31.6	45.5	86%	60%
SW	14.1	15.8	12.9	29.4	122%	54%
1965 FTL	29.8	34.1	38.3	56.2	89%	61%
SW	17.4	22.7	19.3	37.7	118%	60%
1966 FTL	38.3	51.7	58.4	86.0	89%	60%
SW	27.9	29.7	30.5	51.8	97%	57%
1967 FTL	65.1	56.6	61.4	87.0	92%	65%
SW	31.5	30.1	29.8	54.8	101%	55%
1968 FTL	48.0	49.0	53.4	76.7	92%	70%
SW	28.7	34.8	36.5	64.7	95%	54%

[a] Reported on fiscal year basis. Converted to calendar by adding next fiscal year and dividing by two.

SOURCE: U.S. House of Representatives, Subcommittee on Military Airlift, Committee on Armed Services, *Military Airlift* (1970), pp. 6,326 ff.

senger-cargo carriers[4] dominated the cargo industry in terms of shares of cargo ton-miles and revenue. Although they performed scheduled and nonscheduled air freight service, they tended to specialize almost exclusively in scheduled service.

The all-cargo carriers[5] provided scheduled and nonscheduled cargo service and charter passenger service for the military. Because of their relatively low rates, they had a smaller share of the cargo revenue as compared with cargo ton-miles. One of the long-standing public policy controversies has centered on the equipment,

[4] Included were the 11 domestic trunk carriers, 12 domestic local service airlines, and 12 passenger-cargo carriers providing international and territorial service. The Big Four domestic carriers (American, Eastern, Trans World and United), plus Pan American, dominated the combination carriers in terms of freight traffic. For example, of the 2.403 billion scheduled freight revenue ton-miles generated in domestic and international service by the combination carriers in 1968 (Table 2.2), 79% was carried by American, Eastern, United, Trans World, or Pan American.

[5] Included were Airlift International, Flying Tiger, and Seaboard World. Airlift acquired the operating rights of the defunct Slick Airways in 1968. Airlift has had a history of severe financial problems as described in "Airlift Plans Strong Air Freight Emphasis," *Aviation Week and Space Technology* (August 31, 1970), p. 34.

price, route, and service competition between the combination and all-cargo air-lines. The all-cargo carriers fear that the combination carriers will price their freight carried in passenger planes on a low by-product basis and drive the specialized all-cargo carriers out of business. The combination carriers claim that the all-cargo carriers have been artificially protected in one form or another during the past 15 years.[6]

The supplemental airlines,[7] mentioned above briefly, provided no scheduled service, but carried passengers and freight in charter service. In view of the importance of military traffic in their income statements, it is not surprising that the question has arisen frequently as to what percentage of Department of Defense traffic should move via the scheduled carriers, supplementals, or the military's own airlift capability.[8]

Scope of This Study

We will focus primarily on the air freight component of the air cargo industry, rather than explore, in addition, the very different set of problems involving the transportation of mail. As noted, it is anticipated that air freight will provide the bulk of the industry's growth.

Second, the study will be confined to domestic air freight operations for several reasons. Data on foreign carriers competing with U.S. airlines for air freight traffic are less complete than data on U.S. domestic carriers.

International air freight traffic and management strategies are biased by the military conflict in Southeast Asia. Table 2.4 contains time series data for U.S. international air freight traffic, excluding the charter traffic of Flying Tiger Lines.[9] Year-to-year fluctuations in the total nonscheduled service were dramatic, and if the Flying Tiger traffic had been included, the volatility of the series would have increased. Even for the relatively stable scheduled service provided by combination carriers, growth rates varied between 10.4% and 51.3% per year, because of the influence of military traffic.

Finally, international air freight service is performed in an extremely complex environment including bilateral agreements, restrictions in freighter capacity, changes

[6] For a detailed account of the struggles between the all-cargo and combination carriers, see Stanley H. Brewer and James E. Rosenzweig, *The Domestic Environment of the Air Cargo Industry* (Seattle, University of Washington Graduate School of Business Administration, 1967), pp. 22 ff.

[7] In 1968 these included American Flyer Airlines, Capitol International, Johnson Flying Service, Modern Air Transport, Overseas National, Purdue Airlines, Saturn Airways, Southern Air Transport, Standard Airways, Trans International, Universal, Vance International, and World Airways.

[8] See U.S. Congress, House Subcommittee on Military Airlift, Committee on Armed Services, *Military Airlift*, 91st Congress 2nd. Session. Both the supplementals and scheduled carriers were protesting cutbacks in military contracts and the implications of extensive deployment of military C-5s. The carriers said that they had invested heavily in new jet equipment and required military business.

[9] Compare Footnote 2, Chapter 2.

TABLE 2.4. U.S. Air Freight Traffic—International Service
Revenue Ton-Miles
(Data in Millions)

Year	Scheduled Service — Combination Carriers	Percent Change from Previous Year	All-Cargo Carriers	Percent Change from Previous Year	Total	Percent Change from Previous Year	Nonscheduled Service — Combination Carriers	Percent Change from Previous Year	All-Cargo Carriers	Percent Change from Previous Year	Supplemental Carriers	Percent Change from Previous Year	Total	Percent Change from Previous Year	Grand Total	Percent Change from Previous Year
1959	159		36		195		56		13		21		90		285	
1960	191	20.1	35	-2.8	226	15.9	25	-55.4	17	30.8	8	-61.9	50	-44.4	276	-3.2
1961	216	13.1	44	25.7	260	15.0	11	-56.0	36	111.8	45	462.5	92	84.0	352	27.5
1962	264	22.2	66	50.0	330	26.9	23	109.1	46	27.8	100	122.2	169	83.7	499	41.8
1963	296	12.1	86	30.3	382	15.8	13	-43.5	26	-43.5	48	-52.0	87	-48.5	469	6.0
1964	394	33.1	91	5.8	485	27.0	22	69.2	23	-11.5	83	72.9	128	47.1	613	30.7
1965	596	51.3	111	22.0	707	45.8	49	122.7	71	208.7	78	-6.0	198	54.7	905	47.6
1966	721	21.0	126	13.5	847	19.8	201	310.2	309	335.2	171	119.2	681	243.9	1,528	68.8
1967	796	10.4	155	23.0	951	12.3	359	78.6	324	4.9	178	4.1	861	26.4	1,812	18.6
1968	926	16.3	208	34.2	1,134	19.2	478	33.1	238	-26.6	189	6.2	905	5.1	2,039	12.5
1969	1,090	17.7	293	40.9	1,383	22.0	401	-16.1	393	65.1	193	2.1	987	9.1	2,370	16.2

TABLE 2.5. Air Freight Traffic—Domestic Service
Revenue Ton-Miles
(Data in Millions)

Year	Scheduled Service — Combination Carriers	Percent Change from Previous Year	All-Cargo Carriers	Percent Change from Previous Year	Total	Percent Change from Previous Year	Nonscheduled Service — Combination Carriers	Percent Change from Previous Year	All-Cargo Carriers	Percent Change from Previous Year	Supplemental Carriers	Percent Change from Previous Year	Total	Percent Change from Previous Year	Grand Total	Percent Change from Previous Year
1959	290		104		394		3		135		63		201		595	
1960	329	13.4	89	-14.4	418	6.1	2	-33.3	133	-1.5	112	77.8	247	22.9	665	11.8
1961	395	20.1	78	-12.4	473	13.2	2	0.0	180	35.3	114	1.8	296	19.8	769	15.6
1962	486	23.0	82	5.1	568	20.1	3	50.0	348	93.3	115	.9	466	57.4	1,034	34.5
1963	535	10.1	110	34.1	645	13.6	5	66.7	205	-41.1	171	48.7	381	-18.2	1,026	-.8
1964	668	24.9	148	34.5	816	26.5	14	180.0	195	-4.9	185	8.2	394	3.4	1,210	17.9
1965	857	28.3	166	12.2	1,023	25.4	54	285.7	276	41.5	220	18.9	550	39.6	1,573	30.0
1966	1,014	18.3	190	14.5	1,204	17.7	86	59.3	303	9.8	254	15.5	643	16.9	1,847	17.4
1967	1,219	20.2	182	-4.3	1,401	16.4	84	-2.3	320	5.6	264	3.9	668	3.9	2,069	12.0
1968	1,477	21.2	194	6.6	1,671	19.3	65	-22.6	183	-42.9	305	15.5	553	-17.2	2,224	7.5
1969	1,655	12.1	208	7.2	1,863	11.5	107	64.6	184	.5	256	-16.1	547	-1.1	2,410	8.4

SOURCE (for Tables 2.4 and 2.5): CAB, *Handbook of Airline Statistics* and *Air Carrier Traffic Statistics*. For a discussion of the implications of the CAB reported nonscheduled data, see Footnote 2, Chapter 2.

TABLE 2.6

Analysis of U.S. Domestic Air Freight Traffic

(*Adjusted to Exclude Flying Tiger Lines and Pacific and Supplemental Airline Military Traffic*)

1968

Traffic	Revenue Ton-Miles (*Millions*)
Scheduled Freight Traffic	1,671
+ Nonscheduled Combination Carriers	65
+ Reported Nonscheduled All-Cargo	183
− FTL Pacific Charter[a]	157
+ Reported Supplemental[b]	305
− Supplemental Military	268
Total Adjusted Commercial Freight Ton-Miles[c]	1,799
Scheduled as Percent of Adjusted	93%

[a] This assumed that charter passenger load factor was 90% and that military freight load factor was 70%. Thus, of the 351 million international ATMs, 127 million were passenger and 224 million ATMs were freight. Estimated military charter freight was 70% of 224 or 157 million.

[b] CAB, *Handbook,* 1969, p. 193.

[c] No adjustment was made for American Airline's military charter traffic.

in tariffs, and promotional policies designed to stimulate air traffic and/or use of national flag airlines.[10]

Within the domestic air freight sector, we will concentrate solely upon the scheduled service. As indicated in Table 2.5, scheduled freight represented over two-thirds of the total scheduled plus nonscheduled freight traffic, as reported by the CAB.

The scheduled service takes on far greater importance if we concentrate on actual commercial nonmilitary traffic and correct for the inclusion of Flying Tiger's international charter traffic in the domestic data. Table 2.6 displays these adjustments. Over 90% of the actual commercial domestic scheduled plus nonscheduled freight traffic was carried in scheduled freight service in 1968.

Table 2.5 also shows the trends in scheduled domestic freight traffic during the period 1959–1969. The average rate of growth was approximately 17% per year. On the other hand, the year-to-year percentage changes ranged from 6.1% to 26.5%. The traffic growth of the domestic combination carriers was higher, yet less volatile than that of the scheduled all-cargo service. In large measure this reflected the decision of Flying Tiger Line to utilize its aircraft in military charter service.

[10] For a detailed treatment of international air freight opportunities and problems, see Stanley H. Brewer, *The Environment of International Air Carriers in the Development of Freight Markets* (Seattle, University of Washington Graduate School of Business Administration, 1967).

TABLE 2.7

Air Freight Traffic—Domestic and International
Revenue Ton-Miles

(Data in Millions)

	Scheduled Service						Nonscheduled Service								Grand Total Scheduled and Nonscheduled	Percent Change from Previous Year	Percent Nonscheduled to Grand Total
Year	Combination Carriers	Percent Change from Previous Year	All-Cargo Carriers	Percent Change from Previous Year	Total	Percent Change from Previous Year	Combination Carriers	Percent Change from Previous Year	All-Cargo Carriers	Percent Change from Previous Year	Supplemental Carriers	Percent Change from Previous Year	Total	Percent Change from Previous Year			
1959	449		140		589		59		148		84		291		880		33
1960	520	15.8	124	-11.4	644	9.3	27	-54.2	150	1.4	120	42.9	297	2.1	941	6.9	32
1961	611	17.5	122	-.2	733	13.8	13	-51.9	216	44.0	159	32.5	388	30.6	1,121	19.1	35
1962	750	22.7	148	21.3	898	22.5	26	100.0	394	82.4	215	35.2	635	63.7	1,533	36.8	41
1963	831	10.8	196	32.4	1,027	14.4	18	-30.8	231	-41.4	219	1.9	468	-26.3	1,495	-2.5	31
1964	1,062	27.8	239	21.9	1,301	26.7	36	100.0	218	-5.6	268	22.4	522	11.5	1,823	21.9	29
1965	1,453	36.8	277	15.9	1,730	33.0	103	186.1	347	59.2	298	11.2	748	43.3	2,478	35.9	30
1966	1,735	19.4	316	14.1	2,051	18.6	287	178.6	612	76.4	425	42.6	1,324	77.0	3,375	36.2	39
1967	2,015	16.1	337	6.6	2,352	14.7	443	54.5	644	5.2	442	4.0	1,529	15.5	3,881	15.0	39
1968	2,403	19.3	402	19.3	2,805	19.3	543	22.6	421	-34.7	494	11.8	1,458	-4.7	4,263	8.6	34
1969	2,745	14.2	501	24.6	3,246	15.7	508	-6.4	577	37.1	449	-9.2	1,534	5.2	4,780	13.4	32

SOURCE: CAB, *Handbook of Airline Statistics* and *Air Carrier Traffic Statistics*. For a discussion of the implications of the CAB reported nonscheduled data, see Footnote 15.

TABLE 2.8

Analysis of Freighter Traffic Versus Total Freight and Total Cargo Traffic
U.S. Domestic Scheduled Service
1965–1969

	Total Scheduled Freighter Plane				Total Scheduled Domestic Freight		Freighter Plane Percentage of	
	Cargo Revenue (Thousands of Dollars)	Freight Revenue (Thousands of Dollars)	Cargo RTM (Millions)	Freight RTMa (Millions)	Revenue (Thousands of Dollars)	RTMs (Millions)	Revenue	RTMs
1965	91,218	80,360	521	469	209,314	1,023	38.4%	45.8%
1966	124,323	108,003	687	618	243,354	1,204	44.4%	51.3%
1967	157,531	137,348	879	791	278,624	1,401	49.3%	56.5%
1968	200,063	170,528	1,119	1,007	333,562	1,671	51.1%	60.3%
1969	230,882	199,944	1,260	1,134	392,947	1,863	50.9%	60.9%

a 1968 Freight RTMs represent actual data and were 90% of the Cargo RTMs. Inasmuch as in each of the other four years, freight revenue as a percent of cargo exceeded 1968 (85%), it is conservative to estimate freighter freight RTMs as 90% of reported freighter cargo RTMs.
SOURCES: CAB Form 242; Air Transport Association of America, *Airline Facts & Figures*.

Table 2.7 aggregates the domestic and international U.S. air freight traffic. Non-scheduled service as a percentage of total freight traffic is significantly higher than the adjusted domestic 7% figure shown in Table 2.6. The percentage has been declining in recent years, however, and stood at 32% in 1969.

Table 2.8 completes this set of industry statistics by focusing on another definitional term which often leads to confusion. Air freight is carried both in the belly pits of passenger planes (combination service) and in freighter planes, which carry no passengers. The combination carriers operate both freighter and combination planes, but the all-cargo carriers fly only freighter planes.

To avoid confusion between "all-cargo carriers" and "all-cargo planes," we will refer to what some call "all-cargo planes" as "freighter planes" throughout this study.

As if the above definitions were not enough of a problem, a final word of warning is in order. CAB freighter plane statistics normally do not separate out freight from cargo traffic.[11] Fortunately, the overwhelming proportion of freighter traffic consists of freight. A CAB study showed for example that, in 1968, freight carried on domestic scheduled freighters accounted for 90% of the freighter revenue ton-miles and 86% of the revenue.[12] Thus, even though this study is not concerned specifically with the transportation of mail, it must be recognized that freighter plane traffic does not consist solely of freight.

Having expounded the caveat, we can now turn to Table 2.8, which shows the relative importance of freighter planes in the domestic scheduled air freight industry.

Between 1965 and 1969, the percentage of total scheduled domestic air freight which moved in freighter planes increased from approximately 46% to 61%, and

[11] The data analyzed in this study were taken from published reports of the CAB which separate out freighter revenue by the categories of freight, mail, etc., but lump revenue ton-miles into one category. The same policy is followed by the CAB in its annual report *Trends in All-Cargo Service* (1970).

[12] Irving Saginor, "Traffic and Revenue Trends in Scheduled Domestic Air Cargo, 1964–1968" (CAB, Washington, 1969), Mimeo, p. 35.

the percentage of scheduled domestic freight revenue generated by freighter planes rose from 38.4% in 1965, peaked at 51.1% in 1968, and then dropped slightly in 1969.[13]

The Air Freight System

The air freight industry consists of more than airlines. Indeed, one of the industry's major problems is to coordinate policies within what might be termed the air freight system—pick up and delivery, containerization and packaging, billing and collection, airline haul, equipment design, marketing and promotion, and regulation.

Table 2.9 displays a matrix which tabulates a variety of functions which have to be performed and the institutions which are involved directly or indirectly in these functions.

The suppliers to the air freight industry, primarily the aircraft manufacturers, naturally have worked hard to promote the sales of new generations of aircraft. In this capacity they have gone beyond the design of equipment and attempted to assist the carriers in analyzing traffic trends and in designing marketing programs and information systems. The companies also have made presentations to shippers in an effort to strengthen the primary demand for the service. As noted, they have not been successful recently in convincing the carriers to invest heavily in the new large 747-L-500 aircraft; therefore there has been some effort to approach major shippers directly to stimulate the demand for private or contract carriage.

Of course the government as a regulator and promotor of air transportation is involved heavily in the fortunes of the industry. Clearly, government policies affect the performance of the industry; for example, the alleged protection of the all-cargo carriers has preserved substantial competition with the combination carriers. The regulation of pricing by the CAB has been a source of almost constant debate. At times some carriers claim that prices are pegged too high, yet others will assert that the low price policies are bankrupting the industry.

Federal, state, and local governments are active in the promotion of the airports and airways. The recently passed Airport and Airways Bill imposed a 5% tax on air freight shipments to help pay the costs of an improved airport and airways system. Obviously, the continued growth of air cargo depends upon sufficient ground facilities, yet the problems of scarce land, air pollution, and noise are enormous. In one respect, air cargo is more vulnerable to environmental pressures, for freighter planes usually fly at night, when concern for noise is greatest. Some have advocated dedicated air cargo airports located at a distance from heavily populated areas to reduce noise, but this suggestion raises the fundamental strategic question of the ultimate number of air freight airports, air freighter flights, and the magnitude of the ground distribution system.

---

[13] These freight traffic data produce somewhat higher percentages than the cargo data in Saginor's "Traffic and Revenue Trends . . . ," see Footnote 12, Chapter 2.

TABLE 2.9

The U.S. Domestic Air Freight Industry—Functions and Institutions

INSTITUTIONS

Functions	Suppliers to the Air Freight Industry	Federal State and Local Regulatory and Promotional	Local Airport Authorities	Air Carriers Combination, All-Cargo, Supplemental	Air Freight Forwarders	REA Air Express	Air Oriented Surface Carriers (ACI)	Other Surface Carriers	Shippers and Receivers
Design of Equipment	X				X	X	X	X	X
Pick Up and Delivery		X		X	X	X	X	X	X
Billing and Paper Work		X		X	X	X	X	X	X
Consolidation and Terminal		X	X	X	X	X	X	X	X
Flight Operations		X	X	X					X
Marketing-Systems Analysis	X			X	X	X	X	X	
Construct, Finance and Maintain Airports-Airways		X	X						
Pricing		X		X	X	X	X	X	X
Service and Schedule		X	X	X	X	X	X	X	
Choice of Equipment				X	X	X	X	X	

NOTE: X = Overlapping responsibilities.

Other governmental activities will be discussed in connection with topics to be covered separately in this study.

The air freight forwarders are of particular interest, for they relate directly to the question of who is to be responsible for pick up, delivery, and consolidation of freight shipments. Air freight is dominated by small shipments. Almost 60% of the shipments weigh less than 100 pounds, according to several surveys.[14] In addition, most shipments consist of more than one package.

It is extremely expensive to process individual packages on high value airport land, thus most experts see containerization as the means for reducing terminal costs. Although this issue will be discussed more fully under the heading of technology, the structural question arises as to which institutions should be responsible for the pick up and delivery, in addition to the consolidation function.

The air freight forwarders own no planes, but do provide pick up, delivery, and consolidation services. Historically, the air freight forwarder industry was dominated by Emery Air Freight, but also consisted of a large number of relatively small firms, all certificated by the Civil Aeronautics Board and all organized primarily as adjuncts to the airline industry.[15]

Recently, a new trend has developed, whereby the surface carriers have obtained air freight forwarding rights and now threaten the traditional air freight forwarders.[16]

At the same time, the air freight carriers are caught up in the strategic question of soliciting freight directly from shippers or operating through the forwarders. Currently, air forwarders generate about 30% of all domestic air freight traffic.[17] Major forwarders, such as Emery, United Parcel Service, and Airborne, have the power to allocate substantial sums of traffic to individual carriers. It is unclear at this time whether the forwarder share of the market will increase, or whether

[14] See annual surveys reported in *Air Cargo* magazine. See also Lars G. Romberg, "Airfreight: The Billion Dollar Confusion," *Airline Management* (September 1971), p. 24. He reports data showing that 80% of the shipments tendered to one major forwarder were under 100 pounds, whereas approximately 44% of the shipments handled directly by the airlines were under 100 pounds.

[15] For two recent studies of the status of the air freight forwarders, see Civil Aeronautics Board, Bureau of Operating Rights, *An Economic Study of Air Freight Forwarding* (Washington, 1968), and Air Freight Forwarders Association of America, *The New Role of Air Freight Forwarding* (Washington, D.C., the Association, 1970).

[16] In April 1969 the CAB granted three motor carriers—Consolidated Freightways, Pacific Intermountain Express, and Navajo Freight—permission to engage in air freight forwarding for five years as an experiment. It also initiated a rule-making proceeding designed to govern the filing and processing of applications of other motor carriers that desired to become air freight forwarders. The CAB's action was contested bitterly by the air freight forwarders. On March 30, 1970, the U.S. Supreme Court refused to review a lower court ruling which supported the CAB. The Supreme Court said that it was also premature to take the proposed rules for entry under judicial review. In 1970, also, the CAB permitted the Santa Fe and Southern Pacific railroads to initiate air freight forwarding service on an experimental basis.

See also, Norman H. Erb, "Truckers as Air Forwarders: Economic Implications for Shippers," *Transportation Journal* (Spring 1970), pp. 51–56.

[17] AFFA, *The New Role of Air Freight Forwarding* (1970), Exhibit 7. In the New York-Newark market 50.6% of the tons emplaned were tendered by forwarders.

airlines will in effect integrate vertically more aggressively. They might accomplish this vertical integration either by promoting their own industry-sponsored Air Cargo Inc., which performs scheduled pick up and delivery service; by operating their own trucks as individual carriers; or by entering into joint rights with specific surface carriers.[18]

The matrix (Table 2.9) spotlights the particularly difficult structural problem of pick up and delivery service and the competition between air carrier trucking affiliates, surface carriers belonging to Air Cargo Inc., non-ACI truckers, air freight forwarders, and the shippers themselves. One survey of shippers found that over one-third had utilized their own trucks for pick up and delivery, though not necessarily exclusively.[19] The ground distribution function involves difficult jurisdictional questions concerning motor carrier operating rights for air-truck feeder service and the respective roles of the Interstate Commerce Commission and the Civil Aeronautics Board.[20]

The matrix notes the role of REA Express which occupies a unique position as an "indirect air carrier" and provides priority air express service. There is disagreement among experts as to the continued need for air express service today, given the high quality of air freight service and the existence of air parcel post and the forwarders. The future of air express is currently the subject of a CAB investigation, and express as such will not be covered in this book.[21]

Finally, the matrix shows that shippers can engage in private carriage by air either through the operation of their own planes or by chartering freighters. The prospects for private carriage will be discussed in Chapter 5.

The Demand for Air Freight Service

There have been dozens of published and proprietary studies focusing on the question of the consumer demand for air freight. Literally hundreds of thousands

[18] For two recent articles on the status of Air Cargo Inc., see William F. Ryan, "Air Freight on the Road," *Air Cargo* (March 1970); and "Reorganized Air Cargo Inc. Takes on Marketing Role; Denies Financial Problems," *Traffic World* (October 4, 1971), p. 23.

In 1971, ACI was owned by 27 airlines. Its contractors performed the official pick up and delivery service for the carriers at 450 airports. ACI in announcing a 1971 reorganization plan said that it needed to strengthen its relationships with volume commercial shippers, particularly those using house trucks, contract carriers, or "gypsies."

[19] *Air Cargo* Survey (August 1968).

[20] For an excellent review of the regulatory issue see Interstate Commerce Commission, Bureau of Economics, *Air-Truck Coordination and Competition* (Washington, 1967).

In January 1971, the ICC ruled that two air freight forwarders (Emery and Trans Air) could operate as surface forwarders handling any traffic having a prior or subsequent movement by air. This ruling effectively demolished the old policy whereby air freight forwarder surface operation was restricted to a 25-mile radius of an airport. The decision will be printed as 339 ICC 17.

[21] See "CAB to Examine Need for Air Express: New REA Rate Structure is Suspended," *Traffic World* (August 3, 1970), p. 56.

of dollars have been spent on macro and micro forecasts of air cargo traffic. The former try to correlate aggregate industry performance with independent variables which can be forecasted, whereas the latter look at the behavior of individual shippers either by developing theoretical models or through actual surveys.

Macro-Economic Forecasting

In one sense, forecasting aggregate growth rates for air cargo or air freight is deceptively simple. If you eliminate the most volatile sectors (e.g., charter operations, mail, etc.), you find that the growth in U.S. scheduled air freight correlates well with a few variables: real Gross National Product, the price of air freight, and, in one study, a yield service index which blended service and price levels.[22]

A simple yet instructive exercise is to plot domestic scheduled air freight traffic, GNP in constant dollars, and air freight price deflated rates (Exhibit 2.1). Several fundamental conclusions are readily apparent:

(1) Between the end of World War II and 1950, the fledgling domestic scheduled air freight industry grew at a furious pace (over 75% per annum). Air freight rates plummeted by one-third as the scheduled carriers battled a horde of noncertificated contract cargo operators, largely owned and operated by returning servicemen using ex-military cargo aircraft. Unfortunately, the economics of the small capacity piston aircraft could not sustain the low rates, and many of the new firms vanished. In 1949 the scheduled combination carriers were joined by four newly certificated all-cargo carriers, and the basic structure of the air cargo industry began to stabilize.

(2) The 1950s saw the industry growing at a much less rapid (approximately 9%) and somewhat uneven pace. Annual demand was quite responsive to general economic conditions. Gross National Product in constant dollars fell in 1954 and 1958 and scheduled air freight declined in absolute terms in those years. During the Korean War, air freight rates rose, but by the end of the decade had returned to the level of the end of the previous decade. Air freight was being carried in the larger DC-7B and Lockheed Constellation freighter planes, but profits were low. In 1959 the combination carriers introduced the large jet passenger planes. Freight rates began to fall as the carriers worked to utilize the new capacity provided by the belly pits of the jets.

(3) During the 1960s a higher and relatively steady growth pattern emerged. The jet passenger planes were joined by the turbo-prop CL-44 freighter, and the jet freighters. The dramatically reduced operating costs permitted further rate reductions, and the substantial increases in capacity provided by the jet freighters prompted rate cuts to stimulate traffic.

It should not be surprising if macro-economic demand models based on GNP and air freight rates could explain almost all of the variance of the demand during the period.

---

[22] For a review of air freight forecasting equations, see Bernard A. Schreiver and William Seifert, *Air Transportation 1975 and Beyond—A Systems Approach* (Cambridge, M.I.T., 1968), pp. 45 ff.

The Air Transport Association equation utilizing a service index plus GNP and price is found in ATA, *Industry Report* (1969), pp. 46–49.

EXHIBIT 2.1
TRENDS IN U.S. DOMESTIC SCHEDULED AIR FREIGHT TRAFFIC AND YIELD COMPARED WITH GROSS NATIONAL PRODUCT, 1946–1969

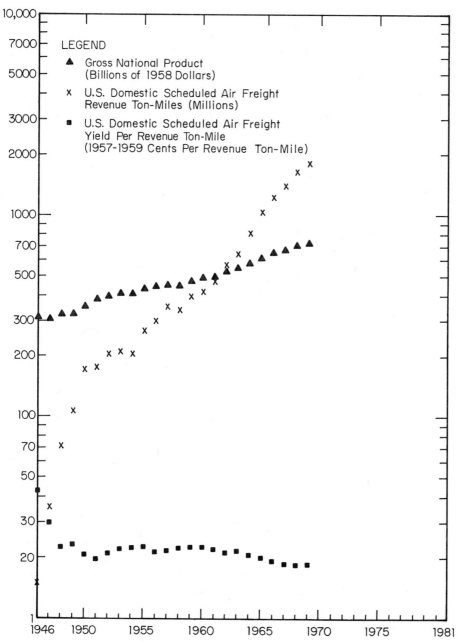

SOURCE: Council of Economic Advisors, *Economic Indicators,* CAB, *Handbook of Airline Statistics.*

A recently published study by the Civil Aeronautics Board developed two equations for forecasting air freight plus express traffic. A level-log equation based on the years 1946 to 1968 for domestic operations in 48 states was as follows:[23]

LOG FTM = .31254 − 1.53860 LOG RTM + 2.78227 LOG GNP where
FTM = Freight plus express revenue ton-miles
RTM = Average air freight revenue per ton-mile deflated by the Wholesale Price Index
GNP = Gross National Product in 1958 dollars.
The standard error was .031 and the R^2 was .995.

The equation implies that a 1% change in GNP will result in a 2.78% increase in air freight traffic, whereas a decline in air freight rates of 1% will produce an increase in traffic of 1.54%. Thus, the model postulates that air freight traffic is both income and price elastic.

In order to reduce problems of collinearity, the CAB used a first difference model for its actual forecasts. The results are impressive in terms of ability to account for past performance.[24] During the period 1947–1969, the variation between forecast and actual values fell within a range of 3% fourteen times. In only three years did the error term exceed 9%.

At this point, despite the excellent fit between historical freight traffic, GNP, and price, the long-range forecasting problem really begins. Most forecasts assume that the "real" price of air freight will continue to fall as new generations of aircraft are introduced. Yet, as will be elaborated at length in this study, air freight rates may well have been too low during the past two decades, and there is no assurance that new generations of freighter equipment will be put into service as quickly as the optimists predict.

Even if prices should fall, it is certainly unreasonable to expect air freight traffic growth to outstrip real GNP by factors of 2.5–3.0, or even more, when transportation as a whole tends to increase at the same or lesser rate as GNP.[25] When will the growth rates of air cargo taper to a more normal level? In effect, when will the industry reach the stage of "maturity?"

Some studies have tried to project total freight traffic and estimate potential air freight traffic by postulating varying degrees of penetration over time using logistics or gompertz curves.[26] The most optimistic studies, such as those published

---

[23] Irving Saginor and David B. Richards, *Forecast of Scheduled Domestic Air Cargo for the 50 States, 1971–1975* (Washington, CAB, 1971) Mimeo, p. 11.

[24] The equation is

Δlog FTM = 0.02834 − 1.20031 (Δlog RTM) + 1.38063 (Δlog GNP)

    R^2 = .710

    Std. Error of Est. = .036

FTM = freight + express revenue ton-miles, RTM = revenue/ton-mile.

[25] TAA, *Transportation Facts and Trends* (1971), p. 2.

Between 1947 and 1970, GNP increased 134%, but intercity ton-miles grew only 89%. If 1960 is used as the base, GNP increased 48% by 1970 and intercity ton-miles grew 46%.

[26] Systems Analysis and Research Corporation, *Air Traffic Growth* (January 1967), as quoted in Seifert and Schreiver, *op. cit.*, p. 46.

by McDonnell Douglas, assume that because the potential air freight traffic is so large, vigorous growth can continue for several decades. McDonnell Douglas has relied on a stage theory of modal traffic growth based on the histories of railroads and trucking and has criticized those who "arbitrarily" assume reduced growth rates following 1975.[27]

Micro-Economic Forecasts

In addition to macro-economic forecasts, air freight management requires an understanding of shipper behavior—micro-economic forecasts—in order to plan for growth in different categories of air freight traffic. The literature consists of theoretical models of shipper decisions based primarily on economic factors, and generalizations arising from shipper surveys.[28]

The theoretical models view the choice of air freight as a function of economic factors including transportation, inventory, packaging, and warehousing costs. These "total cost" models try to identify commodities which, because of cost or value characteristics, can "trade-off" the increased transportation costs of air freight versus reduced inventory, stockout, packaging, and warehousing costs, and thereby reduce total costs. An elaboration of the "total cost" approach is to include demand curves which assume that increased revenue will follow from improved service; therefore, that total profits would rise from the introduction of air freight.

The surveys of shippers are designed to estimate potential air freight traffic by individual markets; define the level of service required; obtain data on commodities and shipping practices (value, density, pieces per shipment, timing of shipments, etc.); and identify the bottlenecks which would restrict the ability of the air carriers to capture potential traffic.

Occasionally shipper surveys use more sophisticated methodological techniques. One study used discriminant analysis and found that the status, education, and background of the traffic manager, in addition to the more common economic variables, explained the likelihood of the shipper choosing air over surface transportation.[29]

Ironically, a deficiency of the micro approach has been its comprehensiveness. In moving from the macro total traffic level to the micro level of individual shippers and individual commodities, the amount of detail becomes overwhelming. The airline is under strong pressure to be all things to all people, and the result is a

[27] McDonnell Douglas, *Advanced Cargo Systems Report*, pp. 23, 43, 45.
Their optimism as to the future of air cargo was captured in the following quote (p. 43):
There is usually a tendency to be conservative in long-term forecasts. . . . This conservatism generally results from a lack of understanding by market analysts and the lack of vision and capability to implement the acceleration factors necessary for growth. The only real constraint to high rates of growth continuing indefinitely is the inertia factor resulting from ever-increasing volume of movement coupled with environmental market maturation. As previously indicated, a transportation mode usually requires 75 years to reach maturity, and air cargo has a long way to go.
[28] Compare Footnote 12.
[29] Henry A. McKinnell, "How to Identify Potential Air Freight Users," *Transportation Journal* (Spring 1968), pp. 5–10.

staggering array of specialized commodity and directional rates, arguments over the rates on and institutional responsibilities for containerized traffic, debates on the treatment of density in the rates structure, etc. It is difficult for the airline to step back and develop broad strategies for meeting the diverse needs of its potential shippers.

A Pragmatic Approach to Classifying Air Freight Traffic

An approach to resolving the problem of designing marketing strategies is to think of air freight traffic as falling into three broad categories: (1) emergency, (2) routine perishable, and (3) routine surface divertible. Exhibit 2.2 lists the types of traffic and compares them with a list of factors which, one might postulate, are of importance to shippers.

Emergency Traffic. Emergency traffic is characterized by the fact that it is not planned in advance. Time is of the essence, and the system must respond quickly to the needs of the customer. Penalty costs of failure may well be significant; therefore price of the service is of little relative importance. Control over the shipment is crucial; indeed the shipper may deliver it to the airline and arrange for delivery himself.

The image of air freight has been built largely on the concept of providing emergency service. There are many who believe that this image has made it difficult for the airlines to tap new markets. As long as shippers perceive air transportation to be expensive premium service for emergency shipments, they will not even consider the service for routine traffic.

Routine Perishable Traffic. Routine perishable traffic is also very time sensitive but, unlike emergency traffic, it is planned. The category includes fresh fruits and vegetables, magazines, cut flowers, samples being flown to trade shows, style merchandise, etc.

The decision to use air freight for routine perishable traffic is usually based on demand and service factors, not cost, for transportation demand is derived from the demand for the basic product. As long as the ultimate customer will pay a cost which reflects premium transportation, the commodity will move. By definition, its dependence on time makes it impossible for it to move via other modes and still meet the needs of the shipper and receiver for service.

Clearly, if technology reduces the cost of air freight and permits lower rates, this type of traffic could grow dramatically as new markets are created, new products brought into being, etc. On the other hand, this traffic is vulnerable to changes in consumer demand. Should the consumer refuse to pay a price which includes the cost of premium transportation, the traffic would cease to move.

Routine Surface Divertible. Routine surface divertible is also planned but, unlike routine perishable, speed is somewhat less important and cost factors take precedence over demand factors. This type of traffic can move by surface modes (usually in combination with field warehousing) and meet the time requirements of the shipper.

EXHIBIT 2.2
AN APPLICATION OF A MARKETING MATRIX TO AIR FREIGHT

	Nature of the Traffic		
	Emergency (Unplanned)	Routine Perishable (Planned)	Routine Surface Divertible (Planned)
Needs of the Customer	*(Entries indicate degree of significance)*		
Costs	Low	Medium	High
Airline or Trucker Pick Up & Delivery	Medium—Customer delivers	High	High
Speed	High	High	Medium
Tracing	Low—It can't afford to get lost	Low—It can't afford to get lost	High
Territorial Coverage by Individual Airline	Low	Medium	High—Wants full coverage
Availability of Capacity from Specific Airline	Medium—Usually space for emergencies	High	High
Information on "Total Cost Approach"	Low	Low	High
Responsiveness of Total System	High	High	Medium
Response by the Airline	*(Entries indicate nature of policy)*		
Pricing	High	Medium	Low
Type of Equipment for Shipment	Belly	Belly or Freighter	Freighter
Personal Selling	Social[a]	Social-Technical	Technical[b]
Schedules	Passenger	Passenger or Evening Freighter	Evening Freighter
Promotion	Schedules and Service Area	Schedules, Price and Markets	Total Cost or Profit Analysis

[a] Social skills include maintaining favorable image, supplying simple information, etc.

[b] Technical skills include training in logistics analysis, knowledge of competitive rates, etc.

The policy question is whether the total costs of the air system might in fact be less than surface. The classic example is the substitution of air freight from centralized locations for a combination warehouse-surface transportation system. In performing such analyses one must not assume that the relevant comparison is air versus current surface costs, for there is no reason to believe that opportunities for improving the surface system have been exploited fully.

For example, a case study developed by the author and included as Appendix B includes an actual analysis performed by one of the domestic carriers which led to the closing of a warehouse and the substitution of air freight. In its surface-warehouse logistics system the customer had been maintaining two months' inventory in the field, notwithstanding the fact that replenishments by truck were made weekly! Further, if total warehouse costs were divided by annual volume moved through the warehouse, the extremely high result suggests that the use of a public warehouse might have been investigated. Finally, the excessive field inventory may have represented either obsolescent stock or seasonal goods which would have to be stored in the central location in any event. Although it is true that the closing of a field warehouse should reduce safety stocks and possibly cycle stock (depending on the relationship between economic lot sizes of production versus shipment), it is also clear that it is dangerous to postulate inventory savings as the difference between inventory levels using air and poorly managed inventories using a surface-warehouse system.[30]

It is important to recognize that routine surface divertible traffic by definition will come to the airlines at the expense of the surface carriers. Although the total tonnage will be relatively small compared to the surface carriers' traffic, the revenue diversions could be substantial.[31]

The critical question will involve the differences in cost and service between the modes of transportation taking into consideration the inventory and warehousing policies of the shippers.

For example, consider the question of choice of mode for transcontinental shipments. In 1971 the East Coast-West Coast air freight general commodity rate, excluding pick up and delivery, was $31.25 per hundredweight. At the highest weight break—3,000 pounds—the rate was reduced to $26.45.

Special commodity rates were available on four commodities with the lowest rate being $18 per hundredweight for shipments of 10,000 pounds of seafood or period-

---

[30] This point was emphasized in a pioneering study of the shippers using air freight, Howard T. Lewis and James W. Culliton, *The Role of Air Freight in Physical Distribution* (Boston, Division of Research, Harvard Business School, 1956). Jack Steele in summarizing one of his detailed case studies which accompanied the text stated:

The reader should note that the principal source of the cost advantage [of air freight] was from interest savings on the capital released from a reduction in inventory levels. Although other factors are involved and discussed herein, the comparison presents evidence that had the Electro-Lab Company established and maintained inventory levels more in line with sales requirements, interest savings comparable to those released when air freight was hypothetically used *might be available regardless of the mode of transportation.* (Italics are the author's.)

[31] Most studies of diversion from truck to air tend to emphasize the small amount of tonnage involved, e.g., American Trucking Associations, Inc. Department of Research and Transport Economics, *American Trucking and the Future of Air Freight* (Washington, D.C., the Association, 1968). Yet, the diversions are far more significant if revenue, instead of tons, is used as the measure.

icals. Pick up and delivery charges at each end totaled from $2.00 to $4.00, depending upon the shipment weight.

The motor carrier class 100 rate including pick up and delivery was $15.64 per hundredweight for LTL shipments and $13.28 for truckload quantities. The preponderance of truck traffic consisted of Class 65-100 commodities.[32] Thus, much of the traffic moved at rates in the $9.00 to $13.00 per hundredweight range at yields to the truck line of approximately 6.5¢ per revenue ton-mile. The differential between air and truck transportation charges often fell into the $12.00 to $16.00 range. Depending upon the railroad Trailer on Flat Car (TOFC) plan chosen, rail rates were below those of truck, increasing the gap between surface and air freight.

The basic question then becomes: Under what conditions will nontransportation charges for "routine surface-divertible" freight be sufficient to offset the premium transportation charges associated with air freight?

The answer requires specification of several inputs: warehousing costs in terms of dollars per hundredweight, the warehouse replenishment order quantity, the order point at which time a replenishment is initiated, the level of safety stock to protect against variability of demand and lead time, the value of the product, and inventory carrying, communications, and order processing costs.

The simplest comparison would be to assume that transcontinental air shipments move direct to customers, whereas surface shipments resupply a warehouse on a hand-to-mouth basis. In effect, relatively small shipments (e.g., 1,000 pounds) would be dispatched daily under either alternative.

Warehousing costs for the surface alternative would probably fall within the range of $1.00 to $3.00 per hundredweight. We will use the higher number, thus reducing the differential between air and surface to $9.00-$13.00.

DeHayes has reported a survey of railroad carload shipments that found average transit times of eight days with a standard deviation of three days.[33] Let us assume that the trucks can do somewhat better, perhaps an average transit time of six days with a standard deviation of two days. Therefore, a reorder point set at ten days' worth of sales would provide 95% protection against stockouts resulting from variability of lead time. For the purposes of this example, we will assume a constant rate of sales during the replenishment period.

Let us assume further that the intransit inventory associated with air is negligible—a maximum of one day. Therefore, the problem is to place a value on the ten days of lead time inventory required by the surface-warehouse system. Table 2.10 calculates the value of the additional inventory in terms of dollars per hundredweight given an inventory carrying cost and commodity value per pound.

The table can be read in one of three ways. If the shipper knows his annual carrying cost and commodity value per pound, he can enter the table to find the additional

---

[32] J. S. Harker, *Freight Transportation Demand U.S. Domestic 1975*, The Boeing Company, Commercial Airplane Group, Cargo Systems Analysis (Renton, May 1970).

[33] Daniel W. de Hayes, Jr., "Industrial Transportation Planning Estimating Transit Time for Rail Carload Shipments," *Papers—Tenth Annual Meeting Transportation Research Forum 1969*, pp. 101–113.

TABLE 2.10

Value of Premium Air Service versus Surface-Warehouse System:
Hand-To-Mouth Inventory Policy—10 Days' Inventory Saved

(Table Entries in Dollars Per Hundredweight)

Inventory Carrying Cost →	10%	18%	24%	30%
Value Per Pound				
$ .50	$ .14	$ .25	$ .33	$ .41
1.00	.27	.49	.66	.82
2.00	.55	.99	1.32	1.64
5.00	1.37	2.47	3.29	4.11
10.00	2.74	4.93	6.58	8.22
20.50	5.62	10.11	13.48	16.85
29.50	8.08	14.55	19.40	24.55

ASSUMPTIONS:

(1) Incremental truck transportation time averages six days with a standard deviation of two days.

(2) Warehouse replenishment policy is based on 95% protection; therefore incremental surface system reorder point is ten days.

(3) Rate of sales during a replenishment period is constant.

(4) Interpretation: If value per pound is $5.00 and inventory carrying cost is 18%, you would be willing to pay $2.47 per hundredweight more for direct air service versus surface transportation plus warehousing.

amount he would be willing to pay for air transportation. For example, assume that his carrying cost is 18% and the value of the product is $20.50. The shipper would be willing to pay air freight charges up to an amount of $10.11 per hundredweight greater than the combined surface transportation plus warehousing costs.

Or, if the transportation and warehousing cost differential and value per pound were known, the shipper would find the appropriate interest rate necessary to achieve parity. The third approach takes the differential and inventory carrying cost as given and solves, for the parity, value per pound.

If the differential between air and surface plus warehouse is in fact approximately $9.00 to $13.00 per hundredweight, the table tells us immediately that air will be more expensive under conditions of equal shipment sizes and the specified transit times, unless either the value of the product approaches $30.00 per pound and inventory carrying costs are at least 10%. If higher inventory carrying costs are used in the analysis, the break-even value per pound drops, but even at a 30% carrying cost factor, the value per pound necessary to justify air freight is in excess of $10.00.

An objection to the above example could be raised, namely, that one would hesitate to resupply field warehouses with a series of small shipments because of the possibilities of poor service. Although an Economic Order Quantity calculation compared with transportation weight breaks might in fact justify a policy of small shipments, the major alternative would be to resupply at intervals associated with minimum transportation costs by the different modes.

TABLE 2.11

Value of Premium Air Service versus Surface-Warehouse System:
Truckload Resupply Policy—21 Days' Inventory Saved

(Table Entries in Dollars Per Hundredweight)

Inventory Carrying Cost →	10%	18%	24%	30%
Value Per Pound				
$ .50	$ .29	$ .52	$ .69	$ .86
1.00	.58	1.04	1.38	1.73
2.00	1.15	2.07	2.76	3.45
5.00	2.88	5.18	6.90	8.63
10.00	5.75	10.36	13.81	17.26
20.50	11.79	21.23	28.31	35.38
29.50	16.97	30.55	40.73	50.92

ASSUMPTIONS:

(1) Incremental truck transportation time averages six days with a standard deviation of two days.

(2) Truckload shipments are equivalent to three weeks' sales, therefore order quantity stock equals 11 days' sales.

(3) Warehouse replenishment policy is based on 95% protection, therefore incremental surface system reorder point is ten days.

(4) Interpretation: See Table 2.10.

For example, a West Coast warehouse could be replenished in the above example with a truckload every three weeks as opposed to 1,000-pound daily shipments. In effect, the lead time inventory of ten days calculated previously would be increased by an additional eleven days (one-half the order quantity). The surface-warehouse system requiring truckload replenishments would thus require an inventory equal to 21 days' worth of sales, where as the air inventory would remain negligible.

Table 2.11 shows the effect of a 21-day differential in inventory costs for varying carrying cost and values per pound. Again, assuming that the differential between air and surface plus warehousing is approximately $9.00 to $13.00 per pound, the range of parity encompasses commodities with values of $20.00 per pound at 10% carrying charges, $10.00 per pound at 18%, and $5.00 per pound at 30%.

Inasmuch as railroad TOFC rates tend to be as much as $2.00 to $3.00 per hundredweight below truck for transcontinental truckload shipments, air's competitive advantage is reduced further.

A recent study of Transoceanic Cargo found that of 402 directional-commodity groupings (the same commodity group would be counted twice if it was imported and exported), only 18 groups had average value per pound greater than $5.00.[34] These are shown in Table 2.12. As would be expected, the list includes "traditional" air oriented commodities, e.g., office machines and parts, scientific instruments, etc. It

[34] U.S. Department of Transportation, Asst. Secretary for Policy and International Affairs, Office of Systems Analysis and Information, *Transoceanic Cargo Study—Forecasting Model and Data Base Vol. I*, prepared by Planning Research Corporation (Washington, 1971) pp. III-60 through III-65.

TABLE 2.12

Transoceanic Commodities with Values in Excess of $5.00 Per Pound

DOTTO Number	Description	Density (*Pounds Per Cubic Foot*)	Value Per Pound
864 I	Watches and clocks, including parts	27	$ 11.80
681 E	Silver, platinum, and platinum group metals, unwrought or partly worked	360	19.31
515 E	Radioactive and stable isotopes, their compounds, mixtures, and radioactive elements, except uranium, thorium ores, concentrates	NA	11.66
681 I	Silver, platinum, and platinum group metals, unwrought or partly worked	360	438.00
212 E	Furskins, undressed	34	12.16
714 E	Office machines and parts, including computers	30	9.41
736 E	Electric apparatus for medical purposes, radiological apparatus, and parts	21	5.22
861 E	Scientific, medical, optical, measuring and controlling instruments, and apparatus, except electrical	30	5.63
614 E	Furskins, dressed, including dyed	11	7.73
726 E	Steam engines, turbines, internal combustion, jet and gas turbines, aircraft and missiles, and parts	21	9.62
746 E	Aircraft and spacecraft, and parts	8	9.82
734 E	Telecommunication apparatus and parts, including radios, TV sets, Naraids	15	7.73
842 E	Fur clothing and other articles made of furskins, except headgear, artificial fur, articles thereof	NA	25.50
212 I	Furskins, undressed	34	6.27
614 I	Furskins, dressed, including dyed	11	6.74
746 I	Aircraft and spacecraft, and parts	8	10.02
842 I	Fur clothing and articles made of furskins and fur, except headgear	NA	6.14
1 I	Live animals, except zoo animals, dogs, cats, insects, and birds	6	9.30

SOURCE: U.S. Department of Transportation, Asst. Secretary for Policy and International Affairs, Office of Systems Analysis and Information, *Transoceanic Cargo Study-Forecasting Model and Data Base,* Vol. I, prepared by Planning Research Corporation (Washington, 1971), pp. III-60 through III-65.

should be noted that the density of these commodity groups is highly attractive. To the extent that the carriers have not exploited the potential for moving these commodities, the marketing implications are obvious, yet the very fact that relatively few commodity groups exhibit value greater than $5.00 per pound puts a limit on the ability of domestic air freight to substitute fully for field warehouses.

It should be recognized immediately that there are still many cases when routine surface divertible traffic should move by air on the basis of economic calculations:

(1) When product obsolescence raises the cost of carrying inventory to relatively high levels.

(2) When product value is extremely high, for example, greater than $7.50 per pound.

(3) When truck or rail service is unsatisfactory.

(4) When surface warehouse costs are unusually high, for example, in excess of $5.00 per hundredweight.

(5) If centralized warehousing plus air freight substitutes for a large number of warehouses, each with relatively small volume. Under such conditions additional safety stock inventory can be saved by combining the volume through one facility.

(6) When truck rates are greater than air freight charges. Over 80% of the truck shipments (not tonnage) move on class rates, and transcontinental air rates are lower than truck class rates in the range of Class 150–200. As indicated in Exhibit 2.3, there are many commodities which move on truck class rates in excess of Class 150.

(7) Finally, routine surface-divertible traffic does not require that the shipper make a decision to close warehouses completely. Herron has shown that an optimal policy may be to keep the slow-moving line items in central locations and ship by air, but stockpile the fast-moving items in the field warehouses. Essentially, the trade-off is between the premium cost of air freight versus the reduced safety stock to support the slow-moving items. Additional savings come from reduction in back-order processing costs and reduced lost sales.[35]

Some of the traffic forecasts pin their hopes for growth on the routine surface divertible business. Lockheed's studies of divertible commodities include automobiles, appliances, machinery, and electronic equipment.[36] McDonnell Douglas estimates that fresh fruits and vegetables alone could provide 20 billion revenue ton-miles by 1980. Although some of this traffic could be considered routine-perishable (e g., would not move at all in the absence of air freight), much would presumably be diverted from the railroads and trucks.[37]

Future cost trends which will determine the ability of the air freight carriers to in fact divert substantial amounts of traffic will be discussed under the heading of technology.

Implications to the Carriers

Exhibit 2.2 has several important implications for air freight managers. Clearly, a universal set of policies—price, pick up and delivery, special services, schedules, etc.—will not meet the diverse needs of the shippers. Also, it is highly unlikely that

---

[35] David P. Herron, "Buying Time and Saving Money with Air Freight."
[36] See Commercial Operations Analysis Department, Lockheed-Georgia Company:
Major Appliances—A Brief Total Cost of Distribution Analysis ER 10520 (1970)
Imported Cars—A Brief Total Cost of Distribution Analysis ER 10519 (1969)
Construction Machinery—A Brief Total Cost of Distribution Analysis ER 10521 (1970)
Electronic Equipment—A Brief Total Cost of Distribution Analysis ER 10517 (1969)
[37] McDonnell Douglas, *Advanced Cargo Systems Report*, p. 58.

EXHIBIT 2.3
ESTIMATED 1975 FOR-HIRE MOTOR TRUCK TONNAGE
(*U.S. Domestic*)

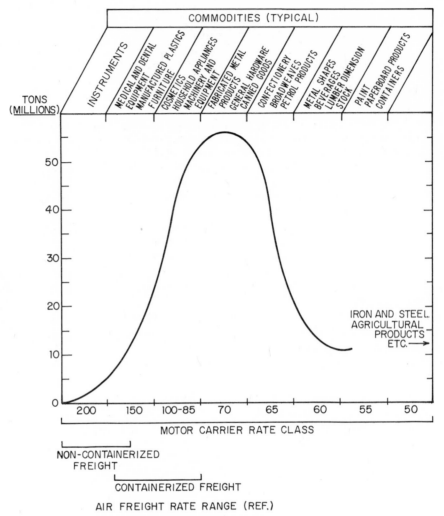

SOURCE: *Freight Transportation Demand—U.S. Domestic 1975,* The Boeing Co., May 1970.

these three classes of traffic today are equally profitable. Finally, the degree to which a carrier decides to concentrate on any particular one or two of the three has important structural implications for the industry.

For example, carriers that strive for routine perishable traffic will not have to make the same investment in educating their sales force in the difficult "industrial marketing" task of selling the service through a total cost analysis. On the other hand, routine perishable traffic is time sensitive, is often seasonal, and can lead to volatile profit performance, even though the traffic as a whole represents routine decisions.

When the spatial as well as the time element is included in the analysis, institutional responsibilities become very important. A shipper who tenders surface divertible cargo destined to off-line as well as on-line points may prefer to work through one of the large forwarders who specializes in controlled routings via several carriers.

Pricing of routine perishable traffic requires knowledge primarily of demand factors, but pricing of routine surface divertible must consider cost trends throughout the alternative distribution systems.

In summary, the degree of sophistication of selling ranges from low to very high as one moves from emergency to routine surface divertible. On the other hand, the response and speed requirements move in the opposite direction: Thus, it would seem reasonable for the airlines to develop broad goals as to what percentage of shipments, tonnage, and revenue fall into these three broad categories, before moving ahead to price out individual shipments. The analogy might be made with the decisions of a manufacturing company to generate a given percentage of its revenue from one broad product line. This strategic decision has major policy implications in terms of selling policies, pricing, channels of distribution, etc. Within the broad product line, more specific individual product decisions can be made subsequently.

Unfortunately, it will not be easy for the airlines to establish these broad policies, for some carriers do not know how much of their traffic is truly emergency, perishable, or could move by surface. In one instance I had the opportunity to ask several airline executives in one company what proportion of the air freight traffic they thought was emergency versus surface divertible. They answered 25% to 40%. The cargo manager then spoke up and said that on the basis of a recent survey, over 75% of the traffic was in fact moving because of a shipper perceived emergency. Without special studies, perceived impressions of traffic may be completely erroneous.

Regardless of the implications of classification schemes on the organization, traffic, and profits, it is still fair to conclude that air cargo managers work within what might be termed a variably optimistic environment. Experts will disagree over the nature of consumer demand, but none predict absolute or even relative declines in traffic over the foreseeable future.

The Technology of the Air Freight Industry

Turning to the studies of technology, we find that the literature is replete with descriptive and analytical material on new aircraft, automated ground handling facilities, new systems for paperwork processing, communications networks, and the like. Inasmuch as technological progress has and will continue to affect in a major way the strategies of airline managers, it would be useful to review briefly the major technological advances.

Aircraft

The most publicized aspect of the air freight industry not surprisingly has been the development of larger and faster aircraft. Table 2.13 compares the specifications of piston, turbo prop, and jet aircraft used in the all-cargo configuration during the past decade. The capacities become more meaningful when it is recognized that standard railroad boxcars have a capacity of 50 tons and trailer trucks carry loads in range of from 28 to 32 tons. Thus, in the space of a decade, freighter aircraft moved from the "half a truckload" category DC-7B to what might be called the "flying boxcar" (707-320) stage (Table 2.13 and Exhibits 2.4, 2.5, and 2.6).

The so-called jumbo jets (Boeing 747F, Lockheed L-500, etc.) feature capacities of two to three boxcars. When it is considered that the average speed of these new aircraft is 30 times greater than that of a freight train, one can envision freight trains in the sky. On the other hand, this potential capacity involves significant costs.

The moment that one mentions cost in the context of airline operations it is important to understand three basic concepts: direct costs, indirect costs, and the manner in which density of the cargo affects air freight costs.

Direct Costs. Direct costs are those associated with flying the airplane and are sometimes referred to as aircraft operating costs. They include crew, fuel, direct maintenance, maintenance burden, and flight equipment depreciation. Inasmuch as direct costs include depreciation, they should not be confused with cash operating expenses.

Table 2.14 shows the range of direct operating costs as actually experienced by

TABLE 2.13
Comparative Freighter Aircraft Specifications
U.S. Carriers

Type of Plane	Type of Engine	Normal Gross Weight	Cargo Capacity (*pounds*)	Best Cruise Speed (*mph*)	Maximum Range
DC-7F	Piston	125,850	33,000	250	3,700
L-1649A	Piston	160,000	33,000	236	5,000
CL-44 D	Turbo Prop	210,000	65,000	386	3,450
B 727 QC	Jet	170,000	46,000	523	3,500
B 707-300C	Jet	332,000	96,800	532	7,440
DC-8F	Jet	325,000	95,124	544	8,720
DC8-63F	Jet	355,000	106,400	555	3,600
B 747F	Jet[a]	775,000	257,858[b]	625	7,475
L-500	Jet[a]	818,500	281,100[c]	505	8,700

   [a] Not in service at time of tabulation.

   [b] Payload based on maximum use of containers drops to about 239,000 pounds.

   [c] Modified versions subsequently raised maximum payload to 320,000 and containerized to 287,500.

   SOURCE: *Aviation Week and Space Technology,* March 10, 1969, and data from manufacturers.

EXHIBIT 2.4
TYPES OF CARGO AIRCRAFT

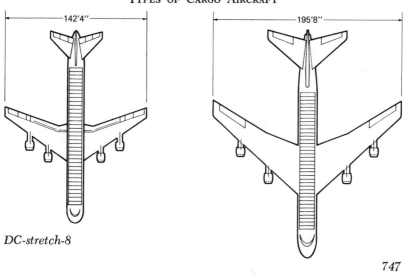

DC-stretch-8

747

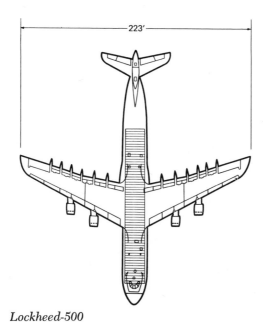

Lockheed-500

SOURCE: *Handling & Shipping,* December 1970, p. 41.

EXHIBIT 2.5
FREIGHTER AIRCRAFT OF THE BOEING COMPANY

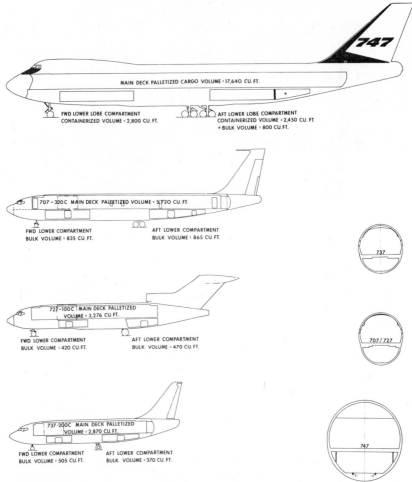

SOURCE: *Boeing, Airborne/Intermodal Pallets and Containers D6-58502$_{R2}$*, Air Freight Development Commercial Airplane Group, Renton, Washington, November 2, 1970.

the carriers in the last full year of significant piston engine freighter service (1966) and the first year of substantial jet freighter operations (1967).

The difference between the direct operating costs per available and revenue ton-mile reflected the load factor, that is, the extent to which the capacity of the plane (weight basis) was utilized.

The reductions in direct operating costs can be described only as dramatic. For example, as indicated in Table 2.14, American Airlines' 707s cut the direct operating costs (DOC) per available ton-mile by 60%, as compared with the piston DC-7

EXHIBIT 2.6
THE LOCKHEED L-500

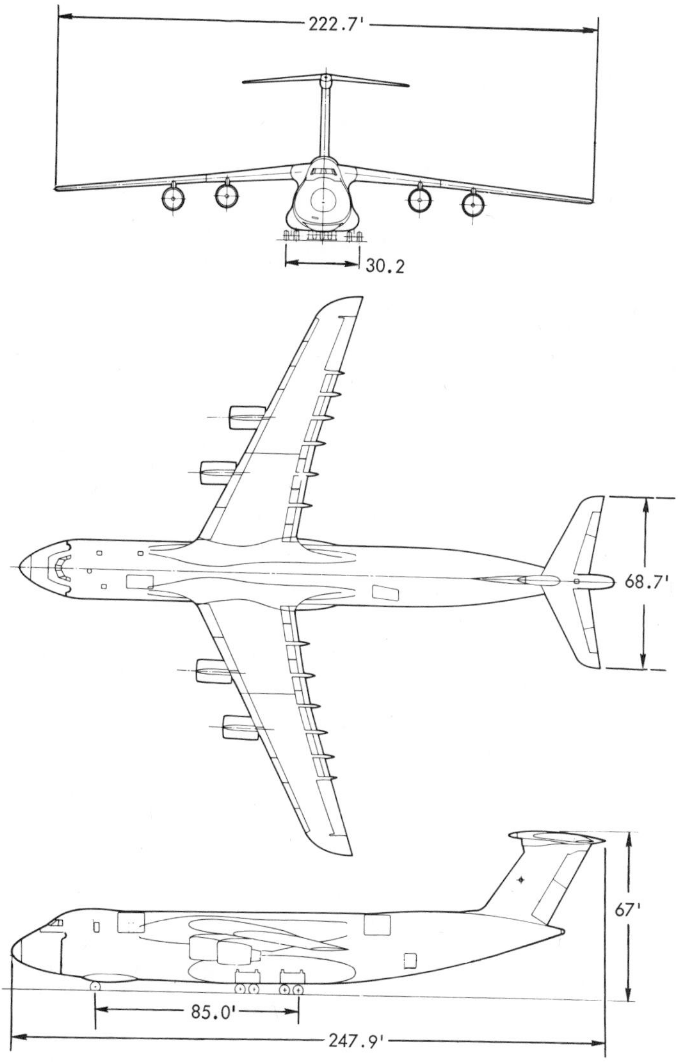

SOURCE: Lockheed-Georgia Company.

freighter. It is true that stage length did increase and aircraft operating costs tended to decline as stage length increased, yet the magnitude of the cost reduction was still overwhelming. For example, even though load factors declined in the face of the great increase in capacity, the direct operating cost per revenue ton-mile was still cut in half.

The desire to reduce direct operating expenses per available and revenue ton-mile

TABLE 2.14

Comparative Freighter Aircraft Performance

(*DOMESTIC U.S. SERVICE*)

Type of Plane	Type of Engine	Airline	Year	Direct Operating Cost			Average Airborne Speed	Average Stage Length	Carrier Freighter Operation Revenue Per RTM
				Per ATM	Per RTM	Per Aircraft Mile			
DC-6A	Piston	United	1965	11.7¢	18.2¢	$1.78	242	418	19.72¢
DC-7B	Piston	American	1965	10.1	15.3	1.81	267	606	17.83
L-1649A	Piston	Trans World	1965	14.3	26.2	2.41	233	283	19.52
C-46	Piston	Delta	1965	15.8	24.3	.97	188	408	25.52
CL-44	Turbo Prop	Flying Tiger	1965	NA	NA	1.78	344	1409	13.54
CL-44	Turbo Prop	Flying Tiger	1967	6.8	10.2	2.04	341	1271	13.29
B 727QC	Jet	United	1967	7.2	11.0	1.30	466	734	20.20
B 707-300C	Jet	American	1967	3.7	7.4	1.64	475	961	15.83
B 707-300C	Jet	Trans World	1967	4.2	10.8	1.92	456	757	18.89
DC-850F	Jet	United	1967	5.0	9.7	1.92	486	1113	20.20

NOTE: Direct Operating Costs (DOC) include Flying Operations, Maintenance-Flight Equipment, and Depreciation-Flight Equipment.

SOURCE: Civil Aeronautics Board, *Aircraft Operating Cost and Performance Report.*

TABLE 2.15

Theoretical Freighter Aircraft Productivity Data at Maximum Load Factor

Type of Plane	Type of Service	Original Cost (Millions)	Capacity (Tons)	Airborne Speed	Utilization Airborne Hours Per Day	Annual Capacity 365 Days (Million Available Ton-Miles)	Ratio Annual Capacity Per Original Cost
707-300C	Domes.	$7.0	40–46	460–480	6.5–9	43.7–72.5	6.2–10.4
707-300C	Inter.	7.0	35–39	500–525	10–13	63.9–94.7	9.1–13.5
DC-8F	Domes.	6.5*	39	475–500	7–9	47.3–64.1	7.3–9.9
DC-8F	Inter.	6.5	37–38	525–530	11–13	78.0–95.6	12.0–15.2
DC-8-63	Domes.	8.8	53–54	485–510	8–10	75.1–100.5	8.5–11.4
DC-8-63	Inter.	8.8	47–49	535–545	11–13	101.0–126.7	11.5–14.4
L-500	Domes.	21.5	140–150	475–490	8–10	194.2–268.3	9.0–12.5
L-500	Inter.	21.5	135–140	485–515	11–13	262.9–342.1	12.2–15.9
B 747F	Domes.	19.0	115–130	550–600	8–10	184.7–284.7	9.7–15.0
B 747F	Inter.	19.0	100–110	600–625	11–13	240.9–326.2	12.7–17.2

SOURCES: Lockheed, Boeing, Trade Journals. These data must be regarded as rough approximations. Specifications change constantly and comparisons are sometimes difficult because of assumptions concerning types of cargo, bulk versus containerized loading, tare weight of containers, length of flight, amount of reserve fuel, density of cargo, actual long-haul cruise speed, etc. Original cost data were obtained from Lloyd's *Aircraft Types and Prices* (1970). Cost data exclude price of spares. Ratio of aircraft cost to aircraft and spares cost ranges from 75% to 86%. Lockheed L-500 cost was estimated by applying the 747 aircraft/aircraft plus spares ratio of 86% to the aircraft plus spares cost supplied by the Air Transport Association of America. Annual capacity is measured in millions of available ton-miles. For illustrations of the 707, 727, DC-8, 747, and L-500 see Exhibits 2.4 through 2.6.

intensified in the late 1960s. First, Douglas produced a stretched version of its passenger and freight DC-8s. Boeing countered with the development of the 747, and Lockheed, as noted, began seeking orders for the L-500.

Tables 2.15 through 2.18 contain data on costs and productivity of the new aircraft. Naturally, the increases in payload and speed produced impressive gains in annual capacity. For example, as shown in Table 2.15 the international version of the L-500 is expected to produce almost four times the available ton-miles annually as the 707-300C. On the other hand, if investment costs are compared to the productivity data, the gains become less dramatic, especially when the 747 and L-500 are compared to the stretched DC-8. In domestic service, the 747F had the capability of providing 2.8 times the available ton-miles as the DC-8-63, but the investment cost was double. Essentially, one had to have confidence of continued substantial increases in traffic, for without this growth the tripling of freighter capacity per plane would be disastrous.

To put the issue another way, Boeing's literature emphasized that whereas 707s required approximately a 50% load factor to break even, the 747F would break even at about a 33% load factor. On the other hand, the average load would have to double in order to maintain break-even loads as a carrier moved from the 707 to 747. The brochures did not compare the 747F with the stretched DC-8.[38]

Yet, as indicated in Table 2.16, the 747s and L-500 did hold out the promise of continued reductions in direct operating (aircraft operating) costs per available ton-mile. On the basis of 1969–1970 costs, the theoretical reduction in expenses per available ton-mile was about 30% for the 747 and 40% for the L-500.

The potential reductions in direct costs were not without substantial risk. When the airlines replaced piston freighters with 707s and DC-8s, aircraft operating expenses per mile *and* per available ton-mile declined (Table 2.14). Yet, the purchase of 747s and L-500s meant that aircraft operating expenses per mile would increase by 75% to 100%. Finally, it was also clear that the direct operating cost reductions would not equal the 50% to 75% drops in DOCs when the carriers switched from piston to jet equipment. In absolute terms, the 1.5¢ to 2.5¢ per available ton-mile difference between the stretched DC-8s and the 747-L-500s would mean little in terms of reducing overall rates.

On what bases, then, could the manufacturers hope to sell new freighters costing from $20 to $25 million apiece? The answers involved the relationship between density and direct costs and a hoped-for revolution in indirect costs.

Density. The density of cargo has a profound impact on air freight costs because the load in an air freighter typically "cubes" out before it "weights out." For example, as indicated in Table 2.17, the design density for a 707 freighter is 12.9 pounds per cubic foot. This means if the density of the containerized cargo equaled approximately 13 pounds per cubic foot, the maximum capacities based on cube and weight would be achieved simultaneously.

[38] See Commercial Airplane Group, The Boeing Company, 747 Division, *747F Freighter D6-13920-R2* (Everett, January 1971), p. 70.

TABLE 2.16

Range of Aircraft Operating Costs Per Available Ton-Mile

Weight Basis—Domestic Operations

2,400-Mile Payload Range—1969 Costs

Range of Aircraft Operating Costs Per Mile		Tons Freight Capacity—Weight Basis—2,400-Mile Range			
		707-DC-8F 45.5 Tons	DC-863 55 Tons	B-747F 119.5 Tons	L-500 144.5 Tons
707	$1.75	3.8	NA	NA	NA
DC-8	2.00	4.4	3.6	NA	NA
DC-8-63	2.25	4.9	4.1	NA	NA
	2.50	5.5	4.5	NA	NA
	2.75	6.0	5.0	NA	NA
	3.00	6.6	5.5	NA	NA
	3.25	7.1	5.9	NA	NA
B-747F	3.50	7.7	6.4	2.9	NA
	3.75	8.2	6.8	3.1	2.6
L-500	4.00	8.8	7.3	3.3	2.8
	4.25	9.3	7.7	3.6	2.9
	4.50	9.9	8.2	3.8	3.1
	4.75	10.4	8.6	4.0	3.3
	5.00	11.0	9.1	4.2	3.5

NOTES: Entries above the heavy line indicate ranges of costs based on 1969–1970 operations. Entries below the heavy line indicate the range of available ton-mile aircraft operating costs in future years. Payload-range data for the 747F and L-500 are based on the assumption that loads will be containerized. Aircraft Operating Costs are also referred to as Direct Costs in this study. NA = Not Applicable.

SOURCE: *Air Transport World,* July 1970, and Boeing Co. 747F Freighter Brochure D6-13920-R2, January 1971.

Unfortunately, airline freight traffic tends to be less dense than the design density of the aircraft. Table 2.17 shows that densities of loaded commodities on board aircraft in a recent survey varied from 5.3 to 20.0 pounds per cubic foot depending on location and/or nature of the shipper. The average density was 8.6 pounds per cubic foot; therefore, a 707's effective cost per available ton-mile on the basis of cube would be 1.5 times that based on weight so long as the density of the cargo remained at 8.6 pounds.

The manufacturers of the 747 and L-500 have responded by designing their aircraft to "weight out" at lower densities. Thus, the L-500's density adjustment factor for an 8.6 pound cargo would be 1.05 versus 1.50 for the 707. On the other hand, should an airline marketing strategy based on the design density of 707s succeed—i.e., cargo densities increase sharply—the 747s and L-500s would weight out, not cube out!

TABLE 2.17

Impact of Density on Operating Costs Per Available Ton-Mile
Domestic Service

(Table Entries Are Factors for Adjusting Design Weight Costs)

	Design Density of Aircraft			
	(Containerized Cargo)			
Igloo-Pallet Densities on Board by Location and Shipper	L-500 9.0 Pounds	DC-8-63 9.9 Pounds	747F 10.9 Pounds	707-320C 12.9 Pounds
(Pounds Per Cubic Foot)	*(Per Cubic Foot)*	*(Per Cubic Foot)*	*(Per Cubic Foot)*	*(Per Cubic Foot)*
5.3 Montgomery Ward	1.70	1.87	2.06	2.43
7.6 Los Angeles	1.18	1.30	1.43	1.70
8.1 United Parcel Service	1.11	1.22	1.35	1.59
8.3 New York City—JFK	1.08	1.19	1.31	1.55
8.6 Average of NYC, Boston, Los Angeles and Chicago	1.05	1.15	1.27	1.50
9.5 Freight Forwarders	W	1.04	1.15	1.36
9.8 Boston	W	1.01	1.11	1.32
10.3 Chicago—O'Hare	W	W	1.06	1.25
20.0 Time Magazine	W	W	W	W

INTERPRETATION: If the aircraft indicated were loaded solely with igloo-pallets having the density shown, the effective cost per available ton-mile would increase by the factor indicated in the table. Thus, Montgomery Ward's traffic has a very low density relative to the design density of 707 freighters. The load would cube out before weighting out. The aircraft operating cost per available ton-mile would be 2.4 times the cost based on design weight. Conversely, a plane-load of *Time* Magazine traffic would have space left over. The extreme density would cause the plane to weight out (W) before cubing out. On the basis of average loadings, the aircraft cost per available ton-mile must be increased by approximately 50% because the effective capacity is determined by cube, not weight.

SOURCE: Lockheed-Georgia Company, *The Density Story*, CMRS 163, 1969.

Table 2.18 shows the range in direct operating costs for the current and proposed jet freighter fleet based on weight and density. The reduction in direct costs per available ton-mile by L-500s and 747s is far more impressive if the density measure is used. In terms of direct operating costs per available ton-mile, adjusted for density, the L-500 would reduce 707 costs by 55%. On the other hand, the design density of the stretched DC-8 is more consistent with current traffic, therefore, the L-500 would reduce direct costs per available ton-mile, adjusted for density, by approximately 30% as compared with the stretched DC-8.

Indirect Operating Costs. Indirect costs include aircraft servicing, traffic servicing, reservations and sales, advertising and publicity, general and administrative, ground equipment maintenance, and ground equipment depreciation. Far too often one hears only the direct operating costs of aircraft cited during discussions of air freight economics. In large measure this reflects confusion within the industry as to the

TABLE 2.18
Aircraft Operating Costs Per Available Ton-Mile
Domestic Operations
(2,400-Mile Range—Adjusted for Density of Cargo—1969 Costs)

Aircraft Type and Design Density	Range of Cost Per ATM (Weight)	Adjustment Factor[a]	Range of Cost Per ATM (Adjusted for density)
707-320C 12.9 pounds per cubic foot	3.8-4.4¢	1.50	5.7-6.6¢
DC-8-63 9.9 pounds per cubic foot	3.6-4.1	1.15	4.1-4.7
747F 10.9 pounds per cubic foot	2.9-3.1	1.27	3.7-3.9
L-500 9.0 pounds per cubic foot	2.6-2.9	1.05	2.7-3.0

[a] Adjustment factor reflects the relationship between aircraft design density and the "on board" igloo density (8.6 pounds per cubic foot) of traffic tendered at New York, Boston, Los Angeles, and Chicago (Table 2.17).

SOURCE: See Table 2.17 for source of design density and Table 2.16 for range of cost per available ton-mile (weight basis).

nature and magnitude of indirect costs. Boeing, in a recent brochure promoting the 747F, stated flatly: "There is no industry accepted standard of computing indirect costs."[39]

Indirect operating costs are not insignificant. During the period 1965–1969, indirect operating costs as a percentage of total operating expenses ranged from Flying Tiger's 37–39% to TWA's 48–50%. American and United's ratios fell into the range of 39–45%. Thus, direct operating costs have to be increased by a factor of 60–85% in order to determine total operating expenses.

For example, when indirect costs and load factor are considered in addition to direct operating costs, it is clear that the profitability of 707s depended heavily upon pricing policy. Adding indirect costs to direct costs produced total operating expenses per available ton-mile in the 8–9¢ range. Load factors, however, for all freighters except Flying Tiger plunged to 40–47% with the advent of the jets, therefore, operating expenses per revenue ton-mile were between 12–15¢ for Flying Tiger, and 16–24¢ for American, United, and TWA during 1965–1969. Of course, these costs made it impossible to cut air freight rates to the "magic" 6¢–8¢ levels that many believed would be necessary to divert substantial traffic from the motor trucks. Indeed, at the actual rate levels of 12–20¢, operating deficits were incurred frequently even with 707s.

The largest component of indirect operating costs was traffic servicing expenses which included terminal operations, billing and collecting, freighter loading, etc.

[39] *Ibid.*, p. 70.

Traffic servicing represented between 45% and 50% of indirect costs and from 16% to 25% of total operating expenses. The aircraft manufacturers are hoping that the introduction of 747 and L-500 freighters will cut traffic servicing costs by 55%, primarily through economies of containerization and increase in shipment size. The implications of reduced indirect operating costs plus the aforementioned reductions in direct operating costs from the L-500 and 747 freighters will be analyzed in Chapter 4.

Terminal Technology

It is almost axiomatic in the transportation industry that once a passenger or piece of freight begins to fly, roll, or float, most of the management's headaches begin to disappear. Much of the poor service performance in the railroad industry can be attributed to delays in terminals. The chaos surrounding the departure of ocean liners has been immortalized in prose and cinema. Despite massive investments in terminal facilities, the nation's air carriers are continually battling the problem of transferring passengers from the security of their automobiles to the security of the aircraft.

The motor carriers appear to have performed a better job in controlling terminal operations. One carrier, United Parcel Service, is well known for its ability to mechanize terminal operations and achieve excellent service at reasonable costs.

The terminal problem confronting air freight is difficult for a variety of reasons. Perhaps most important is the fact that it represents a buffer between a capital intensive, carefully planned system of aircraft operations with a fragmented, chaotic conglomeration of private and common carriers for the most part delivering mountains of packages in relatively small vehicles.

Unlike surface carriers such as United Parcel Service, which controls the flow of its own vehicles into its terminals and thus can plan the flow of packages into its sorting systems, the air freight terminal must adapt to a host of independent deliveries which converge on the terminal within two hours of the departure of a freighter flight. Because there are relatively few freighter flights in a day from any terminal, the carrier is faced with a few periods of intense labor activity and long periods of relative inaction.

The airline consciously trades off capital against labor costs. In order to achieve flight equipment utilization, freighter schedules are established as a "given," and the terminal must then decide whether to hire more labor or risk dispatching partially loaded flights. It usually follows the former policy and builds a labor force to meet peak demands. The results are extremely high costs per ton.

If the pick up, terminal handling, and aircraft loading process weren't difficult enough, the terminal managers face a problem at the unloading and delivery end of the cycle. Many customers prefer to pick up their merchandise at the terminal. Sometimes they fail to claim their goods immediately, and the airline becomes a warehouseman on very expensive airport land.[40]

---

[40] For a good review of the problems of air cargo terminal operations see Simat, Helliesen

Because relatively few air freight terminals account for a large proportion of the industry activity and the fact that air freight is often high value, easily stolen cargo, the terminals face the constant problem of theft. The scandals at New York's Kennedy airport have been publicized heavily.[41] Thus, in addition to difficult functional problems associated with processing air freight, the carriers face the unenviable task of minimizing the problems of theft, labor racketeering, etc.

A further component of the air freight terminal problem is the paperwork processing and billing cycle. A tremendous amount of information is required for calculating weight and balance during the loading of planes, monitoring shipments en-route, determining correct rates, billing customers, deriving statistics for forecasting traffic and judging sales performance, determining costs and profitability of different terminals and different commodities, etc. In the international air freight industry, the problems are compounded by the paperwork requirements of international trade.[42]

The industry has turned to technology to solve most of its terminal problems. Computerized paperwork systems successfully developed for passenger service are being adapted to freight operations.

In order to improve labor productivity, the carriers have tried to mechanize loading and unloading. Interestingly, they have used very different systems. American relies on a "clean floor" in its terminals for sorting and loading igloos (containers), plus the fixed mechanized Astroloader for loading the igloos on the plane. In contrast, TWA's newer terminals have mechanized carts on the floor for sorting, plus a mobile loader.

& Eichner, Inc. and TransPlan, Inc., *Study of Air Cargo and Air Passenger Terminal Facilitation*, prepared for Office of Facilitation, Department of Transportation (March 1969).

Other treatments of the terminal problem include:

International Air Transport Association, Financial and Economic Sub-Committee, *Economics of Air Cargo Carriage and Service* (Montreal, 1969), Sections 6 and 7.

David H. Reeher, "Air Freight Has Problems on the Ground," *Business Horizons* (February 1968), p. 33.

Richard G. O'Lone, "Cargo Slump Laid to Chaos on Ground," *Aviation Week and Space Technology* (June 17, 1968), p. 26.

A. T. Adams, "Ground Handling Problems and Their Costs," *Airline Management and Marketing* (June 1968), p. 24.

Wallace I. Longstreth, "Airports and Terminals are Air Freight's Villains," *Air Cargo* (April 1970), p. 34.

Nieson Himmel, "Freight Handling Evolving Slowly Toward Giant Jet Age," *Aviation Week and Space Technology* (October 26, 1970), pp. 88–94.

[41] Kenneth Marshall, "The Battle for Kennedy," *Transportation & Distribution Management* (July 1970), p. 25.

"Air Freight Problems in New York Gall Shippers, Importers," *The Wall Street Journal* (May 1, 1969), p. 1.

Richard F. Coburn, "New York Seeks Tighter Airport Security," *Aviation Week & Space Technology* (January 1, 1968), p. 35.

[42] See Simat, *op. cit.* for a detailed treatment of the paperwork problem and recommendations for its resolution. For a recent article reviewing information systems see Kenneth J. Stein, "Industry Watches Two Pioneering Freight Data Systems," *Aviation Week & Space Technology* (October 26, 1970), pp. 144–146.

Some carriers have invested in mechanical stackers for storing goods prior to flights or awaiting pick up by customers.[43] Others have installed mechanized sorting systems.

In general the results have been disappointing. Richard Lambert, Vice President-Freight of American Airlines, complained:[44]

> These freight-terminal handling systems, and I include the new ones, have not proved to be the panacea that many had hoped. Not one system has reduced costs. To complicate matters further, some of them are geared to handle only small packages. It is a harsh fact of life that small packages hardly pay their way and frequently don't pay their way, so some of these systems were actually designed to handle traffic that is marginal at best.

The basic problem is that the airlines have been unable or unwilling to adopt policies which would decentralize the loading or consolidation function either under their control or by delegating the responsibility to the forwarders or surface carriers. The hardware which would permit this change in strategy is the container.

Container Technology

The third technological element which has contributed to the dynamic growth of air freight has been the development of the structural container.

An airplane is an ungainly vehicle to load. With the exception of special aircraft designed for military use, cargo cannot be transferred at truck bed height, but must be hoisted to the floor of the plane. When freighter aircraft were put into service, pallets and nets were used to unitize the cargo and speed the loading process. Although pallets were light and cheap, they could not be used easily in intermodal operations. The restraining nets and fabric covers raised problems of security. Pallet rates based on density of the cargo faced the problem that the effective pallet volume was determined in large measure by the stacking efficiency of those loading the pallet. Unlike a structural container, there was no easily measurable "internal volume."

The advent of the 707 and DC-8 freighters saw the development of a family of contoured structural containers, called Type A, ranging in size up to 500 cubic feet. These were supplemented by smaller freighter and belly containers. Table 2.19 and Exhibits 2.7–2.8 show the many varieties of containers which were placed in service.

Although the contoured structural containers greatly facilitated the loading and unloading of cargo and led to increased intermodal service, they still raised several problems:

(1) The awkward shape of the contoured A and B containers resulted in wasted space and difficult intermodal handling. A rectangular container of standard 8-

---

[43] For a description of the problems of introducing the mechanized equipment, see "Airlines, Shippers Battle Break-in Problems," *Aviation Week & Space Technology* (April 15, 1968), p. 34.

[44] Richard Lambert, "Air Transportation," *Proceedings of the NASA Symposium* (Boston, February 10, 1969), p. 51.

TABLE 2.19
Containers Used in Air Freight Service

Name	Capacity	Dimensions	Remarks
A 1	<425 cu. ft.	Base 88″ × 125″	Full contour
A 2	426-475	Base 88″ × 125″	Full contour
A 3	476-500	Base 88″ × 125″	Full DC-8s
			Don't fit in 707s
B	197.7	84 × 58	Half Contour
B 2	99	42 × 58	Half Contour
D	63	42 × 58 × 45	Rectangular
DC-8 Belly	61	34 × 74	
DC-8 Belly	81	41 × 91	
707-720 Belly	75	42 × 98	
727-200 Belly	78	43.4 × 94	
747 Belly	350	60 × 186	
IATA #1	357.5	84 × 102	
IATA #2	404.2	84 × 119	
IATA #4	260.3	84 × 58.0	
IATA #5	197.7	84 × 58.0	
IATA #6	153.7	42 × 84	Same as Type B
IATA A-1 LD3	149	60.4 × 79.0	Belly
IATA A-2 LD1	174	60.4 × 92.0	
10 Foot	570	96.00 × 117.75 × 46.00	Potential 747
20 Foot	1040	96.00 × 238.50 × 96.00	Potential 747
40 Foot	2090	96.00 × 480.00 × 76.00	Potential 747

NOTE: For illustrations of representative containers used in air freight service, see Exhibits 2.4 and 2.5.

SOURCE: *Boeing, Airborne/Intermodal Pallets and Containers D6-58502$_{R2}$*, November 2, 1970.

foot by 8-foot width and height dimensions could be shipped in a Lockheed L-100 Hercules, but not in 707s or DC-8s. The low capacity of the L-100 relative to its operating costs prevented its use by most of the domestic carriers.

(2) The size of the structural container was constrained not only by the contour of the fuselage, but by the fact that it had to be loaded through a side door. The door constrained width of the Type A pallet was 88 inches. As a result, awkward cargo such as carpets could not easily be shipped in 707 or DC-8 freighters. The turbo-prop CL-44 was equipped with a swing tail which permitted end loading, but this feature was not repeated in the 707 or DC-8 family of aircraft.

(3) Containers could not easily be transferred between different classes of equipment. For example, the 707 and DC-8 Type A containers were not interchangeable. Nor were the belly containers for the DC-8, 707, or 727 passenger aircraft. This feature made it difficult for forwarders or large shippers to get interline service without costly rehandling. The wide body aircraft continued the problem. The LD-1 could be handled in the 747 only. Although an LD-3 fitted into both the

EXHIBIT 2.7
AIR FREIGHT CONTAINERS (1)

AIR TRANSPORT ASSOCIATION

A.T.A. TYPE A CONTAINER IS DESIGNED IN VARIOUS CONTOURS
CONFORMING TO CUSTOMER REQUIREMENTS PER USED ON
AIRPLANE CARGO ENVELOPES. THE PALLET BASE IS
88" x 125" x .75" THICK

THE CAPACITY BY CONTAINER TYPE DIVIDES THE TYPE A INTO 3 CATEGORIES -
TYPE A-1, 425 CU. FT. OR LESS
TYPE A-2, 426 TO 475 CU. FT.
TYPE A-3, 476 TO 500 CU. FT.

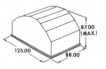

TYPE B
VOLUME - 197.7 CU. FT.

TYPE B - 2
VOLUME - 99 CU. FT.

TYPE C
CANCELLED

TYPE D
VOLUME - 63 CU. FT.

BELLY CONTAINERS

DC8
VOLUME - 61 CU. FT.

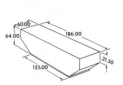

747 FULL-WIDTH CONTAINER
VOLUME - 350 CU. FT.

707/720
VOLUME - 75 CU. FT.

DC8
VOLUME - 81 CU. FT.

727-200
VOLUME - 78 CU. FT.

SEE I.A.T.A. SHEET FOR
LD 1 & LD 3 CONTAINERS

VOLUMES SHOWN ARE REPRESENTATIVE OF CONTAINER TYPE

SOURCE: *Boeing, Airborne/Intermodal Pallets and Containers, D6-58502$_{R2}$*, November 2, 1970.

EXHIBIT 2.8
AIR FREIGHT CONTAINERS (2)

AMERICAN NATIONAL STANDARDS INSTITUTE
INTERNATIONAL STANDARDS ORGANISATION

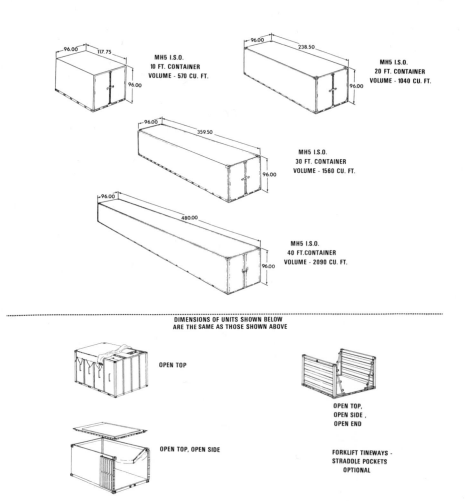

MH5 I.S.O.
10 FT. CONTAINER
VOLUME - 570 CU. FT.

MH5 I.S.O.
20 FT. CONTAINER
VOLUME - 1040 CU. FT.

MH5 I.S.O.
30 FT. CONTAINER
VOLUME - 1560 CU. FT.

MH5 I.S.O.
40 FT.CONTAINER
VOLUME - 2090 CU. FT.

DIMENSIONS OF UNITS SHOWN BELOW
ARE THE SAME AS THOSE SHOWN ABOVE

OPEN TOP

OPEN TOP,
OPEN SIDE,
OPEN END

OPEN TOP, OPEN SIDE

FORKLIFT TINEWAYS -
STRADDLE POCKETS
OPTIONAL

VOLUMES SHOWN ARE REPRESENTATIVE OF CONTAINER TYPE

SOURCE: *Boeing, Airborne/Intermodal Pallets and Containers, D6-58502$_{R2}$,* November 2, 1970.

747 and DC-10, variations in size resulted in different tare weights and payloads depending upon individual airlines.[45]

(4) The carriers have not been able to agree on pricing policies for containers. Disputes have arisen as to incentives for density, tare weight allowances, leasing charges to shippers, and the level of rates themselves. For a time, there was an industry agreement on rates, but it broke down in 1971.[46]

Many hope that the development of a standardized family of rectangular containers for use in the next generation of freighters will not only reduce loading and unloading costs, but resolve questions of pricing and intermodal relationships.[47] As will be discussed in more detail in later sections of this study, the technological development of freighters and standardized containers will not be sufficient. There will also have to be structural changes within the air freight industry to achieve the benefits of containerization.

Conclusions on Technology

It is not surprising that the bulk of the air freight literature is oriented toward technology in view of the fact that the new large aircraft and complex terminal systems are dramatic, represent a substantial investment, and hopefully promise significant increases in productivity with subsequent reduction in costs.

On the other hand, it can be hypothesized, perhaps, that the industry placed too much emphasis on technology as the salvation to its economic problems. One gets the feeling when reading the literature that the "perfect" freighter plane plus a "superautomated" ground handling and paperwork system are all that are necessary to insure economic vitality. It is the contention of the author that technology, though extremely important, is not the crucial variable in the success or failure of the air freight industry. Rather, management strategy will be the decisive element.

[45] See James P. Woolsey, "Airlines Push Containers, But Purchase Program Lags," *Aviation Week & Space Technology* (October 26, 1970), pp. 80–87.

Of the numerous IATA container types only three are common with Air Transport Association container dimensions. LD-1 and LD-3 belly containers for the wide body jets are being manufactured in almost a bewildering number of sizes. One manufacturer reported selling six different LD types and another sold five different LDs to five airlines.

[46] See "CAB Bars Rate Discussion in Approving Airline Talks on Cargo Container Pact," *Traffic World* (May 3, 1971), pp. 80–81.

The first airline container pact was developed under CAB supervision in 1965. In 1971, nine airlines withdrew—American, Airlift International, Braniff, Eastern, Flying Tiger, Northwest Orient, Seaboard World, TWA, and United. New discount belly container rates were proposed immediately following the breakup.

[47] As of 1970 only about 6% of domestic air freight was tendered by shippers, although one CAB official claimed that 20%–30% of the volume moving on freighters represented shipper containers.

See Woolsey, "Airlines Push Containers . . . ," p. 80 and Harold D. Watkins, "Airlines, CAB Grapple with Cargo Tariffs," *Aviation Week & Space Technology* (October 26, 1970), p. 49.

A spokesman for the Air Transport Association of America predicted in 1967 that, by 1975, 80% of air freight would move in containers. (ATA, *American Trucking and the Future of Air Freight*, p. 9.)

Chapter 3

An Analysis of Management Strategy in the Air Freight Industry, 1965-1969

MEASURING MANAGEMENT STRATEGY

WHAT ARE THE BASIC ELEMENTS OF AIR FREIGHT MANAGEMENT STRATEGY; how might they be measured and evaluated; and which will be examined in this study?

The answer lies in a tabulation of the major kinds of decisions that face airline cargo managers:

- Determination of routes and level of service
- Selection of flight equipment
- Development of a ground cargo handling and transportation system
- Planning and implementation of marketing strategies, including pricing, personal selling, promotion, and market research
- Recruiting, training, motivating, and controlling the workforce
- Development of a management organization geared to the specific requirements of the air cargo business with freedom to determine the levels of assets and manpower necessary to achieve corporate financial goals

These strategic types of decisions are clearly interrelated. For example, choice of equipment will affect the cost of operations, feasible prices, frequency of service, and number of locations to be served. Thus, the economics of the 707 and DC-8 freighters are most attractive when long stage lengths are flown, therefore their use might be restricted to relatively few airports coordinated with an extensive feeder truck service. On the other hand, the QC 727 is able to serve more airports directly, albeit at higher ton-mile costs.

The first objective of this study is to analyze the results of management's air freight strategy in the late 1960s. This calls for the identification of major strategic inputs, determination of system outputs, and an understanding of the linkages between inputs and outputs.

For example, the simplest expression of a management input would be the decision to offer a particular type of freighter plane on a given frequency at applicable tariff rates between two points.

The outputs of particular interest in this study are: traffic and competitive position, operating efficiency, and financial performance. Ideally, we would want to know more about other outputs, for example, employee morale and turnover, attitudes of the management group, and quality of service (mean and variance of origin-destination transit times), but more extensive research would be required.

It should be apparent that high performance in each of the three basic categories —volume and competitive position, operating efficiency, and financial performance —is not easy to achieve. Indeed, there may well be conflicts.

For example, a firm might pursue a policy of aggressive increases in capacity to maintain or improve its share of the market even at the expense of profitability or return on investment, if it believed that by doing so it would be in a better position to reap the benefits from the next improvement in aircraft technology.

Or, although share of market and growth are clearly interrelated in this high-growth industry, high rates of growth may not necessarily correlate with efficiency or profitability.

Another trade-off would involve efficiency, profitability, and share of market. A carrier which decided to minimize costs per available ton-mile might schedule equipment in such a manner as to put the carrier at a competitive disadvantage. Thus, costs would be low, yet revenue and market share might be so unsatisfactory as to produce minimal or negative profits.

Clearly, air freight managers would find themselves in a most frustrating position, if they were expected to excel along each of the three dimensions, even though it proved to be impossible.

THE STUDY CARRIERS

In order to analyze the impact of management strategy in the air freight industry a choice had to be made concerning a sample of firms for study. As indicated in the introduction, it seemed desirable to confine the analysis to scheduled domestic air freight service. In turn, because investment in air freighters represented a significant commitment to the concept of air freight, it was decided to analyze the scheduled air freighter operations in the domestic industry. Air freighter service, as noted, represented approximately 50% of the cargo revenue ton-miles and 60% of the cargo revenue during the latter half of the 1960s, the period under study.

Once the study was narrowed to carriers providing domestic scheduled air freighter service, the choice of carriers was clear. Four airlines, American, United, Trans World and Flying Tiger, dominated the industry. In terms of market share, each obtained more than 10% of the air freighter revenue ton-miles. In total, these four carriers accounted for approximately 83–90% of freighter revenue ton-miles and over 70% of total scheduled freight ton-miles (in freighters and combination aircraft) during the period studied.

The fifth most important air freighter operator, Eastern Airlines, had but 5% of the freighter traffic. Therefore, it was decided to concentrate on the "big four" in air freight.

It should be noted at the outset that the carriers had major similarities, but also important differences. Each had operating authority to serve the important trans-continental routes, e.g., New York to Los Angeles, and each operated four-engine jet freighter equipment. All four were recognized for their commitment to air freight. Their marketing and publicity efforts were geared not only to stimulating selective demand (e.g., ship-your-air-freight-via-Carrier-X), but also to generating primary demand, that is, promoting the concept of air freight *per se*.

The differences between the carriers in this study were of two kinds: some were externally created, in the sense that they reflected decisions by the regulatory agencies or prior managements; and others were created as a result of specific management decisions during the 1965–1969 period under study.

The "externally created" differences involved historical commitments, routes, and nature of the airline service being offered.

American Airlines was unique in that it was the first certificated carrier to offer (in 1944) a common carrier air freighter service. As such, it took pride in identifying itself with the growing air freight industry and for years was the number one carrier in terms of air freight traffic.

Trans World was the only one of the carriers to offer extensive international as well as domestic service. Indeed, it was the first carrier to offer trans-Atlantic all-cargo service (1947 in DC-4s). As a result of its domestic plus international scheduled service, it was the only study carrier which had to grapple with the problem of the impact of international freighter schedules on domestic operations.

Flying Tiger Lines had a dynamic controversial history ever since its establishment as one of the certificated all-cargo carriers in 1949. Although it carried no passengers in scheduled service, it did transport military personnel under charter. Yet, being an all-cargo carrier, by definition its future depended upon the promotion of air cargo traffic. Thus, Flying Tiger often found itself taking the initiative as far as the combination carriers were concerned.

United Air Lines was the largest domestic combination carrier during the period under study. Although it served Hawaii, its operations, like American, were primarily in the 48 states. On the other hand, during the early 1960s the company's management had to devote a great deal of attention to the problems of merging Capital Airlines into United. By the mid 1960s, however, United was in a position to increase its commitment to air freight substantially.

Financial Condition of the Study Carriers

In addition to the factors discussed previously (routes, historical involvement with air freight, combination versus all-cargo status), air policies within each of the companies were affected by two sets of financial considerations: the importance of air freight revenue to the company, and the overall financial condition of the company.

Tables 3.1 and 3.2 summarize the relevant data. For the three combination carriers, system cargo and freight revenue as a percentage of total passenger plus cargo revenue were approximately 9–12% and 6–9%, respectively, during the study years. Freighter revenue for the three firms ranged between $14 and $70 million per year, with domestic freighter revenue as a percentage of total passenger

TABLE 3.1

Importance of Air Cargo and Freighter Revenue to Study Carriers, 1965–1969

(Data in Millions of Dollars)

Carrier and Year	Operating Revenue *(Dollars)*	System Cargo Revenue *(Dollars)*	Percent Total	System Freight Revenue *(Dollars)*	Percent Total	Domestic System Scheduled Freighter Revenue *(Dollars)*	Percent Total
American							
1965	612	60.4	9.9	47.3	7.7	28.8	4.7
1966	725	78.6	10.8	61.6	8.5	44.1	6.1
1967	842	76.8	9.1	60.6	7.2	42.1	5.0
1968	957	103.5	10.8	82.3	8.6	54.2	5.7
1969	1033	95.5	9.2	74.3	7.2	53.1	5.1
United							
1965	793	69.2	8.7	45.7	5.8	19.8	2.5
1966	857	109.1	12.7	83.3	9.7	29.4	3.4
1967	1099	111.5	10.1	87.6	8.0	44.9	4.1
1968	1262	117.2	9.3	78.2	6.2	56.3	4.5
1969	1366	130.5	9.6	90.7	6.6	70.3	5.1
TWA							
1965	672	65.1	9.7	42.5	6.3	13.6	2.0
1966	700	67.2	9.6	43.3	6.2	16.2	2.3
1967	873	83.2	9.5	54.0	6.2	22.3	2.6
1968	948	99.9	10.5	62.3	6.6	27.4	2.9
1969	1089	109.9	10.1	74.3	6.8	32.0	2.9
Flying Tiger							
1965	56					17.3	30.9[a]
1966	86					23.5	27.3[a]
1967	87					21.7	24.9[a]
1968	77					21.4	27.8[a]
1969	97					22.5	23.2[a]

[a] The relatively low percentages of freighter revenue to total operating revenue for this all-cargo carrier reflects the fact that most of Flying Tiger's revenue came from military charters. Between 1965 and 1969 the amounts of military revenue were as follows: $30.2, $48.1, $53.4, $43.3, $49.4 million.

SOURCES: CAB, *Handbook of Airline Statistics,* and Moody's *Transportation Manual,* 1970.

plus freight varying between 2% and 6%. Although the percentages of system cargo and system freight total system were similar for the three carriers, TWA's relative reliance on freighter revenue was less than American's or United's.

Table 3.1 reveals another interesting fact about freight revenues in the total picture. Despite the growth in freight traffic, there was no significant increase in cargo or freight revenue as a percentage of total revenue during the period. Indeed, in the case of American, 1969 was a year of relative decline in the importance of freight revenue. Although United's freighters were improving their share of total company revenue, total cargo revenue as a percentage of total company revenue between 1966 and 1969 also declined along with American's. Only TWA displayed any indication of an increasing commitment to air freight but, as will be seen, this trend reflected a lower base as contrasted with definite management strategy. One is therefore left with the impression that the combination carriers by 1970 had made an important though not overwhelming commitment to air freight.

Flying Tiger's data show that a substantial proportion of its activity during the period was devoted to military charter operations.

Table 3.2 gives an overview of the financial environment surrounding the study firms during the last half of the 1960s. In 1965, 1966, and 1967, each of the companies showed positive operating profits and net income despite a major strike at United and TWA in 1966. However, by 1967, operating profits declined in American, Trans World, and Flying Tiger. By 1968 the financial situation worsened, as operating expenses grew at a faster rate than operating revenue; profits plummeted.

In 1969 American was hit by a strike, and its profits continued to decline. Trans World's profit position continued to deteriorate, but United and Flying Tiger experienced substantial improvements in their operating profits. Nevertheless, the reduced growth rates in revenue for American and United did not bode well.

In summary, the study carriers were pursuing freighter strategies during a period in which overall financial performance was deteriorating.

Air Freighter Data Base for the Study Carriers

Appendix Tables C-1 through C-10 contain the basic data which will be referred to throughout the remainder of this study. Most of the statistics come from the Summary Form 242 reports, published annually since 1965 by the CAB.

The data for the combination carriers—American, United and TWA—are based on the statistics furnished to the CAB by the carriers. It is important to recognize that the treatment of indirect expenses by the combination carriers is not consistent. As noted by Brewer and DeCoster, different methods are used to allocate common costs between freighter and passenger services.[1] As is the case in the railroad industry, the questions of joint versus by-product costs and fixed versus variable expenses will probably keep generations of economic consultants and cost accountants busy. On the other hand, despite the problems of the data, they represent the only published statistics on air freighter operations.

[1] Brewer and DeCoster, *The Nature of Air Cargo Costs,* pp. 21–27.

TABLE 3.2
Passenger Plus Cargo Financial Statistics, Study Airlines—Total System
1965–1969
(Data in Millions of Dollars)

Year and Carrier	Operating Revenue (Dollars)	Percent Change from Previous Year	Operating Expense (Dollars)	Percent Change from Previous Year	Operating Profit (Dollars)	Percent Change from Previous Year	Net Income (Dollars)	Percent Change from Previous Year
1965								
American	612	12.5	538	12.1	75	17.2	40	21.2
Trans World	672	16.9	574	17.4	97	12.8	50	35.1
Flying Tiger	56	24.4	47	14.6	9	125.0	4	100.0
United	793	18.5	706	14.8	87	61.1	46	70.4
1966								
American	725	18.5	630	17.5	95	25.0	52	30.0
Trans World	700	4.2	632	10.1	67	−30.9	30	−40.0
Flying Tiger	86	53.6	66	40.4	20	22.2	12	200.0
United	857	8.1	785	11.2	72	−17.2	38	−17.4
1967								
American	842	16.1	759	20.5	82	−12.6	48	−7.7
Trans World	873	24.7	821	29.9	53	−20.9	45	50.0
Flying Tiger	87	1.2	75	13.6	12	−40.0	7	−41.7
United	1099	28.2	988	25.9	111	54.2	73	92.1
1968								
American	957	13.7	893	17.7	64	−22.9	35	−27.1
Trans World	948	8.6	917	11.7	31	−41.5	22	−51.1
Flying Tiger	77	−11.5	74	−1.3	3	−75.0	(5)	NM
United	1262	14.8	1169	18.3	93	−16.2	42	−42.5
1969								
American	1033	7.9	970	8.6	63	−1.6	38	8.6
Trans World	1089	14.9	1064	16.0	25	−19.4	20	−9.1
Flying Tiger	97	26.0	84	13.5	13	333.3	4	NM
United	1366	8.2	1255	7.4	110	19.4	42	0

SOURCES: CAB, *Handbook of Airline Statistics*, and *Moody's Transportation Manual*, 1970.   NM = Not Meaningful.

The data show the magnitude, revenue, expenses, and profitability of cargo traffic carried in freighter planes. In addition, separate information on aircraft fleets give statistics on stage length, and utilization and costs of different types of equipment.

The author has deflated these data by a price index supplied by the Air Transport Association for certain calculations, but otherwise the data are analyzed without modification, e.g., adjustments for strikes. (See Table 3.3.)

Management Strategy of the Study Carriers (Inputs)

Commitment to Air Freight

Perhaps the most important single element of management's air freight strategy is its overall commitment to air freight as a separate business. Traditionally, the airlines have rewarded their managers on the basis of performance in passenger operations. If the air freight organization senses that management has not made a total commitment to air freight, it is not unreasonable to predict that morale and performance could suffer. Many times during the course of the author's interviews comments of this kind were heard: "Air cargo is a second class citizen," and "The passenger group does all the planning, we have to do the selling," etc.

There are several ways of measuring commitment. Perhaps the clearest signal by the combination carriers would be to establish separate air cargo subsidiaries with complete autonomy over equipment purchases, scheduling, personnel, and marketing, etc. No combination carrier has done this to date.

Another important sign of commitment is the investment in freighter aircraft, for once the decision is made by an airline to purchase significant numbers of freighter planes (or convert passenger equipment to freighter operations), air freight ceases to be a by-product of the passenger business.

As noted previously in Table 2.8, air freighter service is not insignificant, for in 1969, 60% of the domestic freight traffic and 50% of the freight revenue resulted from freighter operations. The aircraft manufacturers predict (and hope) that the

TABLE 3.3
Price Deflators Referred to in This Study

Year	GNP Deflator 1958 = 100	ATA Airline Weighted Cash Operating Expense 1958 = 100	Wholesale Price Index 1957–59 = 100
1965	110.9	113.9	102.5
1966	113.8	116.8	105.9
1967	117.3	119.0	106.1
1968	121.8	127.6	108.8
1969	128.1	135.4	113.0

Sources: Council of Economic Advisors, *Economic Indicators,* and Air Transport Association of America.

bulk of the growth in air freight will come from air freighter as contrasted with combination service. Lockheed, in 1965, predicted that, by 1975, 80% of the U.S. domestic cargo traffic would move in all-cargo flights.[2]

In this study, commitment will be measured two ways, each involving freighter plane operations. The first is to analyze the percentage of total cargo carried on freighter planes. In a sense this statistic can be considered an output, that is, the arithmetic calculation made after an accounting period. But, assuming the actual results are consistent with the targets set by management, this statistic perhaps best measures the degree to which management has "cut the cord" from passenger operations.

A second set of commitment statistics would be total capacity of air freighter operations measured in available ton-miles. Carriers which aggressively increase air freighter capacity would be demonstrating commitment to the concept of air freight as a separate business.

Percentage of Cargo Carried on Freighters. Flying Tiger, of course, carried all of its scheduled freight on freighters. American had the strongest commitment in terms of this measure; during the five-year period, freighter share of cargo RTMs increased from 53% to 62%. (Tables 3.4–3.7.)

United's policies are of greatest interest. In 1965 only 34% of its cargo moved on freighters, but by 1969 this percentage had climbed to over 56%. In contrast, TWA's 1965 percentage was similar (36%), yet by 1969 still less than half of its cargo moved on freighters.

In short, American maintained and even increased its commitment slightly, TWA increased its commitment somewhat, and United vigorously introduced air freighter service.

Air Freighter Capacity. Although percentage of cargo moved on freighters is a good indication of air freight commitment, it must be augmented by other data concerning freighter capacity, if meaningful conclusions are to be drawn. For example, a carrier could carry 100% of its cargo on freighters, yet operate so few flights that for all intents and purposes it wouldn't have even entered the market.

Tables 3.4–3.7 contain data on absolute freighter capacity, changes in freighter capacity, and shares of market in terms of freighter capacity.

American Airlines was the leader of the domestic scheduled air freight industry in 1965, by any measure. It had 30% of the freighter capacity, scheduled the greatest number of available ton-miles and, as noted, of the three combination carriers had the greatest percentage of its cargo moving on freighters. During the period studied American took advantage of the 1966 strike among its competitors and increased its share of capacity to almost 39%, but in 1969 it suffered from a strike and its share of capacity fell back to 26%. Its year-to-year percentage

2 E. W. Eckard, *Air Cargo Growth Study* MRS-49 (Marietta, Lockheed-Georgia, 1965), p. 63.

See also McDonnell Douglas, *Advanced Cargo Systems,* p. 27, where it is projected that 90% of world air cargo will move in freighters by 1980.

increases in capacity ranged from a high of 65.3% (1965–1966) to a low of 3.7% (1968–1969).

United during this period pursued a strategy of substantial increases in capacity —27% in 1965–1966 despite the strike (!), 65% the following year, 49% between 1967–1968 (while American's capacity was increasing 29%), and 37% between 1968–1969. As might be expected, these increases in capacity raised United's share of capacity substantially from 21% in 1965 to 30% in 1969.

Flying Tiger's policy was the opposite of United's. The Tigers followed a policy of minimal increases in capacity during 1967 and 1968, preferring to utilize its equipment in trans-Pacific military charter service. However, in 1969 it began operating its DC-8-63Fs in domestic service and its capacity increased 18% in that year. During the period studied, Tiger's strategy resulted in its share of capacity plummeting from almost 19% in 1965 to 11% in 1969.

TWA followed an intermediate strategy, adding capacity but not in sufficient amounts to prevent its share of capacity from declining from 18% to 15%. Its capacity changes in 1966 and 1967 were influenced to a large extent by the 1966 strike; however, in 1968, the fact that its capacity increase lagged behind both American and United indicated that TWA's management was less bullish on the prospects of air freighter service.

Over the period 1965–1969 United led the capacity battle with a 329% increase in capacity followed by American's 160%, TWA's 146%, and Flying Tiger's 79%. The "other" carriers offering freighter service, however, increased capacity 339% and their share of capacity rose from 12% to 17%.

Type of Freighter Equipment

The choice of freighter equipment is an important component of management strategy, for two carriers might have the same total fleet capacity (in available ton-miles) and carry the same percentage of their cargo on freighters, yet have the potential to offer quite different service at different levels of cost. It is testimony to the diversity of thought within the airline community to find that although each of the carriers could have adopted similar equipment strategies, they chose not to do so. (See Tables 3.8–3.10.)

On October 17, 1962, American Airlines entered into a firm commitment for its first 707 freighter planes, again displaying its determination to pioneer in the air freight industry. By 1969 it was operating 37 707 jet freighters, 12 of which were designed with no windows. The remainder could be converted to passenger service, though not at the speed necessary for Quick-Change freighter service.

Almost six months after American, United ordered its first DC-8Fs from McDonnell Douglas, following a policy of operating Douglas aircraft in both long-haul passenger and freighter service. United's commitment to long-range freighter aircraft was significantly less than American's; the United fleet totaled 15 DC-8Fs by 1969.

Trans World was the last in the study of combination carriers to order long-

TABLE 3.4
American Airlines
Operating and Financial Data
Scheduled All-Cargo Service
Domestic
12 Months Ending December 31
(Absolute Data in Thousands)

	1965	Percent Change 1965–1966	1966	Percent Change 1966–1967	1967	Percent Change 1967–1968	1968	Percent Change 1968–1969	1969
Available Ton-Miles (Capacity)	278,901	65.3%	461,061	17.1%	539,748	29.3%	698,093	3.7%	724,047
Revenue Ton-Miles—All-Cargo	161,718	56.7%	253,424	4.8%	265,651	25.4%	333,001	−3.6%	321,009
All-Cargo as Percent of Total Cargo	53.0%		60.9%		60.7%		62.7%		62.1%
Operating Expense Per Available Ton-Mile	9.83¢	−13.7%	8.48¢	−11.1%	7.54¢	2.3%	7.71¢	4.2%	8.03¢
Load Factor	58.0%		55.0%		49.2%		47.7%		44.4%
Share of Market:									
All-Cargo Available Ton-Miles	30.4%		38.8%		31.3%		30.5%		26.4%
All-Cargo Revenue Ton-Miles	31.0%		36.9%		30.2%		29.8%		25.5%

NOTE: NM = Not Meaningful.
SOURCE: Data Base, Appendix C.

TABLE 3.5
United Air Lines
Operating and Financial Data
Scheduled All-Cargo Service
Domestic
12 Months Ending December 31
(Absolute Data in Thousands)

	1965	Percent Change 1965–1966	1966	Percent Change 1966–1967	1967	Percent Change 1967–1968	1968	Percent Change 1968–1969	1969
Available Ton-Miles (Capacity)	193,421	27.4%	246,396	64.7%	405,825	49.1%	605,000	37.2%	829,902
Revenue Ton-Miles—All-Cargo	100,634	35.4%	136,216	63.1%	222,212	36.5%	303,383	23.8%	375,489
All-Cargo as Percent of Total Cargo	33.9%		40.5%		48.6%		52.4%		56.3%
Operating Expense Per Available Ton-Mile	11.66¢	2.6%	11.96¢	−10.3%	10.73¢	−14.4%	9.18¢	.5%	9.23¢
Load Factor	52.0%		55.3%		54.7%		50.1%		45.3%
Share of Market:									
All-Cargo Available Ton-Miles	21.1%		20.7%		23.6%		26.4%		30.3%
All-Cargo Revenue Ton-Miles	19.3%		19.8%		25.3%		27.1%		29.8%

NOTE: NM = Not Meaningful.
SOURCE: Data Base, Appendix C.

TABLE 3.6
TWA
Operating and Financial Data
Scheduled All-Cargo Service
Domestic
12 Months Ending December 31
(Absolute Data in Thousands)

	1965	Percent Change 1965–1966	1966	Percent Change 1966–1967	1967	Percent Change 1967–1968	1968	Percent Change 1968–1969	1969
Available Ton-Miles (Capacity)	165,285	4.3%	172,384	71.2%	295,167	23.4%	364,108	11.6%	406,286
Revenue Ton-Miles—All-Cargo	69,649	15.1%	80,191	47.4%	118,225	22.9%	145,287	13.2%	164,494
All-Cargo as Percent of Total Cargo	36.1%		38.1%		43.0%		45.2%		47.9%
Operating Expense Per Available Ton-Mile	9.84¢	10.0%	10.82¢	−16.8%	9.00¢	−5.9%	8.47¢	9.7%	9.29¢
Load Factor	42.1%		46.5%		40.1%		39.9%		40.5%
Share of Market:									
All-Cargo Available Ton-Miles	18.0%		14.5%		17.1%		15.9%		14.8%
All-Cargo Revenue Ton-Miles	13.4%		11.7%		13.5%		13.0%		13.1%

Note: NM = Not Meaningful.
Source: Data Base, Appendix C.

TABLE 3.7
Flying Tiger
Operating and Financial Data
Scheduled All-Cargo Service
Domestic
12 Months Ending December 31
(*Absolute Data in Thousands*)

	1965	Percent Change 1965–1966	1966	Percent Change 1966–1967	1967	Percent Change 1967–1968	1968	Percent Change 1968–1969	1969
Available Ton-Miles (Capacity)	172,579	31.3%	226,674	8.7%	246,299	6.9%	263,284	17.6%	309,670
Revenue Ton-Miles—All-Cargo	127,611	33.1%	169,811	−3.9%	163,250	1.7%	166,041	5.0%	174,353
All-Cargo as Percent of Total Cargo	100.0%		100.0%		100.0%		100.0%		100.0%
Operating Expense Per Available Ton-Mile	9.81¢	8.1%	9.02¢	5.8%	9.54¢	−1.0%	9.44¢	−13.3%	8.18¢
Load Factor	73.9%		74.9%		66.2%		63.1%		56.3%
Share of Market:									
All-Cargo Available Ton-Miles	18.9%		19.1%		14.3%		11.5%		11.3%
All-Cargo Revenue Ton-Miles	24.5%		24.7%		18.6%		14.8%		13.8%

NOTE: NM = Not Meaningful.
SOURCE: Data Base, Appendix C.

TABLE 3.8

Cargo and Convertible Aircraft Inventory, Study Carriers

	707-300C	DC-8F	727 QC	CL-44D	Propeller	DC-8-63
			American			
1966	12				3	
1967	24					
1968	37					
1969	37					
			United			
1966		9	15		6	
1967		9	30		5	
1968		15	37			
1969		15	37			
			TWA			
1966	7				9	
1967	30		6			
1968	13		8			
1969	12		8			
			Flying Tiger			
1966	4			10		
1967	6	2		10	3	
1968	3	2		10	7	9
1969	4	2		10	1	15

SOURCES: CAB, *Handbook of Airline Statistics; Air Transport World,* December 1969.

range jet freighters signing a commitment ten days after United. By 1965 it was the leader in terms of percentage of revenue ton-miles produced by jet equipment, but this reflected the low absolute level of freighter capacity operated. TWA's less than enthusiastic commitment to air freight can be seen by the manner in which they reported their aircraft inventory to the CAB. In 1967 they included 30 707-300Cs in the category of convertible, but in 1968, 11 had been classified cargo, 2 remained convertible, and the remainder apparently were included in the passenger column.

Two years following the ordering of its long-range jet freighters, United initiated the second phase of its equipment strategy by ordering a fleet of Quick-Change convertible 727QCs from Boeing, on the theory that the ability to convert passenger equipment to freighter service quickly would increase plane utilization substantially and bring freighter service to more cities. By 1969 United had 30 QCs that accounted for over one-third of United's freighter revenue ton-miles. One month later, TWA followed United's lead, but TWA's commitment to the Quick-Change concept was substantially less.

Flying Tiger essentially followed a leap-frog strategy. In the early 1960s, it introduced the CL-44, a relatively inexpensive four-engine turbo-prop freighter and secured a competitive cost advantage over the piston engine freighters flown by the combination carriers. When the combination carriers introduced 707 and

TABLE 3.9
Equipment Strategy—Study Airlines
Scheduled All-Cargo Service
1965–1969

Year and Statistic	Percentage of Revenue Ton-Miles			
	American	Trans World	Flying Tiger	United
1965				
Percent 707-DC-8	78%	85%		70%
Percent DC-8-63				
Percent 727 QC				
Percent Turbo Prop CL-44			83%	
Percent Propeller	22%	15%	17%	30%
Percent Other Jet				
1966				
Percent 707-DC-8	89%	89%		78%
Percent DC-8-63				
Percent 727 QC				
Percent Turbo Prop CL-44			94%	
Percent Propeller	11%	11%	6%	17%
Percent Other Jet				5%
1967				
Percent 707-DC-8	100%	88%		67%
Percent DC-8-63				
Percent 727 QC		10%		28%
Percent Turbo Prop CL-44			96%	
Percent Propeller		2%	4%	5%
Percent Other				
1968				
Percent 707-DC-8	100%	82%		63%
Percent DC-8-63			23%	
Percent 727 QC		18%		36%
Percent Turbo Prop CL-44			77%	
Percent Propeller				1%
1969				
Percent 707-DC-8	100%	85%		65%
Percent DC-8-63			98%	
Percent 727 QC		15%		35%
Percent Turbo Prop CL-44			2%	
Percent Propeller				
Percent Other				

SOURCE: CAB, Form 242.

DC-8 freighters, the Tiger's cost advantage vanished. Instead of purchasing 707s however, it continued to fly its 10 CL-44s in domestic service. In June 1966 it became the only one of the study carriers to order the stretched DC-8-63F and, by 1969, it regained a theoretical cost advantage by placing the aircraft into domestic service.

TABLE 3.10
Comparative Analysis—Study Carriers
Stage Length and Utilization
Jet and Turbo Jet Freighters

	American	United		TWA	Flying Tiger	
	707	DC-8	727	707	CL-44	DC-8-63F
Stage Length (Miles)						
1965	877	1330		828		
1966	882	1054		770	1372	
1967	961	1113	734	757	1271	
1968	930	1139	652	955	1111	1880
1969	950	1195	695	853		1586
Utilization (Hours Per Day)						
1965	5.8	6.69		8.28		
1966	7.06	7.7		8.31	9.52	
1967	8.3	7.22	8.39	8.45	8.71	
1968	6.44	7.23	8.36	7.52	5.6	9.16
1969	6.38	7.04	8.37	6.55		9.15

SOURCE: CAB, *Aircraft Operating Cost and Performance Reports; Air Transport World*, August 1969, June 1970.

Thus, during this period of rapid growth, American and Flying Tiger adopted freighter strategies which had the capability of providing low operating costs, albeit at the expense of serving many cities, for the long-range aircraft were most efficient when flying long-stage lengths. United, and to a lesser extent TWA, invested heavily in equipment that would enable freighters to serve more communities directly, even though the restricted capacity of the equipment resulted in higher operating costs per available ton-mile.

Routes and Service

The power to approve new routes resides in the Civil Aeronautics Board, thus the airlines are unable to make unconstrained decisions for broadening the scope of their air freight service through new routes. But, they can take the initiative in seeking new routes and/or increasing the level of service on existing routes.

Two patterns of service strategy on existing routes are breadth and depth. In the former case, the carrier tries to serve as many origin-destination points as is economically justifiable, whereas in the latter, the carrier allocates his capacity to provide greater frequency in specific markets.

A second element of scheduling strategy relates to the timing of freighter departures. If we assume that a shipper is using air freight primarily to obtain next morning or second morning delivery in major markets, it is to the shipper's advantage to have flights scheduled in the late evening from origin points that arrive at key destinations in time for next morning delivery.

A final scheduling element that affects the quality of service available to a shipper is the percentage of flights which are direct. Although direct service is perhaps most crucial in determining the quality of passenger service, it is important for the movement of freight also. When freight changes planes, it is subject to possible aircraft delays, and even more important, misrouting. Unlike the railroads, who interchange a significant proportion of their traffic, air freighter shipments generally stay within the control of a single carrier. Where connections require a change in airline, the potential impact on quality of service is increased.

The *ANALYZER* Schedule Analysis Program

Early in the planning of this research project, it was decided to investigate the scheduling policy variable as it affected airline competitive performance. The underlying hypothesis was that there was an inherent conflict between scheduling to achieve maximum equipment utilization versus scheduling to meet the demands of individual markets. It is obviously impossible for freighters to depart from all major markets during "prime hours" (e.g., 1900–0300 hours) and keep aircraft operating expenses at reasonable levels.

Ideally, it would be desirable to obtain information on traffic over individual market segments and correlate share of the traffic with different scheduling policies. Current data limitations and budget constraints precluded such an effort. On the other hand, it has been possible to examine the policy input: did the carriers follow different strategies in scheduling their domestic freighter flights?

A computerized program, ANALYZER, was developed to spotlight similarities and differences between the carriers. As noted in detail in Appendix D, the printout contained information on weekly flights for all freighter origin-destination pairs including: time of departure; nonstop, multistop or connecting service; type of equipment; and available ton-miles computed by a payload-range curve for each type of equipment.

Because of budget limitations, ANALYZER was run with but one set of data, the schedules for December 1968. Manual analysis of schedules for the summers of 1964 and 1969 of flight originations by city supplemented the more detailed 1968 data.

It should be recognized at the outset that multiplying the weekly flight data (based on the December schedules) by a factor of 52 to yield annual statistics did not produce the true annual statistics as reported by the CAB. A major problem was seasonality. Other explanations for the variance between projected and actual included the failure of carriers to fly published schedules, differences in factors for converting aircraft flights to available ton-miles, and the fact that the CAB domestic data in 1968 excluded Hawaiian and Puerto Rican freighter service. (See Table 3.11.)

American's reported CAB ATMs were quite similar to those projected by

TABLE 3.11
Comparative Freighter Capacity Data
"ANALYZER" and CAB
(Data in Thousands)

	ATMs on "ANALYZER" 1 Week × 52		ATMs on CAB 242		
Carrier	1968	Share of ATMs	1968	Share of ATMs	Ratio "ANALYZER" to CAB ATMs
American	780,936	21.6%	698,093	30.5%	1.11
TWA	477,828	13.2	364,108	15.9	1.31
United	1,036,204	28.6	605,000	26.4	1.71
Flying Tiger	425,516	11.7	263,284	11.5	1.62
Grand Industry Total	3,611,400		2,291,000		1.576

ANALYZER, whereas United's ANALYZER ATMs appeared to be greatly over-stated. Although part of United's variance can be explained by the inclusion of Hawaiian traffic in ANALYZER, the major reason for the discrepancy could not be ascertained through correspondence.

A second check on the reliability of the December 1968 sample was to compare carrier capacity shares as derived from the nonstop tabulations with capacity shares for 1968 based on the CAB data. As indicated in Table 3.11, this time American's ANALYZER market share was low compared to the CAB, whereas the shares for the other carriers were quite similar to the annual CAB data.

The ANALYZER program grouped the flights into three categories based on departure time. Accounting for time-zone changes made it extremely difficult to tabulate by computer actual origin-destination transit times from timetable data.

- Prime time. Departing between 1900 and 0300. This insures next-morning delivery to almost any major market in the United States in the case of direct service and next-day service to all major markets.
- Secondary time. Departing between 1700–1900 and 0300–0700. Two factors make these departure times somewhat less satisfactory than the prime times discussed above. A shipper wanting next-morning delivery can obtain this service if flights leave between 1700 and 1900, but the shipment may have to be made before the close of the business day. In the other case, departures between 0300–0700 will give next-morning deliveries over medium-length distances, but in many cases the shipment will probably not arrive at the consignee until the second day following shipment.
- Deferred time. Departing between 0700–1700. Most shipments will arrive at the destination too late for same-day delivery, therefore, in most cases the actual service will be second-day delivery.

Tables 3.12 through 3.16 contain the summary data on nonstop and multistop freighter schedules as printed by ANALYZER. The nonstop tabulations were produced primarily to avoid double counting during the determination of available ton-miles. The multistop tabulation, however, gave a more accurate picture of the service available to potential shippers. The tables are self-explanatory, and the major findings are listed below.

(1) The strategies of the individual carriers varied greatly in different markets. The ranges in shares of flights in major multistop markets (Table 3.12) were: American 19%–52%; TWA 8%–33%; United 17%–49%; and Flying Tiger 4%–24%. American was particularly strong in the San Francisco-New York City, New York City-Detroit, Boston-Chicago, and Boston-Los Angeles markets. United, with its corporate headquarters in Chicago and a major maintenance base in San Francisco, dominated the New York-Chicago, San Francisco-Chicago, Chicago-Los Angeles, and Detroit-San Francisco markets. TWA had relatively low shares of flights on a 24 hour basis. Its strongest showings were in the New York City-Los Angeles and Detroit-Los Angeles markets. Flying Tiger's largest market shares were also in the Los Angeles markets, namely Detroit-Los Angeles and Boston-Los Angeles.

(2) If we examine the market shares (in terms of flights) for prime time departures (between 1900–0300 hours) the picture changes. As evident in Table 3.13, United scheduled its service at prime hours to a much greater extent than its major competitor American. For example, in the 10 major market segments studied in detail, United's share of prime departures was greater than its share of 24 hour departures in eight cases. (It offered no service over one of the 10 routes.) TWA also tried to compensate for its relatively fewer flights, by scheduling them at prime hours. In 7 of the 10 markets, its share of prime departures was equal or greater than its share of the 24-hour departures. American, on the other hand, had prime-hour market shares equal to or greater than 24-hour market shares in only 2 of the 10 markets. Flying Tiger's performance was mixed. In several major markets it offered no flights during prime hours, but in the important San Francisco-New York City and New York City-Los Angeles markets, it scheduled a high proportion of its flights during prime hours.

(3) Table 3.14 summarizes the hour-of-day scheduling strategy for the study carriers and the industry, and confirms the findings of the individual market analyses. Overall, the industry tried to schedule the majority of its departures during prime hours. Indeed, 63% of United's freighters left cities between 1900–0300 hours. American's strategy was clearly different, whereas TWA and Flying Tiger's scheduling policies were intermediate and similar.

(4) Tables 3.15 and 3.16 give information on the breadth-and-depth policies of the carriers. As indicated in Table 3.15, United's policies of using quick-change 727s enabled it to serve far more city-pairs than any of the other study carriers, both on a one-way and both-way basis. Yet, no carrier served more than 42% of the total city-pairs with either nonstop or multistop service. This is not surprising, in view of the route patterns of the carriers, and explains why air freight forwarders can help a shipper requiring service to many destinations. The shipper cannot deal with one airline and obtain single-carrier service to all points, but he can work through a major forwarder, such as Emery (if he wants to work with one rather than many firms), and reach many markets.

Table 3.16 divides flights per week by numbers of city-pairs served in an attempt

TABLE 3.12
Analysis of Domestic Air Freighter Schedules
December 1968—Multistop
(*Share of Market—Flights and Available Ton-Miles*)
Total 24 Hours and Selected Markets

	AMERICAN[a]				TWA				UNITED				FLYING TIGER			
	Flights		ATM		Flights		ATM		Flights		ATM		Flights		ATM	
	#	%	#	%	#	%	#	%	#	%	#	%	#	%	#	%
1 SFO-NYC[b]	42	40	4575	40	22	21	2396	21	20	19	1832	16	17	16	2297	20
2 NYC-CHI	18	19	545	22	17	18	434	18	45	47	945	39	5	5	188	8
3 NYC-LAX	22	31	2290	32	22	31	2289	32	12	17	1249	18	5	7	646	9
4 SFO-CHI	16	26	1263	28	5	8	395	9	24	39	1416	32	11	18	1078	24
6 NYC-DTT	17	35	348	39	10	21	205	23	11	23	117	13	5	10	127	14
7 CHI-LAX	12	27	889	28	11	24	815	25	17	38	1055	33	5	11	460	14
8 DTT-SFO	11	26	976	28	5	12	444	13	21	49	1394	40	6	14	661	19
11 DTT-LAX	7	23	590	22	10	33	842	32	6	20	505	19	7	23	732	27
14 BOS-CHI	12	43	432	47	5	18	181	20	10	36	265	29	1	4	45	5
17 BOS-LAX	11	52	1212	50	5	24	551	23	0	0	0	0	5	24	683	28

[a] Indicates flights per week.
[b] Indicates ranking on the basis of flights per week.

CODES: SFO = San Francisco.   CHI = Chicago.
         NYC = New York City.   DTT = Detroit.
         LAX = Los Angeles.   BOS = Boston.

TABLE 3.13
Analysis of Domestic Air Freighter Schedules
December 1968—Multistop
(*Share of Market—Flights and Available Ton-Miles*)
Prime Hours and Selected Markets

| | AMERICAN | | | | TWA | | | | UNITED | | | | FLYING TIGER | | | |
| | Flights[a] | | ATM | | Flights | | ATM | | Flights | | ATM | | Flights | | ATM | |
	#	%	#	%	#	%	#	%	#	%	#	%	#	%	#	%
1 SFO-NYC[b]	21	34	2286	35	11	18	1197	18	14	23	1178	18	11	18	1486	23
2 NYC-CHI	6	11	182	14	12	21	283	21	28	49	511	38	5	9	188	14
3 NYC-LAX	10	23	1041	25	12	28	1249	30	6	14	625	15	5	12	646	15
4 SFO-CHI	6	15	474	18	5	13	395	15	18	45	943	35	6	15	588	22
6 NYC-DTT	5	33	102	40	5	33	102	40	5	33	48	19	0	0	0	0
7 CHI-LAX	5	50	371	69	0	0	0	0	5	50	165	31	0	0	0	0
8 DTT-SFO	0	0	0	0	5	25	444	34	15	75	861	66	0	0	0	0
11 DTT-LAX	1	9	84	9	5	45	421	45	5	45	421	45	0	0	0	0
14 BOS-CHI	0	0	0	0	5	31	181	37	10	63	265	54	1	6	45	9
17 BOS-LAX	11	52	1212	50	5	24	551	23	0	0	0	0	5	24	683	28

a Indicates flights per week.
b Indicates ranking on the basis of flights per week.

TABLE 3.14
Analysis of Domestic Air Freighter Schedules
December 1968—Multistop
(*Distribution of Total Freighter Flights by Hour of Day*)

	Prime Hours[a]	%	Fair Hours	%	Worst Hours	%	Total Flights 24 Hours	%
American	221	36	123	20	270	44	614	100
TWA	241	45	136	25	165	30	542	100
UAL	715	63	246	21	181	16	1142	100
FTL	110	46	34	14	96	40	240	100
Industry Total	2254	55	900	22	972	23	4126	100

[a] Prime Hours (1900–300).
   Fair Hours (300–700 and 1700–1900).
   Worst Hours (700–1700).

to get a crude measure of "depth" or intensity of service. On a total 24-hour basis, American emerges number one, followed by TWA, United, and Flying Tiger. But, United has the highest density in terms of prime-time service, as we might expect from the previous analyses. Thus, United, in 1968, simultaneously appeared to pursue successfully a "breadth" strategy in terms of numbers of city-pairs, and "depth" strategy in terms of flight density during prime hours. TWA served fewer markets and scheduled less flights than American, but did have a higher 24-hour density than United. Flying Tiger, on the other hand, on an overall basis, was weak in terms of both depth and breadth, but chose to allocate its scarce resources in a few major markets.

(5) The analysis of nonstop flights (Tables 3.17–3.21) show quite similar "breadth profiles," compared to the multistop data. Examination of six specific major non-stop markets, where percentage of available ton-miles is a relevant statistic, again displays the variety of strategies employed by the individual carriers. American is the only carrier to have more than 30% of the ATMs in three of the six markets but, again, it tended to schedule its flights in nonprime hours by comparison with United and TWA. Flying Tiger's selective marketing strategy is quite evident, as it scheduled 37% of the ATMs in the Detroit-Los Angeles and 45% of the ATMs in the Los Angeles-New York nonstop markets. United's policy of scheduling at prime times resulted in its having over 30% of the prime-time nonstop flights in five of the six major markets.

In summary, at the risk of oversimplification, the 1968 data suggested that United followed a policy of "breadth plus depth at prime hours"; American, "depth with relatively less concern for prime-hour scheduling"; TWA, overall less commitment than American or United, yet a policy of "depth during prime hours"; and Flying Tiger, "depth in highly selective markets."

In order to supplement the one-shot analysis of schedules, and give some indication of changes in scheduling policy over time, a manual analysis was made of freighter schedules for the summers of 1964 and 1969. Data were obtained on

TABLE 3.15
Analysis of Domestic Air Freighter Schedules
December 1968—Multistop
(Percentage of Total City-Pairs Served by Time of Day)

| | One Way | | | | | | | | Both Ways | | | | | | | |
| | Prime[a] | | Fair | | Worst | | Total 24 | | Prime | | Fair | | Worst | | Total 24 | |
	#	%	#	%	#	%	#	%	#	%	#	%	#	%	#	%
American	21	8	14	9	31	12	44	17	28	11	20	8	34	13	48	19
TWA	23	9	18	11	17	7	41	16	33	13	26	10	20	8	44	17
UAL	78	30	30	19	31	12	104	40	86	33	41	16	40	15	110	42
FTL	14	5	6	4	14	5	24	9	19	7	6	2	18	7	28	11

TABLE 3.16
Analysis of Domestic Air Freighter Schedules
December 1968—Multistop
(Density of Freighter Service—Study Carriers)

| | Flights/Week | | | | City-Pairs—Both Ways | | | | Density | | | |
	Prime[a]	Fair	Worst	Total 24	Prime	Fair	Worst	Total 24	Prime	Fair	Worst	Total 24
American	221	123	270	614	28	20	34	48	7.9	6.2	7.9	12.8
TWA	241	136	165	542	33	26	20	44	7.3	5.2	8.3	12.3
UAL	715	246	181	1142	86	41	40	110	8.3	6.2	4.5	10.4
FTL	110	34	96	240	19	6	18	28	5.8	5.7	5.3	8.6

[a] Prime Hours (1900–300).
Fair Hours (300–700 and 1700–1900).
Worst Hours (700–1700).

NOTE: The bases for the tabulations in Table 3.15 were:
259 origin-destination one-way pairs.
161 origin-destination other-way pairs.
259 origin-destination both-ways pairs.
The percentages for the fair-one-way pairs are based on the 161 other-way pairs. The total-24-hours, prime-hours, and poor-hours statistics are based on the 259 origin-destination one-way pairs.

TABLE 3.17
Analysis of Domestic Air Freighter Schedules
December 1968—Nonstop
(Share of Market-Flights and Available Ton-Miles)
Total 24 Hours

	AMERICAN				TWA				UNITED				FLYING TIGER			
	Flights[a]		ATM		Flights		ATM		Flights		ATM		Flights		ATM	
	#	%	#	%	#	%	#	%	#	%	#	%	#	%	#	%
1 CHI-NYC[b]	16	23	485	28	16	23	324	19	23	32	456	26	5	7	188	11
3 SFO-CHI	16	35	1263	36	5	11	395	11	18	39	1152	33	7	15	686	20
5 CHI-LAX	12	30	890	31	11	28	816	29	12	30	684	24	5	13	460	16
8 LAX-NYC	6	21	625	20	6	21	625	20	5	18	521	16	11	39	1422	45
10 CFO-NYC	11	41	1202	39	5	19	546	18	6	22	656	21	5	19	678	22
11 DTT-LAX	5	23	421	21	5	23	431	21	5	23	421	21	7	32	732	37

TABLE 3.18
Analysis of Domestic Air Freighter Schedules
December 1968—Nonstop
(Share of Market-Flights and Available Ton-Miles)
Prime Hours

	AMERICAN				TWA				UNITED				FLYING TIGER			
	Flights[a]		ATM		Flights		ATM		Flights		ATM		Flights		ATM	
	#	%	#	%	#	%	#	%	#	%	#	%	#	%	#	%
1 CHI-NYC[b]	5	11	152	16	16	36	324	35	17	39	275	30	0	0	0	0
3 SFO-CHI	6	21	474	22	5	17	395	19	12	41	678	32	6	21	588	28
5 CHI-LAX	5	50	371	69	0	0	0	0	5	50	165	31	0	0	0	0
8 LAX-NYC	6	26	625	25	6	26	625	25	5	22	521	20	6	26	775	30
10 SFO-NYC	5	31	546	31	5	31	546	31	6	38	656	38	0	0	0	0
11 DTT-LAX	0	0	0	0	5	50	421	50	5	50	421	50	0	0	0	0

[a] Indicates flights per week.
[b] Indicates ranking on the basis of flights per week.

TABLE 3.19
Analysis of Domestic Air Freighter Schedules
December 1968—Nonstop
*(Shares of Total Freighter Origin-Destination Flights
and Available Ton-Miles by Time of Day)*

	SHARE FLIGHTS (%)				SHARE AVAILABLE TON-MILES (%)			
	Prime Hours[a]	Fair	Worst	Total 24	Prime	Fair	Worst	Total 24
American	10	12	24	14	21	19	26	22
TWA	11	14	15	13	15	12	12	13
United	33	30	19	29	30	30	26	29
Flying Tiger	5	5	11	6	11	9	16	12
Other Carriers	41	39	31	38	23	30	20	24
Total	100	100	100	100	100	100	100	100

[a] Prime Hours (1900–300).
Fair Hours (300–700 and 1700–1900).
Worst Hours (700–1700).

flights per week, number of cities (not city-pairs) served, and the direction of service. As indicated in Table 3.21, the analysis indicates that Flying Tiger actually reduced the number of flights per week during this period, American increased its service 103%, TWA 143%, and United 278%.

Both Flying Tiger and American essentially served the same cities during the five-year period, but United and TWA increased their city coverage by 38% and 55% respectively.

The table also includes density measures, flights per week per origin city served. This measure of density differs significantly from that used in the ANALYZER program, flights per week per city-pair served.

Between 1964 and 1969, Flying Tiger flights per week per city served actually declined. Each of the others increased their density significantly with United reaching an average of 20 originating flights per week per city served. Again, the breadth strategy of United is confirmed, although the different measure of depth (i.e., density) masks the depth strategy of American relative to United. United's origin densities were high, but its city-pair densities were lower than American and TWA according to 1968 data.

Pricing Policy

Inextricably linked with the service feature of air freight is the question of price. Air freight prices, reported as yield per revenue ton-mile, reflect a variety of demand and cost factors. On the demand side, yield is affected by the nature of the commodity (high value commodities or emergency shipments can bear greater transportation charges than low value), the direction of the shipment (airlines often quote low "backhaul" rates), and seasonality.

TABLE 3.20

Analysis of Domestic Air Freighter Schedules

December 1968—Nonstop

(Number and Percentage of City-Pairs Served by Time of Day)

	One Way								Both Ways							
	Prime[a]		Fair		Worst		Total 24		Prime		Fair		Worst		Total 24	
	#	%	#	%	#	%	#	%	#	%	#	%	#	%	#	%
American	16	10	11	11	17	11	26	16	20	13	14	9	18	11	30	19
TWA	18	11	11	11	8	5	30	19	22	14	15	9	11	7	31	19
UAL	48	30	24	24	19	12	66	42	50	31	32	20	24	15	69	43
FTL	8	5	6	6	10	6	16	10	9	6	6	4	13	8	20	13

[a] Prime Hours (1900–300).

Fair Hours (300–700 and 1700–1900).

Worst Hours (700–1700).

TABLE 3.21
Comparative Analysis—Freighter Schedules
1964, 1969

	1964 (Summer)			1969 (Summer)		
	East-bound	West-bound	Total	East-bound	West-bound	Total
American						
Flights/Week	94	74	168	162	179	341
Cities Served	12	10	22	11	12	23
Density	7.8	7.4	7.6	14.7	14.9	14.8
TWA						
Flights/Week	62	62	124	145	156	301
Cities Served	9	9	18	12	16	28
Density	6.9	6.9	6.9	12.1	9.8	10.8
United						
Flights/Week	78	80	158	289	308	597
Cities Served	11	10	21	14	15	29
Density	7.1	8.0	7.5	20.6	20.5	20.6
Flying Tiger						
Flights/Week	99	98	197	67	63	130
Cities Served	9	10	19	9	11	20
Density	11.0	9.8	10.4	7.4	5.7	6.5

SOURCE: Official Airline Guide and *Air Cargo Magazine*.

Cost factors include size and weight of the shipment, length of haul, nature of the commodity (perishability, susceptibility to damage, etc.), and type of flight equipment in which the shipment moves, and whether or not the shipment is containerized.

In view of the many variables which affect the rates of individual shipments, some might consider it inappropriate to utilize a carrier's average yield per revenue ton-mile as a proxy for its pricing policy. Obviously, the average yield is affected directly by changes in traffic mix, rate changes following the introduction of new equipment, differences in length of haul as the result of new schedules and services, etc.

On the other hand, carrier and industry average yields per ton-mile are routinely reported in the trade press and regulatory reports and, as such, reveal major changes in industry behavior as well as differences between carriers. Some of the differences are beyond the control of individual airlines; for example, a carrier's route structure may force reliance on short hauls with attendant high costs and the need for relatively high yields per revenue ton-mile.

But, it is the thesis of this study that the carriers have a great deal of discretionary power with respect to choice of equipment, scheduling, designing a marketing strategy so as to achieve a target traffic mix, maintaining relationships with air freight forwarders, promoting containerization, etc. To the extent that the average yield per revenue ton-mile reflects these controllable factors, it is a legitimate proxy for the pricing component of a total air freight strategy.

During the study period, United had the highest average unweighted freighter yield, 19.8¢, per revenue ton-mile. TWA's average was almost the same, 19.4¢, but American's 16.8¢ per revenue ton-mile was 15% below United's. Flying Tiger was the consistently low price carrier even though it utilized relatively expensive (by comparison with jets) CL-44s during four of the five years. Its average yield of 13.3¢ was 33% below United's.

Part of the differences in pricing strategy can be explained by equipment. Yields tended to be high for American, United, and TWA, during 1965 and 1966, as they phased out high-cost propeller planes. United's high yields also reflected the policy of operating a substantial number of 727 QC freighter planes over relatively short-stage lengths. Without more detailed data for freighter yields on similar routes, it is difficult to determine precisely the proportion of the difference between carrier yields attributable to sales policies and the resulting traffic mix, yet the evidence does suggest that American and Flying Tiger tended to carry lower yield traffic.

Equally as significant as the differences in yields between the carriers was the trend in freighter pricing. Each of the study carriers reduced their freighter yields per revenue ton-mile between 1965 and 1969. American's average reduction in yield was 1.9% per year followed by 1.3% per year reductions by Flying Tiger and United. TWA's yield remained about the same.[3]

These freighter average price reductions of 1.3%–1.9% per year can be compared to the trends in freight yields per revenue ton-mile during the period when the jet passenger planes were introduced. The 707 made its debut in domestic passenger service in late 1958. By the end of 1959 almost 20% of the domestic truck revenue passenger miles were handled by jets. Between 1959 and 1965, the freight yield per revenue ton-mile for the Big Four domestic trunk combination carriers plummeted 12.4%, from 22.53¢ to 19.73¢, an average annual reduction of approximately 2.2%.[4]

Thus, major reductions in air freight yields took place while the combination carriers were trying to fill the greatly increased belly capacity of their new passenger jets. In many cases the decline in yields during the pre-jet freighter period exceeded the declines in freighter yields during the later 1965–1969 period.

Notwithstanding these price reductions, the average freighter yields per revenue ton-mile were two to three times those of the long haul motor carriers. Many in the industry felt that still greater price reduction would be necessary if air freight's true potential were to be exploited.

Other Elements of Marketing Strategy

In addition to price, air freight marketing strategies relied heavily on personal selling and promotion. Comparative information on selling and promotion was developed through interviews and analysis of statistical data.

---

[3] See Appendix C, Table C-4. In the period 1965–67 American's yield declined at an annual rate of 6% per year, but increased yields during 1968 and 1969 reduced the annual reduction over the period 1965–69 to 1.9% per year.

[4] CAB, *Handbook of Airline Statistics, 1969 Edition*, p. 93.

One case study, included as Appendix A, documented the effort by American Airlines to implement its "selective marketing strategy" whereby a combination of field selling supported by a national marketing group focused on specific potentially profitable air freight commodities. In the case it was noted that TWA preferred to decentralize its staff support by using "regional engineers" to back up the field sales effort. An international carrier went so far as to provide computerized analysis of total logistics costs for prospective shippers.

Another way of describing the marketing strategy inputs is to analyze actual expenses on the assumption that they reflect budgeting decisions. For example, difference in advertising expense versus personal selling expense per available ton-mile would give clues as to the relative weights put on each by management. Analysis of the advertising, publicity, reservation, and sales accounts for freighter operations, during the period studied, revealed some rather surprising facts.

(1) In terms of percentage of total expenses, TWA and Flying Tiger tended to devote a higher proportion of its resources to reservations and sales (R&S) and advertising and publicity (A&P) as compared with United and American (Appendix C, Table C-10). Flying Tiger's performance can be explained in part because it was the only all-cargo carrier in the group. It could not benefit from passenger-oriented sales and promotional programs. TWA's experience—almost 8% of its expenses accounted for by R&S + A&P—may have reflected its relatively low scale of operation by comparison with American and United. Thus, if sales and promotion required a threshold level of costs, a carrier with relatively low traffic would tend to have a higher percentage of expenses devoted to R&S + A&P than a carrier with heavy traffic. Yet, if one compares American's 1965 with TWA's 1967 capacity figures (essentially the same level of operations in both years), TWA's percentage of R&S + A&P expense is still 2.8 times greater than American's.

(2) A further indication of TWA's relatively high commitment to marketing expenses is the fact that in terms of absolute dollars TWA actually outspent American and United in all but one year even though its capacity and traffic were significantly less. For example, in 1969, TWA spent $2.8 million on the combined R&S + A&P domestic freighter accounts versus American's $1.8 million, even though American's traffic was almost double TWA's and its revenue was more than 50% greater.

(3) If we examine costs per available ton-mile as another measure of marketing commitment on the assumption that as capacity increased, budgeted marketing expenses might also increase in some predetermined proportion, we again find TWA and Flying Tiger's reservations and sales costs more than double those of American's and United's. But advertising and publicity expenses per available ton-mile are quite similar for United, TWA, and Flying Tiger—all being approximately four times higher than American. Total marketing expenses per ATM for TWA and Flying Tiger on the average during the five-year period were about 75% greater than United and more than triple that of American.

(4) Even though the absolute dollar amounts devoted to marketing were low—no carrier spent more than $4 million for freighter marketing in 1969—Flying Tiger and TWA tended to commit relatively larger proportions of their resources to marketing. The fact that American and United spent less than 5% of their op-

erating expenses on marketing is also significant when it is noted that almost 12% of the total expenses of the domestic trunk carriers in 1970 were devoted to reservations and sales.

Of course, one can argue that the greater emphasis on passenger marketing reflects the competitive struggle to stimulate and accommodate primary and selective demand. Yet, the marketing task for air freight carriers is not inconsequential, particularly if it is hoped to attract "surface divertible" traffic. As mentioned previously, a more sophisticated industrial marketing strategy is called for, and marketing costs as a percentage of total costs could well increase.

Traffic Servicing and Terminal Strategy

Terminal expenses represent approximately 20% to 25% of the cost of air freighter operations, thus it would be useful to compare major differences in the way that the carriers planned and implemented terminal strategies. With the exception of scattered bits of research, terminal strategy is not well documented. An analysis of terminal strategies would include data on capital and labor productivity ratios, the degree of mechanization, the characteristics of the traffic at classes of terminals, the extent of shipper tendered containers, and freighter schedules.

Again, the percentage of traffic servicing expenses to total operating expenses serves as a rough proxy for the importance of terminal commitment in the overall air freight strategy. This percentage was similar for the combination carriers during most of the study years. Flying Tiger, however, exhibited lower percentages than the combination carriers in four of the five years.

Another measure of terminal commitment is the ratio of investment in ground property and equipment per available ton-mile. As of 1969, the ratios for the study carriers were as follows: American 6.85×10^{-3}, United 11.33×10^{-3}, TWA 13.094×10^{-3}, and Flying Tiger 6.91×10^{-3}. United's relatively high figure may reflect the breadth of its freighter service, whereas TWA's ratio indicates that its level of investment in ground facilities was high relative to its commitment to freighter operations.

Summary

Thus, the survey of carriers' inputs reveals that management had a remarkable degree of discretion and exercised it. There were major differences in capacity, percentage of cargo carried on freighters, equipment, scheduling, pricing, and, to a lesser extent, "other" marketing expenditures.

United stands out as the carrier which changed its inputs significantly during the period as it pursued a strategy of expanding capacity heavily, serving many markets, and scheduling flights at prime departure hours, yet carrying traffic at relatively high yields per revenue ton-mile.

Flying Tiger, on the other hand, refused to allocate substantial amounts of capacity to domestic service and maintained a policy of "selective competition" in a few major markets, but did maintain significantly lower prices during the period.

American began the study period as the undisputed leader in terms of traffic and capacity linked with a policy of lower yields as compared with TWA and United. Yet, by the end of the five years, it found itself challenged severely by United.

TWA remained consistently weak in terms of capacity and commitment to air freight, except ironically in the percentage of expenses devoted to reservations, sales, advertising, and publicity.

The purpose of the next section of this chapter is to examine the results of these different strategies and to link the outputs with the aforementioned inputs.

The Outputs of Management Strategy

The analysis of the results of the management strategies will be presented in two stages. The first will be an overview using rank order analysis of the five-year performance as a whole. Rank order analysis will also be used to spotlight the trends in relative performances.

The second stage will be to examine the three basic outputs: (a) traffic and share of the market, (b) operating efficiency, and (c) financial performance in detail. This will involve analysis of year-to-year changes in input and output data, interpretation of two dimensional graphs showing key inputs and outputs, and the use of multiple regression analysis to determine functional relationships.

The Results of Rank Order Analysis

Table 3.22 displays the ranking of the unweighted average values of the basic input and output data for the four study carriers over the five-year period. An exception to the unweighted ranking was used in the reporting of profit before taxes. The ranking reflects the absolute total profit during the five years.

On the basis of output measures, American clearly emerged as the leader. Even though its prices were relatively low, its high capacity and traffic, above average load factor, and low operating expenses per available ton-mile combined to yield the best operating ratio and profit performance.

Flying Tiger's policy of diverting its capacity from scheduled to charter operations meant that its share of scheduled traffic was relatively low. Low operating expenses and high load factors, combined with very low prices, enabled it to move into the number two profit position.

United's aggressiveness in capacity and relatively high prices were offset by relatively high operating expenses. In absolute terms it ranked third in profits.

TWA was the weakest of the study carriers. Despite its relatively strong commitments to publicity and sales, it refused to follow United's lead in challenging American's share of capacity. Its high operating costs plus poor load factors, combined with low traffic levels, left it with the worst profit performance.

TABLE 3.22
Ranking of Average Input Plus Output Data
Study Carriers, 1965–1969

| | RANK | | | |
	High Performance 1	Above Average Performance 2	Below Average Performance 3	Low Performance 4
INPUTS				
Share of Capacity	AAL	UAL	TWA	FTL
Capacity	AAL	UAL	TWA	FTL
Percent Freight on Freighters	FTL	AAL	UAL	TWA
Price (High rank = low price)	FTL	AAL	TWA	UAL
% Reservations & Sales	FTL	TWA	AAL	UAL
% Advertising & Promotion	FTL	TWA	AAL	UAL
% General & Administrative	FTL	TWA	UAL	AAL
% R & S + A & P	FTL	TWA	UAL	AAL
% R & S + A & P + G & A	FTL	TWA	UAL	AAL
OUTPUTS				
Share of Traffic	AAL	UAL	FTL	TWA
Traffic	AAL	UAL	FTL	TWA
Operating Expense/ATM	AAL	FTL	TWA	UAL
Load Factor	FTL	AAL	UAL	TWA
Operating Expense/RTM	FTL	AAL	UAL	TWA
Operating Ratio	AAL	UAL	FTL	TWA
Profit Before Tax	AAL	FTL	UAL	TWA

Tables 3.23 and 3.24 amplify the average five-year data by showing the ranking of the important inputs and outputs for each of the five years.

In terms of inputs, no carrier's rank changed by more than one level during the five-year period. The major shift involved United. It achieved number one rank in share of capacity and capacity by 1969, and simultaneously moved from fourth to third place in level of rates.

TABLE 3.23
Rank Order Analysis—Study Carriers
Scheduled Freighter Operations—Inputs
1965–1969

Management Inputs	1965	1966	1967	1968	1969
(1) Share of Market—Capacity					
American	1	1	1	1	2
United	2	2	2	2	1
TWA	4	4	3	3	3
Flying Tiger	3	3	4	4	4
(2) Capacity					
American	1	1	1	1	2
United	2	2	2	2	1
TWA	4	4	3	3	3
Flying Tiger	3	3	4	4	4
(3) Percent Freight on Freighters—Combination Carriers					
American	1	1	1	1	1
United	3	2	2	2	2
TWA	2	3	3	3	3
Flying Tiger	a	a	a	a	a
(4) Price—Yield per Revenue Ton-Mile					
American	2	2	2	2	2
United	4	4	4	3	3
TWA	3	3	3	4	4
Flying Tiger	1	1	1	1	1

a Flying Tiger's percent was always 100.

An analysis of the output trend rankings reveals a great deal more volatility. United, for example, began the period with the worst profit level of the four carriers. By 1968, it had moved to the number one profit position, but in 1969 it dropped back into a deficit number four position.

During this same period, United's ranking in terms of market share moved from number three to number one. It became the leader in share of revenue and improved its relative position in terms of operating expense per available ton-mile and load factor.

In contrast, American's position weakened somewhat. It slipped into the number two slots in terms of traffic and revenue market shares and profit before tax. Although it ranked first in operating expense per available ton-mile throughout the period, the combination of lower load factor and low prices prevented it from holding on to the number one profit position by the end of the period.

Flying Tiger's profits fluctuated. By the end of the period it exhibited the best profit performance, albeit the lowest of the deficits. Its consistently high load factors (even with stretched DC-8s in 1969) meant low operating expenses per revenue ton-mile. Unfortunately, its yields per revenue ton-mile were lower still and the results were deficits in 1967–1969.

TWA's only relative strength was in operating expenses per ATM, but its chronically low load factors made profits impossible.

The rank order analysis shows clearly that market and revenue shares were

TABLE 3.24
Rank Order Analysis—Study Carriers
Scheduled Freighter Operations—Outputs
1965–1969

System Outputs	1965	1966	1967	1968	1969
(1) Share of Market—Traffic					
American	1	1	1	1	2
United	3	3	2	2	1
TWA	4	4	4	4	4
Flying Tiger	2	2	3	3	3
(2) Share of Market—Revenue					
American	1	1	2	2	2
United	2	2	1	1	1
TWA	4	4	3	3	3
Flying Tiger	3	3	4	4	4
(3) Profit Before Tax					
American	1	1	1	2	2D
United	4D	3D	2	1	4D
TWA	3D	4D	4D	4D	3D
Flying Tiger	2	2	3D	3D	1D
(4) Traffic					
American	1	1	1	1	2
United	3	3	2	2	1
TWA	4	4	4	4	4
Flying Tiger	2	2	3	3	3
(5) Operating Expense/ATM					
American	2	1	1	1	1
United	4	4	4	3	3
TWA	3	3	2	2	4
Flying Tiger	1	2	3	4	2
(6) Load Factor					
American	2	3	3	3	3
United	3	2	2	2	2
TWA	4	4	4	4	4
Flying Tiger	1	1	1	1	1
(7) Operating Expense/RTM					
American	2	2	2	2	2
United	3	3	3	3	3
TWA	4	4	4	4	4
Flying Tiger	1	1	1	1	1

NOTE: D = Deficit.

correlated with shares of capacity. Explanations of profit, however, are more difficult. On the one hand, American and Flying Tiger used similar combinations of low prices and low operating costs which resulted in 1–2 profit rankings in most of the years. In contrast, United's strategy of pouring on capacity resulted in dramatic improvement in its profit position even though its operating expenses and prices were high—until 1969, that is—when as noted, it simultaneously achieved first place in traffic and dropped to last in profit before taxes.

A Word on Methodology

Although the rank order analysis permitted some generalizations as to the relationship between inputs and outputs, it would be useful to investigate the absolute values of the input and output data in order to understand the strategy of the study carriers more clearly.

The data base, as noted, was developed from reports filed with the CAB by carriers operating air freighter service. A major statistical problem arises from the fact that in a given year, four carriers accounted for approximately 80% to 90% of the air freighter activity. Thus, any attempt to use regression analysis to determine cross-sectional functional relationships would immediately encounter the problem of limited degrees of freedom.

Yet, regression analysis would be useful in determining functional relationships between inputs and outputs; for example, market shares of traffic versus capacity shares, costs as a function of capacity, etc.

In order to provide more observations for a statistical analysis, a combination of cross-section and time-series data was used. For each of the five years, 1965–1969, data for the four major study carriers—American, United, TWA, and Flying Tiger—plus a fifth category "other carriers" were arrayed. To reduce the impact of price changes, the dollar values were deflated by indices supplied by the Air Transport Association.[5] It should be noted that the deflators were based on total industry factor prices during the period, not air freighter factor prices. Nevertheless, the adjusted dollar values (in 1958 dollars) were considered a reasonable approximation of deflated factor costs necessary for a cross-section analysis.

The net result is that the statistical cross-section analysis is based on a maximum of 25 observations, four carriers, and the grouped "other carriers" for each of the five years.

Although the number of observations relieves the problems of degrees of freedom, the nature of the sample raises a host of questions about the validity of regression analysis. For example, is the cross-section analysis of time-series data legitimate or are the data points the results of shifting functions over time? Although much of the data reflect the cost and operating performance of jet equipment, there were also propeller and turbo-prop operations during the study

---

[5] See Table 3.3 for a comparison between the ATA index, the wholesale price index, and the GNP deflator.

period. A further question pertains to the nature of the functions. Could curves be better fitted to the data points?[6]

In the face of the rather formidable statistical problems, it was decided to take a relatively pragmatic approach, that is, focus on the most important inputs and outputs, plot the relationships, and use regression analysis in a descriptive rather than predictive sense to supplement the analysis of the graphs.

In several instances the analysis will focus on a sub-sample of 25 observations, for example the performance of American, United, and TWA alone. Regressions on so few data points would be meaningless, but visual examination of the graphs proves to be quite useful in explaining functional relationships.

Competitive Position and Traffic

Market Share and Capacity Share. Recent research has disclosed that the desire to achieve or protect market share has been a dominant factor in passenger airline management strategies.

In turn, passenger market shares in individual markets (usually two carrier) are related to shares of capacity through an "S" shaped function which tends to reward those who aggressively increase capacity, but penalizes those who follow a policy of maintaining relatively low shares of capacity. For example, a carrier increasing its capacity share from 40% to 60% might find its market share moving from 30% to 70%. It has been suggested that this quest for market share has given rise to the periods of overcapacity that have plagued the airline passenger sector in the past.[7]

Does the "S" curve phenomenon hold true in the air freight industry? Exhibit 3.1 implies not, for if the "S" curve existed, one would expect disproportionate increases in market share relative to capacity (i.e., a concave upward curve) in the range shown. A straight line fitted to the data had an R^2 of .8834 and the equation showed that for every 10% increase in capacity share there was a 9.5% increase in market share.

Deviations from the straight line can be explained largely in terms of the individual carriers. For example, it's clear that TWA's market share always lagged behind its capacity share, whereas Flying Tiger's market share exceeds its capacity share. The explanation of Flying Tiger's performance is relatively easy—its prices were significantly lower than the other carriers.

---

[6] For a detailed discussion of the problems of combining cross-section and time-series data in transportation economic studies see Planning Research Corporation. *Transoceanic Cargo Study—Forecasting Model and Data Base Vol. I,* prepared for the U.S. Department of Transportation (March 1971), pp. V97–V110.

[7] See N. N. Taneja, "Airline Competition Analysis," M.I.T. Flight Technology Laboratory *FTL Report R-68-2* (September 1968), as cited in William E. Fruhan, Jr., *The Fight for Competitive Advantage: A Study of the United States Domestic Trunk Air Carriers,* Division of Research, Graduate School of Business Administration, Harvard University, 1972.

EXHIBIT 3.1
U.S. DOMESTIC AIR FREIGHTER SERVICE
1965–1969
MARKET SHARES—CAPACITY VS. TRAFFIC
STUDY CARRIERS

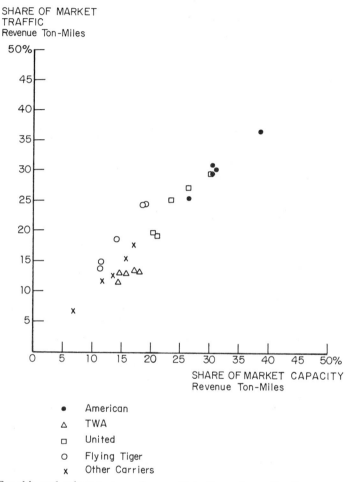

SHARE OF MARKET
TRAFFIC
Revenue Ton-Miles

SHARE OF MARKET CAPACITY
Revenue Ton-Miles

•   American
△   TWA
□   United
○   Flying Tiger
x   Other Carriers

SOURCE: For this and subsequent graphs, see Data Base, Appendix C.

TWA's performance is more difficult to explain. As noted earlier, TWA tried to schedule its limited capacity at prime hours and also spent relatively more money on the marketing function. On the other hand, it had the lowest management commitment to cargo in terms of percentage of traffic carried on freighters. Perhaps this lack of clear management commitment inhibited the marketing effort.

A modification of the regression equation cited above can be developed to take carrier effect into consideration. The regression model uses dummy carrier variables and explains more of the variability between the actual performance and the regression line.[8]

Equation Number 2 (Appendix E) shows the results of using dummy variables. By comparison with Equation Number 1 (Appendix E) the R^2 increases from 88.34 to 97.94, and the dummy variables have logical coefficients, that is, all other things being equal, TWA's market share is 3 points less than the regression line, whereas Flying Tiger's market share is 4 points greater than the regression line.[9]

In short, the statistical analysis indicates that regardless of what the carriers may have hypothesized as they made their capacity decisions, market shares were essentially proportional to capacity shares.

The same graphical and statistical approach can be used to explain share of the market in terms of revenue with capacity shares. Again, there appears to be a linear relationship overall (Exhibit 3.2) with American and Flying Tiger lagging because of their lower prices, and United benefitting from its higher prices. TWA still falls below the 45 degree line despite the fact that its prices were relatively high, testimony to its weak competitive position.

Absolute Traffic and Capacity. If market shares were proportional to capacity shares, it is not surprising to find that traffic levels were highly correlated with absolute levels of capacity, with the coefficient being the incremental load factor. In the cross-section static analysis, the incremental load factor coefficient was .4319 implying that for every increase of 100,000 available ton-miles, revenue ton-miles increased 43,190.[10]

Average system load factors declined for the individual study carriers during the period, partly because of the shift from smaller capacity propeller equipment to the jets, but also reflecting the fact that capacity increases exceeded traffic

[8] The equation with dummy variables takes the form of
$$Y = a + b(X_1) + c(X_2) + d(D_1) + e(D_2) \text{ etc.,}$$
where D_1, D_2 etc. have a value of either 1 or 0.
In effect, the dummy variables add a constant to the equation associated with the particular carrier represented by the dummy variable. This model has problems, however, for it assumes that the regression lines for each carrier have the same slope but different intercepts, that is a constant difference in performance. It is difficult to imagine a positive intercept in an equation linking traffic shares with capacity shares, for surely if capacity share were zero, there would be no market shares. The constant differences, therefore, exist within the range of the data points, and extrapolation in either direction would be hazardous.

[9] Unfortunately, the dummy variable coefficients display relatively high standard errors. It is also interesting to note that the SOM capacity coefficient changes in the dummy equation version. Now, share of the market in terms of traffic increases at a slightly faster rate than capacity share in the ranges studied. Yet, returns to capacity increases are still not significantly high.

[10] The R^2 was 92.83 and the standard error of estimate was 23.8 million revenue ton-miles. Thus, 95% of the time the results of the estimating equation applied to the 1965–1969 time period would be within 47 million of the actual freighter revenue ton-miles by carrier. The use of dummy variables (Equation Number 19—Appendix E) increased the R^2 to 98.32 and reduced the values of the coefficient and standard error. The constant differences in actual traffic from the regression line are reasonable, that is, TWA is weak and Flying Tiger is strong.

EXHIBIT 3.2
U.S. DOMESTIC AIR FREIGHTER SERVICE
1965–1969
MARKET SHARES—CAPACITY VS. REVENUE
STUDY CARRIERS

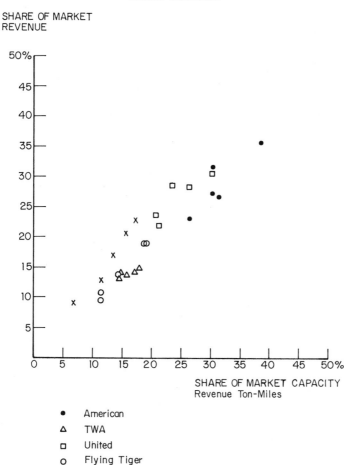

increases in most years. The overall pattern for the combined carriers excluding Flying Tiger's high load factors when it flew CL-44s is deceptively level, insofar as it balances the declines in American and United with the continually weak performance of TWA. The decline in individual carrier load factors, of course, contributed to the adverse economic performance of the carriers. (Exhibit 3.3)

Traffic, Price, and Capacity

If traffic appeared to be associated with capacity to a large degree, what about price? The literature has suggested that the price elasticity of demand for air

EXHIBIT 3.3
U.S. DOMESTIC AIR FREIGHTER SERVICE, 1965–1969
STUDY CARRIERS
RELATIONSHIP BETWEEN LOAD FACTOR AND CAPACITY

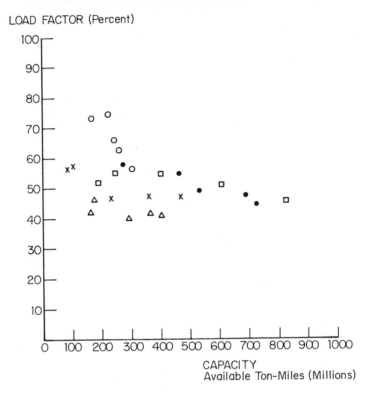

LOAD FACTOR (Percent)

CAPACITY
Available Ton-Miles (Millions)

- American
△ TWA
□ United
○ Flying Tiger
x Other Carriers

freight is very high, indeed one study implied that if rates reached the level of 6¢ per revenue ton-mile, the demand would be infinitely elastic. But there are strong differences of opinion.[11]

11 See Stanley H. Brewer, *The Complexities of Air Cargo Pricing* (Seattle, University of Washington Graduate School of Business Administration, 1967), p. 11 for the chart plotting traffic against cents per revenue ton-mile. At 6¢ the demand becomes infinitely elastic.

See, Lockheed-Georgia, Commercial Marketing Research Department CMRS 59, p. 3, for another study of air freight price elasticity. It concluded that the rate elasticity factor was 3.0, that is, for every 10% decline in rates there would be a 30% increase in traffic.

The CAB's level log forecasting equation including Gross National Product and price as

Simply plotting price versus traffic to determine price elasticity can be dangerous, for it ignores the capacity decision of the carriers. United's yield per revenue ton-mile was relatively high, yet its traffic increased substantially as it increased capacity.[12] Flying Tiger's prices were low, but its traffic reflected its low capacity.

Inasmuch as elasticity pertains to the percentage change in traffic versus a percentage change in price, the evidence on elasticity can best be summarized by a tabulation of percentage changes in capacity, price, and traffic for the study carriers. The deflator used for air freight prices was the wholesale price index rather than the ATA airline expense deflator, on the assumption that the real price changes should be stated in terms of prices experienced by air freight consumers.

As indicated in Table 3.25, dividing percentage changes in traffic by percentage changes in price alone would lead to extremely high elasticities in many cases. In addition, the change in response to price are not always consistent with theory. Thus, in 1967–1968 American's real prices went up slightly, but traffic increased at a substantial rate reflecting capacity increases.

In short, price appears to be important yet must be evaluated in conjunction with capacity responses. Changes in real GNP produce incremental potential traffic, and the airline capacity and price decisions determined the traffic. The evidence appears to indicate that capacity decisions outweighed price. In this case, a regression equation in the logarithmic form for the 25 observations yielded an R^2 of 18.32, when price was the sole independent variable. However, when capacity was added as an independent variable, the R^2 climbed to 93.44 (Equations Number 16 and 17—Appendix E).[13]

Thus, capacity increases appeared to be the most dynamic element affecting air freighter traffic during the period 1965–1969. The rank order and traffic analyses suggested that during "good times" benefits appeared to flow from capacity increases, but that capacity in and of itself might guarantee traffic, but not profits. The next section will investigate the subject of operating efficiency with particular attention focused on costs as a function of capacity.

independent variables implies a price elasticity of −1.54, that is, a 10% decline in rates will increase volume 15.4%. (See Irving Saginor and David B. Richards, *Forecast of Scheduled Domestic Air Cargo for the 50 States*, p. 11.)

On the other hand, a spokesman for Flying Tiger has claimed that 80% of the cargo market is *not* elastic with respect to price within plus or minus 30% of the given rates. (See Harold D. Watkins, "Airlines, CAB Grapple with Cargo Tariffs," p. 43.)

A further study which postulates that the demand for air freight is price inelastic within price ranges of ±10% is W. Bruce Allen and Leon N. Moses, "Choice of Mode in U.S. Overseas Trade: A Study of Air Cargo Demand," *Papers Ninth Annual Meeting, Transportation Research Forum* (Oxford, Indiana, 1968), pp. 235–248.

[12] Compare text, Chapter 3, Management Strategy of the Study Carriers, Pricing Policy. The higher yields reflected different mixes in traffic, stage lengths, and type of equipment flown.

[13] As indicated in the equations, the use of price alone resulted in an elasticity coefficient of −1.207. When capacity was included the elasticity coefficient became inelastic, namely, −.475.

TABLE 3.25
Percent Changes in Capacity, Price, and Traffic
1965–1969
Study Carriers

	Percent Change in Price (*1957–59 Dollars*)	Percent Change in Capacity	Percent Change in Traffic
American			
1965–66	−5.6	+65.3	+56.7
1966–67	−9.1	+17.1	+ 4.8
1967–68	+ .13	+29.3	+25.4
1968–69	−2.0	+ 3.7	− 3.6
United			
1965–66	+5.8	+27.4	+35.4
1966–67	−6.4	+64.7	+63.1
1967–68	−8.1	+49.1	+36.5
1968–69	−2.8	+37.2	+23.8
TWA			
1965–66	+ .4	+ 4.3	+15.1
1966–67	−6.9	+71.2	+47.4
1967–68	−2.8	+23.4	+22.9
1968–69	− .5	+11.6	+13.2
Flying Tiger			
1965–66	−1.1	+31.3	+33.1
1966–67	−4.1	+ 8.7	− 3.9
1967–68	−5.3	+ 6.9	+ 1.7
1968–69	−3.8	+17.6	+ 5.0

Operating Efficiency

Most of the economic literature has agreed with the proposition that there are few inherent economies of scale in the airline industry given a particular type of aircraft technology. Thus, the Department of Transportation included in its testimony before the Civil Aeronautics Board in 1970 the following:

> In summary, we may say that the results of our regression analysis indicate a tendency toward constant returns to scale (i.e., constant costs over the relevant range of service) when available ton-miles and market density are increased proportionately and increasing returns (i.e., falling average costs when expansion takes place over new routes). In both cases, however, the effect on average cost is barely perceptible, stage length being a much more important determinant of the level of average cost. For practical purposes then, we can conclude that the industry is characterized by constant returns to scale.[14]

The DOT's testimony raises a definitional question: What are returns to scale? Declining average costs may simply reflect the spreading of fixed costs over more

14 Testimony of James C. Miller III Before the Civil Aeronautics Board, Domestic Passenger Fare Investigation (Fare Level) Docket 21866-7 (August 25, 1970), p. 26.

activity units. Although this might be considered one definition of scale, a second test is more rigorous. It associates returns to scale with declining marginal costs in response to activity increases. The DOT tended to refer to average costs throughout its discussion of scale. Our analysis will look at the question from both points of view: How did average and marginal costs change for important components of air freight expenses?

Total Operating Expenses. Exhibit 3.4 shows total operating expenses in con-

EXHIBIT 3.4
U.S. DOMESTIC AIR FREIGHTER SERVICE, 1965–1969
STUDY CARRIERS
OPERATING EXPENSE DEFLATED VS. CAPACITY

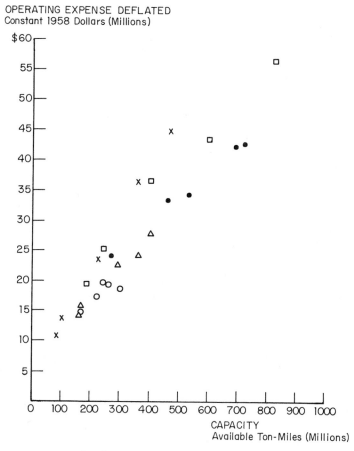

OPERATING EXPENSE DEFLATED
Constant 1958 Dollars (Millions)

CAPACITY
Available Ton-Miles (Millions)

- ● American
- □ United
- △ TWA
- ○ Flying Tiger
- x Other Carriers

stant 1958 dollars versus capacity for the period 1965–1969. A linear regression equation can be fitted to the data with fairly good results, namely, an R^2 of 87.3 and a standard error of $4.3 million. The intercept was $7.2 million, indicating on the basis of the 25 observations that fixed costs were $7.2 million and variable costs were 5.7¢ per available ton-mile within the activity range studied (Equation Number 5—Appendix E).

The implications of the equation are most interesting. Were it to go unchallenged it would indicate that average costs would decline as capacity increased to the extent that the fixed costs of $7.2 million were spread over the available ton-miles.

And, indeed, this appears to be true, for when average costs are plotted against capacity, there is a downward but bottoming-out drift in the function (Exhibit 3.5).

More important, the linear function in Equation Number 5 (Appendix E) also implies no economies of scale in the sense that marginal costs decline. By definition, marginal costs would equal the slope of the function, 5.7¢ per available ton-mile, at all capacity levels.

If, in fact, the functional relationship were as stated, the air freight industry could be characterized as one with relatively low threshold costs. For example, American Airlines' operating expenses at a scale of 724 million available ton-miles are reported as $42.9 million (constant 1958 dollars). If the intercept of $7.2 million is correct, only 17% of American's costs in 1969 would be considered fixed, with the rest being variable.

Perhaps this was indeed the case, yet if one looks at American's data points alone, the intercept appears to fall in the $10–$15 million range and its variable costs appeared to be approximately 4.5¢ per available ton-mile versus the general regression's 5.7¢.

Flying Tiger's total operating expenses followed the linear function with the exception of 1969's value. The introduction of the stretched DC-8 resulted in a shift in the total cost function.

TWA's costs followed the function well. There were no clear indications of economies of scale in the sense that marginal costs decline.

United, on the other hand, had fixed costs in the $10–$15 million range with variable costs of approximately 5¢ per available ton-mile.

In summary, there was some evidence that fixed costs increased and marginal costs declined as capacity increased, particularly in the case of American. Yet, the economies of scale, if present, were certainly not overwhelming. The overall pattern of Exhibit 3.4 is distinctly linear. Thus, given the technology of the 707-DC-8 generation of aircraft, we tend to find relatively low threshold costs in the range of $7–$15 million (1958 dollars) with incremental costs in the range of 4.5¢–6.0¢ per ATM depending on the carrier.

Inasmuch as aircraft operating expenses (crew, fuel, maintenance, depreciation, and maintenance burden) comprise the largest portion of freighter direct plus indirect operating expenses, it is appropriate to ask the question of the extent to which operating efficiencies were achieved in aircraft operations.

EXHIBIT 3.5
U.S. Domestic Air Freighter Service, 1965–1969
Study Carriers
Relationship Between Operating Expense Per Available Ton-Mile
and Available Ton-Miles
(*Constant 1958 Dollars*)

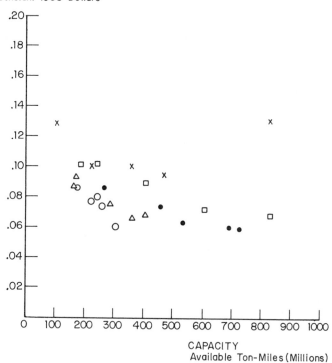

A simple tabulation of aircraft operating expenses per available ton-mile versus stage length by type of aircraft reveals some useful insights as to the economics of the industry and the importance of scheduling decisions on costs.

As indicated in Exhibits 3.6 and 3.7 the 727 QC and CL-44 were high-cost aircraft even though each was used in quite different markets. United was willing to accept the high operating costs in order to serve new short-haul markets. Flying Tiger operated the relatively expensive CL-44s over long-stage lengths and then leapfrogged to the stretched DC-8.

The data on 707 performance show rather dramatically declining operating

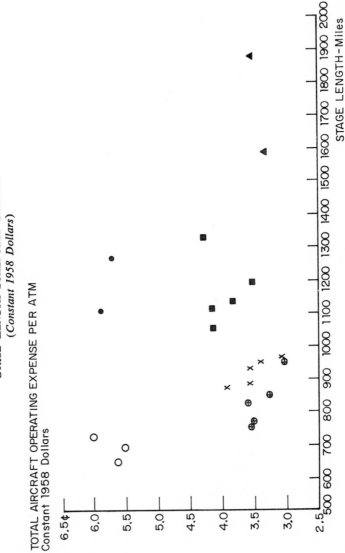

EXHIBIT 3.6

TOTAL AIRCRAFT OPERATING EXPENSES PER AVAILABLE TON-MILE VS.
STAGE LENGTH SCHEDULED SERVICE
(Constant 1958 Dollars)

TOTAL AIRCRAFT OPERATING EXPENSE PER ATM
Constant 1958 Dollars

STAGE LENGTH–Miles

x   707 American
⊕   707 TWA
■   DC8 United
◄   DC-8-63F Flying Tiger
●   CL-44 Flying Tiger
○   727 QC United

EXHIBIT 3.7

TOTAL AIRCRAFT OPERATING EXPENSES PER AVAILABLE TON-MILE VS.
STAGE LENGTH SCHEDULED SERVICE

(*Actual Dollars*)

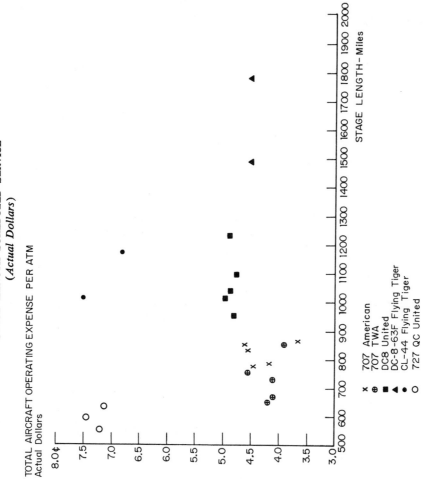

TOTAL AIRCRAFT OPERATING EXPENSE PER ATM

TOTAL AIRCRAFT OPERATING EXPENSE PER ATM
Actual Dollars

STAGE LENGTH—Miles

x   707 American
⊕   707 TWA
■   DC8 United
◄   DC-8-63F Flying Tiger
●   CL-44 Flying Tiger
○   727 QC United

costs per ATM as stage length increased. TWA's costs were even lower than American's, but its very low load factors, as noted, eliminated its competitive cost advantage.

United's DC-8s operated over longer stage lengths, but did not produce lower costs. Essentially the cost function shifted in response to change in aircraft type and company.

Flying Tiger's stretched DC-8s flew very long-stage lengths, but were unable to lower available ton-mile costs on a deflated dollar basis appreciably as reported to the CAB. This fact is somewhat surprising in view of the physical capability of the aircraft to produce lower ton-mile costs, but, as indicated previously in Table 2.16, crossovers between stretched DC-8s and 707s could occur depending upon specific carrier operating environments.

Looked at as a whole, the industry does not seem to have reduced aircraft operating expenses in response to changes in stage length but, in individual companies, economies of scale as a function of stage length do appear.

Flight Operations. One major explanation for the apparent linear relationship between operating expenses and available ton-miles is seen in Exhibit 3.8 which compares flying operations expense with capacity.

In view of the different types of aircraft represented during the period, the failure of curve to be convex upward indicates that flight crews have succeeded in gaining the lion's share of productivity increases stemming from larger and faster aircraft. A possible exception is revealed in the American data which can be interpreted as flattening out in response to capacity increases.

Traffic Service. A major opportunity for the industry to benefit from capacity increases and volume lies in the traffic service function, which includes the bulk of the terminal charges. Unit declines in terminal costs are assured as the size of the shipment increases, the ultimate saving being realized when loose packages are tendered in containers. As indicated previously, relatively few shippers tender containers, thus major cost reductions have not been achieved through this route. And, there has been some questioning of the worth of automated terminals for handling loose packages.

Nevertheless, as the industry has grown and increased its capacity, traffic service expenses on a deflated basis have shown a quite different pattern from that of flight operations. As indicated in Exhibit 3.9, there appears to have been an "S" shaped cost curve within the range of data collected.

When average traffic costs per available ton-mile are plotted against capacity, the downward slope is more pronounced than that for average operating expenses per ATM versus capacity. For individual carriers such as American and United, the reduction in constant dollars ranged from 31% to 60% (Exhibit 3.10).

Thus, there is definite evidence of economies of scale in the traffic service category on the basis of the admittedly "soft" data. The ability of the air freight industry to continue to improve its competitive position will depend in large measure on further reductions in "real" traffic service costs.

Marketing Expenses. As one moves from an analysis of flying operations through

EXHIBIT 3.8
U.S. Domestic Air Freighter Service, 1965–1969
Study Carriers
Flying Operations (Deflated) Vs. Capacity

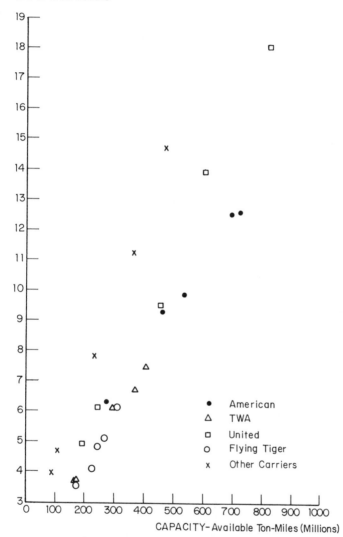

traffic service expenses to marketing, the relationships between the expense account and scale of operation (in terms of available ton-miles) become much less
clear. Earlier we noted that the major carriers (American and United) spent
relatively less of their total budget on marketing than the weaker carriers. Thus,
it is not surprising to find that if marketing expenses (advertising plus publicity

EXHIBIT 3.9
U.S. DOMESTIC AIR FREIGHTER SERVICE, 1965–1969
STUDY CARRIERS
TRAFFIC SERVICE EXPENSE (DEFLATED) VS. CAPACITY

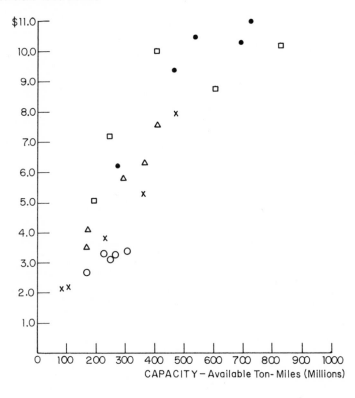

TRAFFIC SERVICE EXPENSE DEFLATED
Constant 1958 Dollars

•	American
□	United
△	TWA
○	Flying Tiger
x	Other Carriers

plus reservations plus sales) are plotted against capacity, two patterns emerge. TWA, Flying Tiger, and the "other carriers" increased marketing expenses sharply in response to changes in capacity, whereas in the cases of American and United, the function shifted to the right. American's conservative strategy is confirmed by the graph. United becomes quite bullish as it pours on the capacity. Extrapolation from this graph would be at one's peril! (Exhibit 3.11.)

Year-to-Year Changes in Operating Expenses. The analysis of operating expenses to this point has concentrated on relationships of absolute and average data

EXHIBIT 3.10
U.S. DOMESTIC AIR FREIGHTER SERVICE, 1965–1969
STUDY CARRIERS
TRAFFIC SERVICE EXPENSE PER ATM VS. CAPACITY

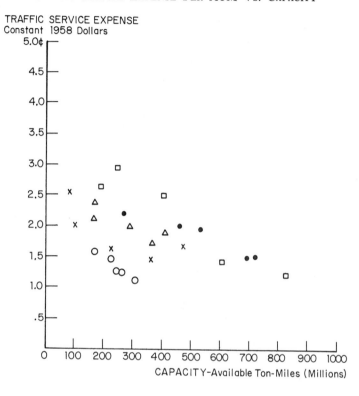

NOTE: Traffic Service Expense is cents per Available Ton-Mile.

to absolute levels of capacity. Yet, managers developing operating budgets and monitoring performance, more often face the problems of differential or percentage changes. For example, if capacity is increased by 10%, what is likely to happen to the flight operations account, maintenance, marketing, etc.?

Although we could perform a regression analysis in terms of differences rather than absolute values, it is more useful to simply look at the percentage changes in the individual accounts by carrier and attempt some generalizations. Tables 3.26 through 3.29 take the basic data from Appendix C and display ratios of percentage changes in operating revenue and selected operating expense accounts versus per-

EXHIBIT 3.11
U.S. DOMESTIC AIR FREIGHTER SERVICE, 1965–1969
STUDY CARRIERS

Advertising and Publicity Plus Reservations and Sales Expense Vs. Capacity

(*Constant 1958 Dollars*)

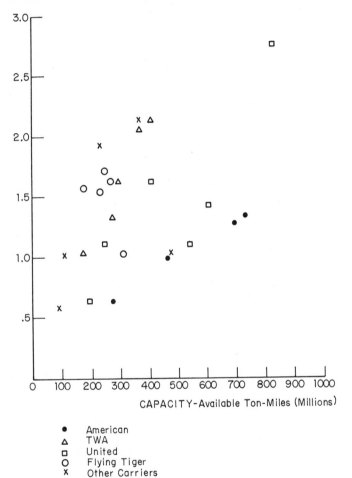

centage changes in capacity, in effect a kind of capacity elasticity measure on a year-to-year basis.

Upon analyzing these tables one is immediately struck by the volatility in the year-to-year data induced by a variety of factors including wage agreements, introduction of new equipment, strikes at United and TWA during 1966, and American during 1969, etc. One looks in vain for the patterns found on the

TABLE 3.26

Relationship Between Percentage Changes
in Operating Revenue, Selected Operating Expenses,
and Changes in Available Ton-Miles
1965–1966

△%Capacity	American 65.3%	United 27.4%	TWA 4.3%	Flying Tiger 31.3%
△%Fly.Op./△%Cap.	.767	.982	.674	.604
△%Maint./△%Cap.	.228	.412	4.279	.470
△%Tfc. Svce./△%Cap.	.848	1.693	4.698	.882
△% Res. & Sales/△% Cap.	1.003	2.409	8.883	−.054
△%Adv. & Pub./△%Cap.	.599	3.150	6.884	.137
△%Total Oper. Exp./△%Cap.	.652	1.120	3.418	.665
△%Oper. Rev./△%Cap.	.808	1.75	4.511	1.15

TABLE 3.27

Relationship Between Percentage Changes
in Operating Revenue, Selected Operating Expenses,
and Changes in Available Ton-Miles
1966–1967

△%Capacity	American 17.1%	United 64.7%	TWA 71.2%	Flying Tiger 8.7%
△%Fly.Op./△%Cap.	.456	.899	.956	2.34
△%Maint./△%Cap.	−1.39	.580	.021	3.25
△%Tfc. Svce./△%Cap.	.818	.658	.617	−.517
△% Res. & Sls./△% Cap.	.918	.802	.417	.184
△%Adv. & Pub./△%Cap.	.526	.768	.233	5.29
△%Total Oper. Exp./△%Cap.	.239	.739	.596	1.71
△%Oper. Rev./△%Cap.	.263	.818	.528	−.874

NOTE: In 1966 TWA and United suffered a 43-day strike.

TABLE 3.28

Relationship Between Percentage Changes
in Operating Revenue, Selected Operating Expenses,
and Changes in Available Ton-Miles
1967–1968

△%Capacity	American 29.3%	United 49.1%	TWA 23.4%	Flying Tiger 6.9%
△%Fly.Op./△%Cap.	1.26	1.14	.808	1.86
△%Maint./△%Cap.	2.21	.507	.350	−.493
△%Tfc. Svce./△%Cap.	.191	−.163	.675	1.78
△% Res. & Sls./△% Cap.	.352	.399	1.68	.869
△%Adv. & Pub./△%Cap.	2.26	−.519	.94	−.957
△%Total Oper. Exp./△%Cap.	1.10	.560	.688	.841
△%Oper. Rev./△%Cap.	.983	.519	.962	−.174

TABLE 3.29

Relationship Between Percentage Changes
in Operating Revenue, Selected Operating Expenses,
and Changes in Available Ton-Miles
1968–1969

△%Capacity	American 3.7%	United 37.2%	TWA 11.6%	Flying Tiger 17.6%
△%Fly.Op./△%Cap.	1.70	1.06	1.55	1.57
△%Maint./△%Cap.	2.00	.925	3.52	−1.57
△%Tfc. Svce./△%Cap.	3.43	.653	2.54	.653
△% Res. & Sales/△% Cap.	3.59	4.83	.922	−1.27
△%Adv. & Pub./△%Cap.	2.78	.288	.914	−3.10
△%Total Oper. Exp./△%Cap.	2.16	1.02	1.93	.107
△%Oper. Rev./△%Cap.	−.541	.669	1.47	.284

NOTE: In 1969 American suffered a 20-day strike.

graphs comparing absolute values of operating expenses or flight operating expenses or flight operating expenses in deflated dollars versus available ton-miles.

On the other hand, useful generalizations can be made. In 1966 and 1967 the changes in flying operations expenses tended to lag behind percentage changes in capacity, yet in 1968 and 1969 the reverse became true as wage increases took effect.

Changes in maintenance expenditures bore almost no relationship to capacity changes. In most years, increases in maintenance expenses lagged far behind changes in capacity, but there were sharp exceptions, for example, TWA in 1966, Flying Tiger in 1967, American in 1968, and American and TWA in 1969.

Between 1966 and 1968, traffic service percentage changes in expenses almost always lagged significantly behind percentage changes in capacity, but in 1969 increased wages, and American's strike perhaps decreased productivity and resulted in major increases for American and United.

Marketing expenses gyrated wildly. In 1966 they tended to exceed capacity increases, but in 1967 and 1968 they lagged behind. Between 1968 and 1969, however, they climbed sharply with the exception of Flying Tiger, which we may assume had embarked upon a budget-cutting campaign to control deficits.

Overall total operating expenses tended to lag behind percentage increases in capacity during 1966–1968, but for all carriers except Flying Tiger capacity increases proved disastrous in 1969.

A final statistic of interest concerns the percentage changes in operating revenue in response to capacity changes. The operating revenue reflects two factors: change in price and change in volume. Between 1965 and 1966 percentage changes in operating revenue tended to equal or exceed percentage increases in capacity. But, with few exceptions during the remaining years, percentage changes in revenue failed to equal percentage changes in capacity. Clearly, the industry was caught in a price-cost squeeze, the implications of which will be examined in more detail in the following section.

Financial Performance

In early 1968 Lockheed-Georgia published a report entitled *Air Cargo Profitability Study 1957–1966* which contained the following somewhat guarded conclusions:[15]

> Although no effort is made to conclude that profitability from the cargo service is higher than from the passenger service our evidence does indicate that those airlines that have expended substantial effort for the development of the air cargo market have enjoyed increased cargo revenues and, proportionately, increased profits.
>
> * * * * *
>
> Since we do not have cost allocation data we have been unable to determine accurately the relative profitability of the passenger service and the cargo service. Nevertheless, the airline groups which have taken the lead in the development of the cargo market through use of large turbine aircraft in the scheduled all-cargo service have experienced the highest profitability of our three groups during the past three years. The Top Four Airlines after adjustments to compensate for adverse changes in the passenger market, have shown higher profitability than the Other Airlines.
>
> In summation, it appears that the airline which neglects to develop its air cargo business is missing a highly profitable source of revenues.

Our analysis leads to opposite conclusions, for, in domestic-scheduled freighter service, the rewards for increased investment during the period 1965–1969 were minimal or nonexistent profits. During the five years, American was the only one of the four study carriers to show a cumulative freighter profit before tax, $3.0 million on an investment of $104 million, as of 1969 (Table 3.30). United and Flying Tiger suffered cumulative deficits in the $4 million to the $7 million range, whereas Trans World lost $18.5 million on its domestic freighter service.[16]

These statistics are even more discouraging when it is recognized that operating profits or losses of freighter service do not include interest charges on the investment. They do, however, include depreciation.

It is important to recognize that the profitability figures for the combination carriers reflect allocated costs between belly freight and freighter operations. Flying Tiger's domestic freighter profits are likewise affected by the difficulty in separating common costs incurred in charter and domestic scheduled freighter services. Thus, there are undoubtedly differences of opinion within the airline community as to the actual level of freighter profits or losses.

Yet, these are the only published data, and if public policy decisions are to be made on the basis of reported freighter profits or losses, these data will be the ones utilized.

---

[15] E. W. Eckard, *Air Cargo Profitability Study 1957–1966*, CMRS 93 (Marietta, Lockheed-Georgia Commercial Marketing Research Department, 1968), pp. 1, 31.

[16] In 1970 freighter losses increased still further. The domestic trunk and all-cargo carriers suffered an operating loss before taxes for the year ending December 31 of $45.2 million, compared to $27.6 million in 1969. Losses before taxes for the individual study carriers were: American $6.6 million, TWA $7.7 million, United $19.8 million, and Flying Tiger $1.7 million

TABLE 3.30

Cumulative Profits Before Tax, 1965–1969,

and Investment in Air Freighter Operations, 1969

Study Carriers

	Air Freighter Operations Cumulative Profits Before Tax 1965–69 *(Millions of Dollars)*	Net Investment in Scheduled Air Freighter Operations 1969 *(Millions of Dollars)*
American	$3.022	$104.4
United	−6.981	142.2
TWA	−18.530	54.7
Flying Tiger	−4.679	54.8

NOTE: Net Investment includes working capital, flight and ground equipment, investments and special funds, long-term prepayments, developmental and pre-operating costs, and unamortized discount and expense on debt.

SOURCE: CAB.

Clearly, it is to the advantage of airlines and regulators alike to have more accurate data on profits. But, said one official of a major airline: "No one has been able to calculate the overall profitability of air freight. If you asked 200 accountants, you'd get 200 answers."[17]

A second approach to the analysis of profitability is to note its volatility in response to changes in capacity, traffic, revenue, and expenses. Table 3.31 shows these data for each of the study carriers during each of the years 1966–1969 in terms of percentage change in profits versus percentage change in capacity, traffic, etc.

In seven of the sixteen observations, changes in operating revenue lagged behind changes in traffic. In seven instances the percentage change in operating revenue exceeded the percentage changes in traffic, yet somewhat surprisingly, an "operative revenue-traffic elasticity" greater than 1.0 did not always mean an increase in profits. For example, in 1969 United's traffic increased 24% and its operative revenue increased 25%, yet its profit plummeted by $7 million.

When percentage changes in operating expenses exceeded percentage changes in capacity, the results usually were sharp drops in profits. But not always. In 1966 United reduced its deficit sharply even though its operating expenses increased at a faster rate than capacity, for its revenue increases were even more spectacular.

In short, the carriers were subject to extreme changes in profits resulting from relatively small changes in the differences in the rates of change between capacity, traffic, revenue, and expense.

Profitability could not be correlated with capacity, that is, those who pursued a vigorous policy of capacity expansion were subject to the same financial uncer-

[17] Richard P. Cooke, "Passenger Airlines' All-Cargo Operations Result in Drag on Profit, Reports Show," *The Wall Street Journal*, April 15, 1968, p. 3.

TABLE 3.31

Selected Operating and Financial Statistics—Study Carriers
Percentage Change from Previous Year and Impact on Profits
Scheduled All-Cargo Service, 1966–1969

(All changes are positive except where indicated)

Carrier & Year		Capacity	Traffic	Operating Revenue	Operating Expenses	Profit Before Tax	Absolute Change Profit Before Tax ($ Millions)
American	1966	+65%	+57%	+53%	+43%	+251%	+3.5
	1967	17	5	− 5	4	− 73	−3.6
	1968	29	25	29	32	− 75	−1.1
	1969	4	− 4	− 2	4	NM	−5.3
United	1966	+27%	+35%	+48%	+31%	NM	+2.6
	1967	65	63	53	48	NM	+1.4
	1968	49	37	25	28	− 41	− .5
	1969	37	24	25	38	NM	−7.0
Trans World	1966	+ 4%	+15%	+19%	+15%	NM	+ .3
	1967	71	47	38	42	NM	−1.8
	1968	23	23	23	16	NM	+ .7
	1969	12	13	17	22	NM	−2.7
Flying Tiger	1966	+31%	+33%	+36%	+21%	+763%	+2.6
	1967	9	− 4	− 8	15	NM	−4.8
	1968	7	2	− 1	6	NM	−1.6
	1969	18	5	5	2	NM	+ .6

NOTES: All percentages are rounded to the nearest percent.
American strike 27 Feb.-19 March 1969.
TWA and United on strike 43 days in 1966.
NM = Not Meaningful.
SOURCE: Data Base, Appendix C.

tainties as those who were more conservative. In terms of deflated 1958 dollars (Exhibit 3.12) American's profits seemed to fall as its capacity increased. For the remaining airlines, the pattern was extremely mixed and generalizations are impossible. In any event, there was certainly no evidence that increases in freighter capacity were associated with increases in profits.

Throughout the study we have focused on percentage of cargo carried on freighters as an indication of management commitment. To what extent was this statistic associated with profits? Here, the evidence is somewhat more intriguing. If we eliminate Flying Tiger on the grounds that the basic nature of its business required it to focus on cargo, we find that profitability tended to follow commitment most of the time. For example, as United increased its commitment, its deficits decreased, then became profits. TWA with its low commitment, never

EXHIBIT 3.12
U.S. DOMESTIC AIR FREIGHTER SERVICE, 1965–1969
STUDY CARRIERS
PROFIT BEFORE TAX (DEFLATED) VS. CAPACITY

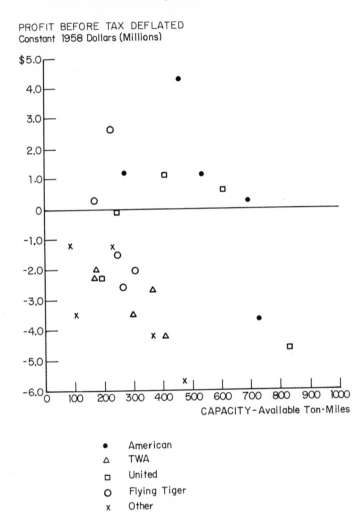

moved into the black. American, with its high percentage of cargo carried on freighters was profitable four of the five years. Yet, commitment alone could not save United and American from the harsh economic penalties suffered in 1969 (Exhibit 3.13).

A further important financial statistic is the operating ratio; calculated by dividing operating expenses before interest and taxes by operating revenue. The advantage of utilizing the operating ratio for financial analysis is the absence of negative numbers. On the other hand, the operating ratio obscures the magnitude

EXHIBIT 3.13
U.S. Domestic Air Freighter Service, 1965–1969
Study Carriers
Profit Before Tax (Deflated) Vs. Percent Freighter

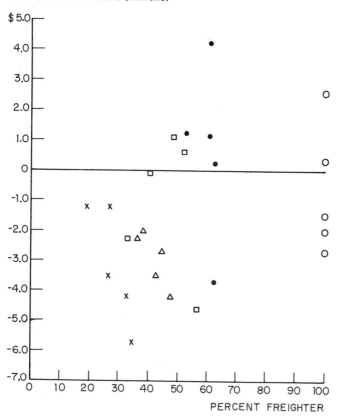

of the data being studied. A carrier with $100 million in operating revenue and $90 million in expenses would show the same operating ratio as a $10 million revenue carrier with $9 million in expenses.

As indicated in Appendix Table C.1, air freighter service tended to display high operating ratios throughout the five-year period. If we compare the air freighter operating ratios with those of railroads and motor carriers we find that they are more similar to the motor carriers, that is, they tend to fall in the range of 90 or above (Table 3.32).

When operating ratio is plotted against capacity, there appears to be evidence that the ratio falls (improves) as capacity increases. But, the profit margin remains extremely thin, and when the ratio climbs above 100 at high levels of capacity the results as experienced by United and American in 1969 are extremely disheartening (Exhibit 3.14).

An operating ratio is a financial measure that cannot be viewed in isolation if one wants to obtain a true picture of the profitability of the enterprise. For example, trucking companies with operating ratios of 95.0 earn quite respectable

EXHIBIT 3.14
U.S. Domestic Air Freighter Service, 1965–1969
Study Carriers
Operating Ratio Vs. Capacity

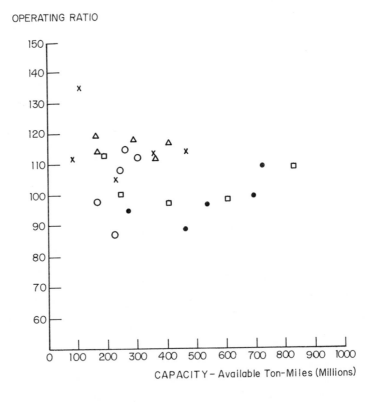

OPERATING RATIO

CAPACITY – Available Ton-Miles (Millions)

●   American
△   TWA
□   United
○   Flying Tiger
x   Other Carriers

TABLE 3.32
Comparative Operating Ratios
Rail—Truck—Air Freighter

(*SELECTED YEARS*)

	High Profit Year		Low Profit Year	
U.S. Railroads	.7618	(1966)	.8118	(1970)
Class I and II Motor Carrier	.947	(1965)	.962	(1970)
Air Freighter Operations:				
American Airlines	.8875	(1966)	1.095	(1969)
United Airlines	.970	(1967)	1.136	(1965)
Trans World	1.127	(1968)	1.196	(1965)
Flying Tiger	.871	(1966)	1.160	(1968)

NOTE: Operating Ratio = Operating Expense divided by Operating Revenue.
SOURCES: Association of American Railroads, *Yearbook of Railroad Facts & Figures, 1971;* American Trucking Association, *American Trucking Trends, 1970–71;* Appendix Table C.1 for Air Freighter Operating Ratios.

returns on equity or investment, whereas railroads with operating ratios in the 80–85 range find that their return on investment is pitifully small.

The reason is a second factor, capital productivity, that is, the relationship between revenue and investment. If capital productivity is high, a dollar of investment generates $2.00, $3.00, or even $4.00 of revenue. Under such conditions, 5% profit margin before interest and taxes (i.e., an operating ratio of 95.0) in effect generates returns on investment before interest and taxes of from 10% to 20%.

But, if capital productivity is low, the operating ratio must be extremely low in order to generate an adequate return on investment.

TABLE 3.33
Comparative Capital Productivity
Truck, Rail, Domestic Air Freighter Service
1969

	Operating Revenue	Net Investment in Operating Property	Ratio Revenue to Net Investment in Operating Property
	(*In Billions of Dollars*)		
Class I & II Truck	$ 7.339	$ 1.670	4.39
Class I Rail	11.451	27.734	.413
American Airlines	.053	.098	.541
TWA	.032	.045	.711
United	.070	.114	.614
Flying Tiger	.022	.043	.512

SOURCES: American Trucking Association, *Trucking Trends; The American Railroad Industry, A Prospectus* (ASTRO), 1970; CAB, Form 242.

Table 3.33 compares the capital productivity of railroads, motor carriers, and the study air freight carriers. The evidence is unmistakable. The airlines operating air freighter service had relatively poor capital productivity, that is, a dollar in net operating property generated less than a dollar in revenue in all cases.

The implications of the above observations are startling to say the least, for during the period 1965–1969 air freighter service displayed the *operating ratio of the motor carriers yet the capital productivity approaching that of the railroads.*

SUMMARY

The first objective of this study is to analyze management strategy during the high growth years 1965–1969 to determine (1) the degree to which different strategies were employed by the companies during this period, and (2) the success or failure of these strategies.

The findings can be summarized as follows:

(1) The four major carriers operating freighter equipment (American, United, Trans World, and Flying Tiger) competed in an environment of dramatic traffic growth utilizing quite different strategies in terms of pricing, scheduling, equipment selection, marketing budgets, etc.

(2) There was strong evidence that market shares were related to capacity shares, although in contrast to the passenger business, not disproportionately in the sense that increases in capacity would lead to even greater increases in market share.

(3) Overall operating expenses on a deflated basis climbed proportionately to increases in capacity. With the possible exception of traffic service expenses, there were no substantial indications of economies of scale, given the 707-DC-8 generation of flight equipment.

(4) Air freighter load factors on a weight basis normally were less than 50% during the period, therefore reported operating costs per revenue ton-mile were more than double the costs per available ton-mile.

(5) Insofar as average air freight traffic had densities lower than the design densities of the aircraft, the cube load factors were higher than weight load factors, but the problem of capacity utilization persisted and even worsened as weight load factors declined.

(6) Freighter financial performance for each of the carriers during this period of growth was poor, despite differences in strategy. Air freighters exhibited the low capital productivity of the railroads and the high operating ratio of the trucking industry.

How could management continue to make substantial investments in the face of such unappealing economics? Was it in effect following a "buy in" strategy so as to achieve strong market shares before the introduction of the jumbo jet aircraft and, further, hoping that the jumbo jets would generate the adequate return on investment so conspicuous by its absence in the history of the industry?

Perhaps more important, what in fact will be the enivronment facing the air freight industry in the next decade? Will the economic payoff materialize? What are the implications for air freight managers and the other interest groups associated with or competing with the industry? The answers to these important questions will be the subject of the next chapter of this study.

Chapter 4

The Outlook for U.S. Domestic
Air Freight in the Coming Decade

THE SECOND OBJECTIVE OF THIS STUDY IS TO ANALYZE THE FUTURE environment of the U.S. domestic air freight industry and make recommendations which might be of use to airline managers and others as they plan their domestic air freight strategy for the coming decade.

The analysis of the environment includes: (a) a further look at the traffic potential for the industry, (b) a projection of comparative operating costs of air and surface modes for domestic shipments, and (c) the economics of investment in the next generation of freighter including questions of costs, pricing, industry structure, and intra-industry competition.

The conclusions and recommendations, which incorporate the findings of the historical analysis plus the analysis of the future environment, are reserved for the final chapter.

DOMESTIC AIR FREIGHT TRAFFIC POTENTIAL

During the 1960s, as noted in the beginning of this study, most of the air freight traffic forecasts featured dramatic growth rates in the range of 19%–25% per year during the period 1968–1980. The economic slowdown of 1970 and 1971 and its aftermath have produced significant revisions in the forecasts.

For example, in 1971 the CAB in its macro-economic forecasting study cited earlier projected domestic scheduled air freight plus express ton-mile growth rates ranging from 10.4% to 15.8% over the period 1971 to 1975.[1] The forecasts assumed a 4% rise in real GNP in each of the years. The differences in growth rates reflected air freight pricing policies.

---

[1] Saginor and Richards, *Forecast of Scheduled Domestic Air Cargo for the 50 States, 1971–1975*, p. 18.

The high forecast was based on a 1971 8% increase in the yield per revenue ton-mile and a decline in "real" air freight prices of 2% per annum in the years following. The low forecast projected that yields increase 12% in 1971 and 2% in current dollars per year thereafter. Inasmuch as the freight rates will depend upon the level of operating costs, a critical question is the future level of air freight operating costs. The freight rate projections were based on historical trends in "real" air freight prices. In turn, the reductions in "real" air freight prices followed from the introduction of more efficient jet equipment. Thus, the question becomes: Will in fact a new generation of air freighter equipment be put into operation with the capability of reducing "real" costs and "real" prices?

In addition to prices, the forecasting equations rely heavily on the level of the GNP and the relation between GNP and air freight traffic. We speculated earlier how long air freight would be able to grow at levels two and three times that of real GNP.

For the 12 months ending December 31, 1971, domestic air freight revenue ton-miles increased 1.6%, but real GNP climbed 2.7%. Thus, as the economy emerged slowly from the mini-recession of 1970–1971, air freight traffic lagged behind.[2]

Is domestic air freight entering a new phase of reduced growth, or will the growth surge reappear as the economy strengthens? Recently the manager of economic research for United Airlines addressed the question directly. He challenged the prevailing theory that air freight growth would exceed passenger growth. Indeed, he predicted that domestic air passenger travel would grow at an annual rate of 10% with cargo traffic lagging behind. His key point was that the conditions which gave rise to cargo growth during the period 1960–1970 would not be repeated during the 1970s. His reasons included:[3]

First, jet freighters provide a massive increase in speed and total capacity; much of the market growth domestically consisted of development of the fresh produce market as a backhaul load for jet freighters. Second, the Post Office put a great deal of nonpriority mail in the air. Third, the Viet Nam war was obviously a major stimulant which we hope is being phased out. I doubt that we will see significant new investments in more cargo airplanes because, so far, none of the past investments in cargo planes have paid off in commercial service. A few passenger planes might be converted to cargo use if the trade-offs are right.

About two-thirds of the air cargo consists of emergency shipments and much of the balance is perishables requiring speed. These markets are already well developed; penetration of other markets will require air freight to become cost competitive with surface freight; although this is a physical possibility within this decade, the risks may be so high that no one will really try to bring it off.

The remarks are of great interest for several reasons. The Postal Service is mentioned as a source of cargo traffic and, indeed, it is rumored that the Postal Service

---

[2] Transportation Association of America, Supplement, "What's Happening in Transportation: Transport Review for 1971," January 31, 1972, p. 2; and Council of Economic Advisors, *Economic Indicators*, February 1972.

[3] "Airline Economist Gloomy on Cargo Traffic Growth: Sees Passenger Upturn," *Traffic World* (June 21, 1971), p. 16.

may establish its own fleet of private freighter planes. Although this policy would not have a severe impact on freighter traffic, it would reduce total cargo revenue and further intensify the industry's financial plight.[4]

As we noted in the first section of this report, military traffic was of great importance to the all-cargo and supplemental carriers operating freight service. To the extent that the winding down of the Viet Nam war reduces direct and indirect (dependents' travel and shipments) traffic, the growth prospects of air cargo will be dampened.

His statement that most of air cargo is either what we termed earlier emergency or routine perishable traffic and that these markets are largely tapped has even greater implications. If true, this means that future growth must come from the routine surface divertible sector. Not only is it more difficult to "sell" this type of traffic, the trade-offs between service and costs are more complex. The ultimate ability of the air freight system to capture this traffic will depend upon the future costs of the surface versus the air system. These will be explored shortly.

Before turning to competitive costs, it is appropriate to spotlight an important research question stemming from the United prediction. Do we in fact know what proportion of air freight falls into the emergency, routine perishable, and routine surface divertible categories? Is emergency traffic really two-thirds of the current business? If so, the implications with respect to pricing are obvious, for emergency traffic by definition should exhibit low price elasticity.

The industry is embarking upon a major data gathering project which will attempt to display air freight traffic by routes, carriers, commodities, etc. Unless specific attention is paid to the three basic classifications, management will have a major gap in data necessary for planning.

Interestingly enough we can hypothesize that emergency and routine perishable shipments should increase faster than real GNP, in an increasingly affluent economy, in response to product proliferation and/or the demands for new services. If inflation is controlled and real GNP growth returns to the 4%–5% level the United forecast is unduly pessimistic.

Routine surface divertible traffic, on the other hand, affords an immense "one-shot" growth potential, but once tapped will increase more in line with surface transportation and the real GNP.

Thus, the traffic picture remains clouded. Most likely growth rates will remain in the 8%–12% range pending development of routine surface divertible traffic. This still places air freight in the category of a high growth industry, for the U.S. Department of Labor's tabulation of high growth industries through the 1970s includes annual output ranges between 5.9% and 10.2% per year.[5] In turn, the develop-

---

[4] See Boeing Study *Post Office Parcel Post System* (not dated, circa 1970) which recommends that the Post Office invest in a system of private 747s. Ironically, the study shows that most of the benefits could be achieved with 707s. For example, 707s could capture 92% of the transcontinental parcel mail traffic, with 747s handling 100%.

[5] U.S. Department of Labor, Bureau of Labor Statistics, *Patterns of U.S. Economic Growth,* Bulletin 1672 (1970), p. 44.

ment of routine surface divertible traffic requires a more detailed look at the comparative costs of the modes of transportation.

PROJECTIONS OF TRANSCONTINENTAL TRANSPORTATION COSTS

This section of the chapter will project transportation costs for the trucks, railroads, and airlines performing transcontinental freight service during the next decade. The objective is to get an idea of the cost relationships between the modes on the assumption that rates ultimately will reflect relative costs. This is but one part of a total cost analysis. Unfortunately, the costs on warehousing are extremely difficult to obtain and project, and these costs are important in determining total costs. Nevertheless, it is the author's opinion that the projections of transportation costs will provide useful insights as to the ultimate competitive position of air freight in the domestic transportation picture.

The basic approach in projecting costs was to focus on the line haul and terminal costs separately. The line haul costs were derived by identifying the basic unit of production if possible, that is, plane miles for air freight and truck miles for motor freight. Train-mile costs were not available in the form necessary for the analysis, so car-mile costs were utilized.

In each case, the line haul costs represented costs per available ton-mile. Thus, each of the carriers was analyzed on the basis of lowest potential costs. In effect, the costs are in terms of per revenue ton-mile assuming that 100% load factors (weight basis) are achieved. If a carrier had a poor load factor because of imbalanced traffic, weak sales efforts, poor scheduling, etc., the costs per revenue ton-mile would be higher than the costs per available ton-mile.

In addition, the costs per available ton-mile were reported on the bases of both weight and density, with the density basis reflecting the traffic typically being carried by the mode.

Rather than try to project point estimates of carrier costs in the decade ahead, a parametric approach was taken. Historical cost trends were analyzed, and future costs were projected on several assumptions: continuation of past trends, more likely increases in costs, and an upper limit based on competitive position, government policy, etc. The result is a band of possible costs rather than precise statements of costs. Thus, we can more easily answer questions of the form: "What if the railroads should hold their costs in line, but the trucking industry lets costs get out of hand?"

Projection of Line Haul Costs

Trucking. The projection starts from a historical analysis of line haul vehicle-mile out-of-pocket costs experienced by motor carriers in the Transcontinental Territory during the years 1963–1968. Line haul vehicle-mile costs should not be confused with the term "Transportation" costs as reported to the ICC. Line haul costs include labor, fuel, maintenance, depreciation, etc. The out-of-pocket expenses are based on 90% of the total operating expenses, rents, and taxes, excluding income taxes, but include a 5% allowance for return on depreciated investment.[6] Out-of-pocket costs were chosen for the analysis to reduce the problems of allocation of general overhead in the comparative analysis.

As indicated in Table 4.1 line haul out-of-pocket vehicle costs during the period 1963–1968 increased from 37.8¢ to 43.3¢ per vehicle-mile, a rate of approximately 3% per year. If we assume that these data represented a reasonable approximation of the true average cost of operating a vehicle in transcontinental service, we can compute the cost per available ton-mile on weight and density bases by applying payload and cubic capacity factors of the trailer. Our analysis assumes that the tractor pulls a 40-foot trailer. To the extent that the tractor pulls a larger payload, for example, twin 27-foot trailers, the cost per available ton-mile falls accordingly.

Projections have been made on three bases: continuation of the past trend, cost increases of 8% per annum, and an upper limit of 10% cost increase per annum.

These projections might well be biased against the trucking industry—conversely in favor of the competitive carriers. One recent transportation study predicted that trucking costs per revenue ton-mile would fall over the next several years because of heavier loads stemming from liberalization of size and weight laws.[7]

In any event, the author believes that line haul trucking costs will increase at an annual rate of approximately 7%–8% per annum during the 1970s, primarily because of the wage settlement negotiated in 1970. In 1968 wages and fringe benefits accounted for 58.2% of the Class I inter-city common motor carriers, carriers of general freight, and a slightly higher percentage of total operating expenses. The agreement between the Teamsters and the Trucking Industry in 1970 provided for a three-year wage agreement ending in an hourly wage which amounts to a 13% per annum increase compounded over the period.

Thus, the most likely costs per vehicle-mile in 1975 and 1980 will be 70¢–74¢ and $1.00–1.09 respectively, if in fact the cost increase factors materialize. The corresponding costs per available ton-mile for 40-foot trailers are shown in the table.

A major uncertainty regarding this forecast was introduced in August 1971, when President Nixon inaugurated his new economic program by freezing wages and prices for 90 days. On October 7, the President announced his plans for Phase II of the program. The fundamental objective was to reduce the rate of inflation to the 2%–3% per annum range by the end of 1972, and the key institutions for achieving this goal were the Cost of Living Council, Price Commission, and Pay Board.

---

[6] See Bureau of Accounts, Interstate Commerce Commission, *Costs of Transporting Freight by Class I and Class II Motor Common Carriers of General Commodities by Regions or Territories for the Year 1966* (Washington, 1967), p. 183.

Trucking line haul and terminal costs used in this study are taken from the relevant annual issues of this ICC report.

[7] Westwood Research, Inc., *Commercial Air Freight Rate Analysis and Forecast Project WR 144.* Prepared for Douglas Aircraft Company (Los Angeles, 1970), p. 40 and Figure 2.

This study assumes that a 25% liberalization of size and weight restrictions will reduce direct operating costs 10%. Their data also include pick up and delivery and overhead costs, therefore are not directly comparable with data in this study.

TABLE 4.1
Line Haul Trucking Costs Per Available Ton-Mile
Weight and Density Bases—Transcontinental Territory
1963–1968, 1975, 1980

Year and Out-of-Pocket Line Haul Cost Per Vehicle Mile		Out-of-Pocket Cost Per Available Ton-Mile		
		Weight Basis 20-Ton Capacity	Adjusted for Density (*Pounds Per Cubic Foot*)[a]	
			15.0	*8.6*
1963	37.8¢	1.89¢	2.52¢	4.40¢
1964	38.9	1.95	2.60	4.53
1965	39.8	1.99	2.65	4.63
1966	41.5	2.07	2.76	4.81
1967	42.9	2.15	2.87	5.0
1968	43.3	2.17	2.89	5.05
1975				
Alt I	53.3	2.67	3.56	6.21
Alt II	74.2	3.71	4.95	8.63
Alt III	84.4	4.23	5.64	9.84
1980				
Alt I	61.7	3.08	4.11	7.16
Alt II	1.09	5.45	7.27	12.67
Alt III	1.36	6.81	9.08	15.85

[a] Density calculations based on truck design density of 20 pounds per cubic foot.

NOTES: 1963–1968 data from Interstate Commerce Commission, *Costs of Transporting Freight by Class I and Class II Motor Common Carriers of General Commodities.*
Projections based on following assumptions:

Alternative I: Continuation of 1963–1968 cost increase trend, approximately 3% per annum.
Alternative II: Assumes cost increases of 8% per annum during period 1969–1980. More realistic in view of the 39-month 46% wage increase agreement negotiated in 1970.
Alternative III: Assumes average cost increases of 10% per annum, which would appear to be an upper limit.

In November 1971, the Pay Board announced its general policies which called for a normal limit of 5 1/2% per year for pay increases, but provided increases up to 7% in unusual situations.

As of the writing of this study, it is uncertain whether wage controls will become a permanent fixture during the next decade. It is highly probable, however, that the rate of wage increases will be significantly below the 1970 13% per annum settlement. Should the cost increase factors be reduced to the historical 3% level, primarily through increases in productivity, the line haul cost per vehicle-mile of truck service will be in the low 50s in 1975 and the low 60s in 1980.

The density projections are based on two values. The first, 15.0 pounds per cubic foot, is the density of truck traffic as reported in a study by Lockheed-Georgia. The second, 8.6 pounds per cubic foot, is the density of on-board air cargo surveyed by Lockheed-Georgia.[8] Thus, the very high costs in the last column of Table 4.1 are predicated on the unrealistic assumption that the truck is filled with the kind of freight that now moves by air cargo. The costs per available ton-mile on a density basis might well fall into the 5¢–6¢ range in 1975 and 8¢–10¢ range in 1980 if cost increases average 8% per annum during the period.

Railroad TOFC Costs. The methodology for projecting Railroad Trailer on Flat Car (TOFC) costs was similar to that used for the trucks, but the line haul costs were based on TOFC costs per car-mile as reported by the Interstate Commerce Commission, rather than per train-mile. Only three years' history was available, during which time line haul costs increased approximately 5.5% per annum (Table 4.2).

It should be noted that the 30¢ per car-mile line haul costs were consistent with train-mile costs of $14–$17 during the period. The car-mile costs implied that the average train length was 47–57 TOFC cars, which if anything biased the costs upward against the railroad. For example, if train-mile costs were $15, a 70 car TOFC train might experience car-mile costs of 21.4¢.

Line haul costs were reported on an out-of-pocket basis for reasons cited earlier. Out-of-pocket costs include 80% of freight operating expenses, rents and taxes (excluding Federal income taxes), plus a return of 4% after Federal income taxes on 50% of the road property and 100% of the equipment used in freight service.[9]

The projections were based on cost increase rates of 5.5% and 8%. The former assumes continuation of past trends, whereas the latter seems more relevant in view of recently negotiated labor contracts. The resulting line haul costs per ton-mile are approximately 1.3¢ in 1975 and 1.8¢ in 1980. A combination of heavier loads and wage increase rollbacks might well reduce the values. On the other hand, deferred maintenance might have resulted in unreasonably low historical costs which were used as the basis for the projection.

Air Freighter Costs. Transcontinental air freighter line haul costs were projected by focusing on the Total Aircraft Operating Expenses shown in Table 4.3. These costs, also known as air freighter direct operating costs, including flight crew, fuel, maintenance, and depreciation. The base figures for the projections were the 1969 available ton-mile costs computed earlier and displayed in Table 2.18.

[8] P. F. Calkins, T. H. Baker, and E. J. Joiner, *The Density Story*, CMRS 163 (Marietta, Lockheed-Georgia, November 1969), pp. 42, 53.

The 8.6-pound figure for air cargo density might be too low. American Airlines in two special studies reported on-board densities of 9.6 and 9.8 pounds per cubit foot. See American Airlines' testimony in CAB, *Docket 21866-7* (*Domestic Passenger Fare Investigation, 1970*) Exhibit No. AA78, p. 1.

The trucking density figure might be too high. See Peter W. Schutz and Max J. Reinhart, *Economic Analysis of Power Options for Line Haul Vehicles*, National West Coast Meeting, Society of Automotive Engineers (1970), p. 5, where an average truck density of 13 pounds per cubic foot is assumed for a simulation of long haul trucking costs.

[9] U.S. Interstate Commerce Commission, Bureau of Accounts, *Railroad Carload Cost Scales by Territories for the Year 1967* (Washington, 1969), p. 4. Rail TOFC data are taken from this source for the years indicated.

TABLE 4.2

Rail Trailer on Flat Car (TOFC) Line Haul
Out-Of-Pocket Costs Per Available Ton-Mile
1966–1968, 1975, 1980

Year	Line Haul Cost Per TOFC Car-Mile	Line Haul Cost Per Ton-Mile
1966	28.92¢	.723¢
1967	29.96	.749
1968	32.25	.806
1975 I	46.91	1.173
II	55.27	1.382
1980 I	61.31	1.533
II	81.21	2.030

ASSUMPTIONS:

   (1) Two trailers per flat equal 40 ton load.

   (2) Mountain Pacific and Trans-Territory experience.

   (3) Projection I based on 5.5%, the line haul increase during 1966–1968.

   (4) Projection II based on 8%.

   (5) Allowance for circuitry not included.

   (6) Density equals 14.6 lbs./cu. ft.

SOURCE: ICC, *Rail Carload Cost Scales by Territories.*

TABLE 4.3

Projection of Air Freighter Aircraft Expenses Per
Available Ton-Mile at Varying Cost Increase Factors
Transcontinental Service 1975, 1980

			Total Aircraft Operating Expenses Per ATM			
			Weight Basis		Density Basis	
			1975	1980	1975	1980
707-320C	@	3%	5.25¢	6.09¢	7.88¢	9.14¢
		6%	6.24	8.35	9.36	12.53
		8%	6.98	10.26	10.47	15.39
DC-8-63	@	3%	4.90	5.67	5.61	6.51
		6%	5.82	7.78	6.67	8.92
		8%	6.51	9.56	7.46	10.96
747F	@	3%	3.70	4.29	4.66	5.40
		6%	4.40	5.88	5.53	7.40
		8%	4.92	7.23	6.19	9.09

NOTES:

   (1) Weight basis based on design density. Density basis based on average loaded density. See Tables 2.17 and 2.18.

   (2) Aircraft operating expense projections based on highest values in Table 2.18.

Projections were made for 707, DC–8–63, and 747 freighter aircraft. The costs per available ton-mile (weight basis) were converted to density costs through the use of factors shown in Table 2.18.

Cost increase factors of 3%, 6%, and 8% were tested. Assuming no rollback of wage increases, the actual cost increase factor for line haul aircraft operating expenses per available ton-mile will probably fall within the range of 3%–6% per annum during the 1970s. For example, American Airlines predicted in data submitted to the CAB in 1970 for the Domestic Passenger Fare Investigation that average annual freighter aircraft operating expenses per available ton-mile would increase at a rate of 4½% per year between 1970 and 1972.[10] American's cost estimates were predicated on annual increases in ground and pilot payrolls of about 7% per year. The Air Transport Association of America reported in mid-1970 that three-year wage settlements negotiated during 1969–1970 would increase wages 11% annually.[11]

On the other hand, line haul cost increases for 747 freighters, if put into service, might well be lower than 707s and DC–8s based on the operating experience of the passenger 747s. Crew costs are a smaller proportion of 747 costs, whereas depreciation is a much higher percentage by comparison with 707 and DC–8 freighters.

The above calculations assume that the aircraft will weight rather than cube out. But, as stressed throughout this study, air freight tends to be less dense than surface shipments. After adjusting theoretical line haul costs per available ton-mile (weight basis) for density, the costs per available ton-mile climb sharply.

Comparison of Surface and Air Line Haul Costs. Exhibit 4.1 displays data drawn from Tables 4.1–4.3 and permits an easy comparison of the probable line haul cost ranges that the modes competing for transcontinental traffic will experience in 1975. In addition to the range of costs, the most likely levels have been indicated.

The data indicate that if 707s are used in air freighter service "most likely" line haul costs per available ton-mile (weight basis) will be 60% greater than those of trucks. The "most likely values" assume that air costs will increase at an annual rate of 5%, whereas truck costs will increase at 6%. On a density basis, however, 707 line haul air freight costs per available ton-mile will be almost double those of trucks if the same traffic mix continues to be handled.

The use of stretched DC–8s narrows the gap between truck and air particularly in terms of density.

If 747 freighters were introduced, they might well operate at lower line haul costs per available ton-mile than trucks handling 40-foot trailers in 1975, depending on the cost increase factors chosen. It is more likely that there will be a 5% to 10% differential in favor of trucks, however.

Perhaps the most interesting aspect of Exhibit 4.1 is that rail out-of-pocket TOFC costs will remain substantially below those of air or trucks. Although there has been

[10] American Airlines Testimony in *Docket 21866-7*, Exhibits AA 43, AA 44 and AA 45.

[11] Air Transport Association of America, Economics and Finance Department, *Major U.S. Airlines Current Economic Review and Financial Outlook* (Washington, by the Association, July 1970), p. 18.

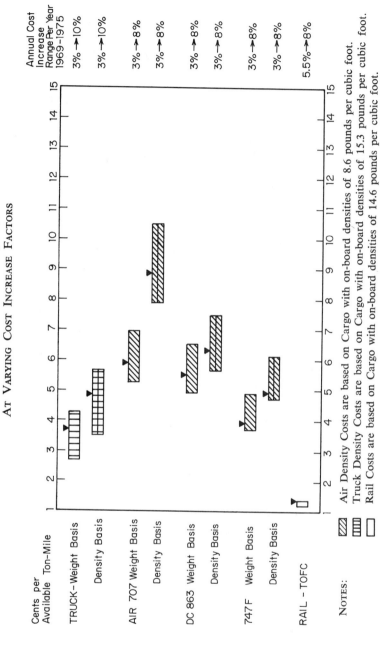

EXHIBIT 4.1
COMPARATIVE LINE HAUL COSTS PER AVAILABLE TON-MILE
AIR—TRUCK—TOFC
TRANSCONTINENTAL SERVICE, 1975
AT VARYING COST INCREASE FACTORS

NOTES: Air Density Costs are based on Cargo with on-board densities of 8.6 pounds per cubic foot.
Truck Density Costs are based on Cargo with on-board densities of 15.3 pounds per cubic foot.
Rail Costs are based on Cargo with on-board densities of 14.6 pounds per cubic foot.

▶ Indicates most likely value in 1975.

some criticism of the ICC's approach to costing TOFC traffic,[12] the evidence still indicates that the railroads have a significant competitive cost advantage over trucks and air for transcontinental service. It remains to be seen whether the railroads can provide the level of service necessary to attract transcontinental traffic now moving by the other modes.

Projection of Terminal Costs

Terminal costs for the different modes of transportation are much more difficult to project than line haul costs for a variety of reasons. Line haul costs tend to vary directly with the scheduling of the vehicle, whereas terminal costs are a function of a variety of inputs: number, weight and density of shipments, whether packages are tendered loose or in containers, productivity and flexibility of the workforce, etc.

In some instances terminal costs are almost fixed in the short run once line haul schedules are developed. For example, an air freight terminal might well hire enough men to fully load all departing freighters without delaying the planes. If the actual load factors on a given night were less than 100%, terminal expenses would be substantially the same as if 100% load factors had been achieved.

On the other hand, many motor carriers are able to adjust terminal expenses proportional to traffic flows. Lower load factors would not necessarily mean higher terminal expenses per revenue ton-mile within reasonable ranges. The question of the true variability of terminal expenses remains vexing.

Even though it is difficult to determine future terminal costs, they cannot be ignored, for, particularly in the case of air freight service, they represent an important component of total shipment costs.

Again, a pragmatic approach has been taken. Average cost data from the three modes will be presented and projected at varying cost increase factors. The resulting costs per ton will be divided by transcontinental mileages in order that a cost per ton-mile figure can be developed.

Trucking Terminal Costs. The ICC reports out-of-pocket trucking terminal costs broken down into pick up and delivery service, platform handling, and billing and collection. Pick up and delivery costs have been excluded from the comparative tabulations, because airline freight rates generally exclude pick up and delivery, and many rail TOFC rates are published on a ramp to ramp basis. To the extent that the cost comparisons suggest relative spreads in rates, it was felt that the costs should not include pick up and delivery.

Platform handling and billing and collection costs for carriers operating in Transcontinental Territory were obtained for the years 1963–1968. The costs for an

---

[12] Aaron J. Gellman, "Surface Transportation," *Technological Change in Regulated Industries,* ed. by William M. Capron (Washington, Brookings, 1971), pp. 170–171.

The rail's comparative advantage is also emphasized in a study done for Pacific Intermountain Express by A. T. Kearney & Co. and reported in Carl Glines, "Trucking's Stake in Air Freight," *Commercial Car Journal,* March 1968, pp. 69–80. Rail line haul costs are shown to be approximately one-third those of air on the basis of cube in 1975.

average shipment (generally 1,000 pounds during this period) were used for the analysis. As indicated in Table 4.4, the costs per ton ranged from $6.39 to $7.84 per platform handling operation. On an origin-destination basis, the total platform and handling costs would be doubled. It should be noted that these terminal costs per ton figures are higher than those reported by the American Trucking Association, for the costs used in this study are based on tonnage actually moving over the platform, whereas the ATA statistics divided terminal expenses by total intercity tonnage.[13] The ICC reports indicate that shipments weighing more than 5,000 pounds will probably not move over the dock.[14]

Platform handling costs per ton increased at about 4.2% annually during 1963–1968. Even if these handling costs should increase at a 10% rate (Table 4.4), the handling cost per revenue ton-mile for a shipment moving 2,500 miles would amount to less than 2¢ in 1980.

Billing and collecting costs per ton for a 2,500-mile shipment were small according to the ICC average cost data. Although they appear understated in the author's opinion, even if they were doubled, the cost per revenue ton-mile would still be insignificant (Table 4.5).

In total, therefore, platform handling plus billing and collecting costs per revenue ton-mile will fall into the 1.2¢ to 2.2¢ range during the 1970s. In 1975, the most likely value for out-of-pocket terminal costs on transcontinental shipments excluding pick up and delivery will be 1.1¢ per revenue ton-mile.

Projecting Rail TOFC Terminal Costs. The out-of-pocket terminal costs for rail TOFC service as reported by the ICC include billing, tying and untying of loaded trailers on the rail car, special service costs applicable to TOFC traffic, switching cost at origin and destination, and trailer rental based on three days. The terminal costs do not include pick up and delivery.

The reported costs per ton are based on a shipment and therefore do not have to be doubled as was the case with the motor carrier platform costs.

Data were available only for the years 1966, 1967, and 1968, during which time the costs per ton moved from $3.07 to $6.09 and back to $5.89. As was the case with motor carriers, spreading these costs over a 2,500-mile haul produced very low terminal costs per revenue ton-mile. On the other hand, the costs do not include actual loading of the container, whereas motor carrier terminal costs included platform handling charges. Therefore, Table 4.6 shows the TOFC costs per revenue ton-mile with and without the "most likely" motor carrier platform handling charges added in.

If the platform handling costs are excluded, out-of-pocket rail TOFC terminal costs per revenue ton-mile for a 2,500-mile haul will probably fall within the .3¢ to .6¢ range during the decade. If platform handling costs are included, the total terminal costs per revenue ton-mile would range between 1.28¢ and 1.85¢. Thus,

---

[13] American Trucking Associations, *American Trucking Trends 1970–71* (Washington 1971), p. 24.

[14] ICC, *Costs of Transporting Freight . . . by Motor Common Carriers*, p. 187.

TABLE 4.4

Average Platform Handling Costs Per Ton
Average Shipment Weight
Class I and II Motor Carriers—Transcontinental   Territory
1963–1968, 1975, 1980

(Shipment Distance 2,500 Miles)

Year	Platform Handling Cost Per Ton	ORIGIN & DESTINATION Platform Handling Costs	
		Per Ton	Per Ton-Mile
1963	$6.39	$12.78	.51¢
1964	6.77	13.54	.54
1965	7.21	14.42	.58
1966	7.73	15.46	.62
1967	7.38	14.76	.59
1968	7.84	15.68	.63
1975 I	10.32	20.64	.84
II	11.79	23.58	.94
III	13.44	26.88	1.23
1980 I	12.55	25.10	1.03
II	15.77	31.54	1.26
III	19.74	39.48	1.97

NOTE: 1963–1968 data from Interstate Commerce Commission, Costs of Transporting Freight by Class I and Class II Motor Common Carriers of General Commodities. The cost data are based on average shipment weights, which for transcontinental shipments were approximately 1,000 pounds during this period. As shipment sizes increase, platform costs per hundredweight fall, primarily because the percentage of shipments handled over the platform decrease as weight increases. If the shipment weighs more than 5,000 pounds, it will probably not be handled over a platform. In computing platform costs per ton-mile, platform costs per ton have been doubled to reflect origin and destination handling. The projections have been based on the following:

Alt. I	4%	Historical trend.
Alt. II	6%	Most likely rate of increase.
Alt. III	10%	Most likely upper limit.

including platform handling would raise TOFC terminal costs almost to the level of line haul costs for a 2,500-mile haul.

Projecting Air Freight Terminal Costs. There are a host of problems associated with projecting air freight terminal costs, not the least of which are definitional. Some studies focus on total Indirect Operating Costs (IOCs), which as noted include terminal expenses, aircraft servicing, ground equipment maintenance and depreciation, marketing expenses, general and administrative, etc.[15]

---

[15] Boeing *747F Freighter, D6-13920-R2*, p. 70.

TABLE 4.5
Billing and Collecting Costs Per Ton-Mile
Transcontinental Territory
1963–1968, 1975, 1980

(1,000-Pound Shipment, 2,500 Miles)

Year	Billing and Collecting Cost Per Shipment	Billing and Collecting Cost Per Ton-Mile
1963	86.858¢	.070¢
1964	89.709	.072
1965	88.013	.070
1966	89.951	.072
1967	110.588	.088
1968	115.183	.092
1975 I	173.192	.138
II	197.403	.158
1980 I	231.770	.186
II	290.050	.232

NOTES: Projection I assumes cost increases of almost 6% per year, the rate experienced during 1963–1968.

Projection II assumes increases of 8% per year.

Other treatments isolate the so-called "freight handling costs" per shipment, which include traffic servicing, servicing administration, sales, advertising and publicity, and an allocation of general overhead.[16]

Still others look at only a portion of the traffic servicing costs, namely, the direct loading and terminal expenses, excluding billing and collection, accounting and information, etc.[17]

For the purposes of a comparative analysis of terminal costs versus the surface modes, it is perhaps most useful to concentrate solely on traffic service expenses (CAB account number 6200), which include freighter loading and unloading, freight accounting and information services, building and equipment rental, utilities and supplies, and freight storage.

In 1969 average traffic servicing expenses per revenue ton-mile for the study carriers ranged from a low of 2.3¢ (Flying Tiger) to a high of 6.4¢ (TWA). Average hauls per shipment for total freight service in 1969 were 1,147 miles. Shipments moving on air freighters tended to move longer distances, for example, American's average length of haul for total freight shipments in 1969 was 940 miles, whereas freighter shipments moved 1,494 miles on the average.[18]

[16] See Letter dated December 18, 1969, from American Airlines to Civil Aeronautics Board applying for a 3-level rate structure for freight general commodities, Exhibit B entitled "Freight Handling Costs—250 Pound Shipment, 1968."

[17] A. T. Adams, "Ground Handling Problems and Their Costs," p. 26.

[18] American Airlines Testimony in CAB *Docket 21866-7* (1970), Exhibit AA 22, p. 2.

TABLE 4.6
Rail Trailer on Flat Car (TOFC)
Average Terminal Costs Per Revenue Ton and Per Ton-Mile
1966–1968, 1975, 1980

(2,500-Mile Haul)

Year	Origin Plus Destination Terminal Cost Per Ton	Origin Plus Destination Terminal Cost Per Revenue Ton-Mile	Motor Carrier Platform Handling Per Revenue Ton-Mile	Total Terminal Including Platform Handling Per Ton-Mile
1966	$3.07	.123¢	.62¢	.74¢
1967	6.09	.244	.59	.83
1968	5.89	.234	.63	.86
1975 I	8.57	.343	.94	1.28
II	10.09	.404	.94	1.34
1980 I	11.20	.448	1.26	1.71
II	14.83	.593	1.26	1.85

ASSUMPTIONS:
(1) Costs based on Mountain Pacific Trans Territory experience.
(2) Projection I based on 5.5%, the line haul increase between 1966–1968.
(3) Projection II based on 8%.
(4) "Most Likely" Motor Carrier Platform Handling Costs used. (See Table 4.4.)
SOURCE: ICC, *Railroad Carload Cost Scales by Territories.*

If we apply an estimate of 1,500 miles for freighter shipments' lengths of haul to the traffic servicing expenses per revenue ton-mile, we obtain traffic service costs per ton ranging from Flying Tiger's $34.50 to TWA's $96.00. These rough average cost values per ton can be compared with other data cited in the literature. Boeing estimated that 1970 costs per ton enplaned for the total cargo handling, reservations and sales, advertising, administration, ground property, equipment maintenance, and depreciation were $80.00.[19] Traffic service costs based on the Boeing average would be approximately 60% of these costs, or $48.00 per ton.

A 1969 survey by the International Air Transport Association found that ground handling costs per shipment averaged $115.00 per ton, but that average reflected an extremely wide range of costs, from as low as $30.00 per ton to $129.00 per ton.[20]

A student report written at the Harvard Business School found that in early 1969, freighter traffic servicing costs for three of the carriers providing service from Boston ranged between $30.00 and $37.00 per ton, which if doubled for origin plus destination would indicate total traffic handling costs per shipment of $60.00 to $74.00 per ton.[21]

[19] Boeing *747F Freighter, D6-13920-R2*, p. 70.
[20] IATA, *Economics of Air Cargo Carriage and Service*, p. 22.
[21] Victor W. Dahir, "A Comparative Study of Three Ground Handling Systems for Air

The reason for the difficulty in pinning down average traffic service costs with any degree of confidence is that they vary significantly with the weight of the shipment. For example, Flying Tiger claimed that in 1969 its traffic servicing costs for a 100-pound shipment were $209.00 per ton, but that a 3,000-pound shipment incurred traffic servicing costs of but $40.00 per ton.[22]

When these figures are compared with the rail and truck terminal charges per shipment of $6.00–$15.00 per ton, it is easy to understand the statements in the literature of which the following is typical:[23]

> Particular potential for cost reduction is represented by the traffic servicing cost, which in some cases is as much as five or ten times that experienced by motor carriers.

Projections of traffic service costs were made with these assumptions in mind:

(1) Assuming that standard 707 and DC-8s, rather than 747s, L-500s, etc., are used, there will be no chance of achieving the hoped-for efficiencies of handling large rectangular containers through terminals.

(2) Labor costs are a major component of terminal operations. They account for over 80% of the direct expenses of loading, unloading, and handling. Labor unit costs, in the absence of wage controls, might well increase at annual rates of 8%–12% during the decade of the 1970s.

(3) Opportunities for productivity increases are hampered by the peaking of relatively few air freighter flights in a given terminal. Much of the processing takes place within one or two hours of flight time. It is difficult to spread the workflow more evenly during the day.

(4) Notwithstanding the above statement, our previous analysis indicates that deflated traffic service expenses did not increase proportionately with air freighter capacity increases. Increased capacity and traffic have apparently produced some economies of scale, although these economies of scale can evaporate in the face of exorbitant labor settlements.

All things considered, it appeared that an estimate of future traffic service costs per revenue ton-mile made by American Airlines (in conjunction with CAB Docket 21866-7) seemed reasonable. American assumed that increased labor costs would offset improved productivity and that traffic service costs per revenue ton-mile would increase 2.5% per year during the early 1970s. If the 2.5% increase factor were applied to American's 1969 costs, the 1975 projections per ton and revenue ton-mile would be $78.00 and 3.1¢, respectively. The same 2.5% increase factor, applied to Flying Tiger's 1969 average traffic service expenses per revenue ton-mile, yielded estimates of 2.7¢ per revenue ton-mile in 1975.

Therefore, a range of 2.7¢–3.1¢ was used for projecting 1975 traffic service expenses per revenue ton-mile in 707-DC-8-63 type equipment. How great a reduc-

Freight," A Research Report Submitted in Partial Fulfillment of the Requirements for the Degree of Master in Business Administration (Boston, Harvard Business School, 1969), p. 48
[22] Wallace I. Longstreth, "Airports and Terminals are Air Freight's Villains," p. 34.
[23] Westwood Research, *Commercial Air Freight Rate Analysis and Forecast*, p. 23.

tion might be achieved in these costs were shipment weights to increase substantially and/or 747-L-500s introduced?

Here, the evidence becomes very difficult to interpret. Boeing says that total tonnage related indirect operating costs (traffic servicing plus marketing, general, and administrative, etc.) would be reduced to $45.00 per ton by the introduction of 747 freighters. This would imply traffic service expenses (1970 costs) of perhaps $20.00–$25.00 per ton.[24]

One often-cited paper claims that increasing shipment weights from 200 to 2,000 pounds would reduce traffic handling costs 75%–80%.[25] In 1969 American stated that its traffic servicing expenses per ton for 250-pound shipments were $94.72.[26] A reduction of 75% would reduce costs to $23.68 per ton. And as noted, Flying Tiger said that if 3,000-pound shipments were tendered to its DC-8-63s, it could handle them for $40.00 per ton in 1970 costs.

If all of these estimates were projected at 2.5% over the 1970s, it was found that traffic servicing costs per air freighter revenue ton would fall into a broad range of from $25.00 to $90.00 or 1.0¢ to 3.6¢ per revenue ton-mile for transcontinental flights, depending on equipment technology, size of shipment, productivity of labor, size of wage settlements, etc.

Comparative Analysis of Surface Vs. Airline Haul plus
Terminal Costs During the 1970s

By gathering the data developed in the previous two sections, a general picture emerges of the comparative cost relationships between the modes which will be competing for transcontinental traffic during the 1970s.

The data are displayed in Table 4.7. In the analysis of direct operating expenses, a significant spread was found between rail, truck, and 707 air freighter costs. When stretched DC-8s or 747s were substituted for 707s, the gap between air and truck closed or vanished, but rail continued to be quite attractive.

If the terminal costs are now included, the spread between air and surface increases, as does the gap between truck and rail. For example, "most likely" rail line haul plus terminal costs are projected to be 37% of the costs of transcontinental trucking, and truck costs will be 56% of 707 air freighters, assuming 100% weight load factors.

The use of 747s at 100% load factors will reduce line haul plus terminal costs to within 10% of the level of trucking, and, depending on differential increases in factor costs, could drop below those of the motor carriers.

The 747 and rail TOFC costs both require containerized shipments. If container "stuffing" costs are added to the TOFC and 747 data on the assumption that they

[24] Boeing *747F Freighter, D6-13920-R2*, p. 70.

[25] Lockheed Aircraft Corporation, "Economics of Air Cargo Ground Handling and Control," International Forum for Air Cargo (Montreal, 1964), as quoted in Systems Analysis and Research Corporation, *Air Cargo Cost Study, CC-617-68* (October 1967), pp. 52–53.

[26] Before the Civil Aeronautics Board, *Complaint of Trans World Airlines, Inc.,* "Three-level Freight Rates Proposed by American Airlines," December 30, 1969, Exhibit C.

TABLE 4.7
Range of Line Haul Plus Terminal
Out-Of-Pocket Costs Per Revenue Ton-Mile
Surface Vs. Air Transportation
1975

	Line Haul[a]	Terminal[b]	Total Range	Most Likely
Trucking	2.67–4.23¢	.97–1.39¢	3.64–5.62¢	4.9¢
Rail TOFC	1.17–1.38	.34–.40	1.51–1.78	1.8
Air Freight				
707	5.25–6.98	2.7–3.1	8.0–10.08	8.8
DC-8-63	4.90–6.51	2.3–2.7	7.2–9.21	8.0
747	3.70–4.92	1.0–2.0	4.70–6.92	5.4

[a] Truck plus Air based on 100% load factor (weight basis). Rail based on 70,000-pound shipments.

[b] Rail Terminal excludes platform handling (see text). Air Terminal includes only traffic service expense.

would ultimately be passed on to the shipper, the spread between motor carriers and rail would diminish and that between trucks and air would increase by 1.0¢ per ton-mile.

If average air freighter traffic continues to be less dense than truck or rail traffic, air freight on a density basis would be even more unfavorable in terms of cost per available ton-mile. Of course, if the same commodity were shipped by either mode, the density argument would be moot. But, to the extent that the overall average density of commodities by mode affects the cost and rate structure, air freight would be substantially handicapped by the average density of its traffic.

Throughout this discussion of cost projections, reference has been made to factors which might affect the values shown in Table 4.7. Following is a summary of these and other factors:

(1) The imposition of wage and price controls might reduce the magnitude but not the spread between the modes.
(2) If motor carriers operate equipment larger than 40-foot trailer, either singly or in multiple, direct operating costs will fall.
(3) If depreciation on 707 aircraft were excluded, aircraft operating expenses per available ton-mile would fall approximately 20%. The author believes that it is dangerous to disregard depreciation, as Eastern discovered in pricing its air shuttle service. Eventually, new equipment has to be obtained, or significant maintenance expenses will be incurred to keep the service going.
(4) Rail TOFC costs might well be lowered if longer trains than those implied in the calculations were operated.
(5) Rail and 747 costs are biased downward by excluding the costs of stuffing containers.

In all, it is reasonable to conclude that unless jumbo air freighters are put into service, motor carriers and rail will continue to maintain a significant competitive advantage over domestic air freighter service even at 100% load factors.

The Financial Prospects for Air Freighter Service in the 1970s and 1980s

This analysis of the domestic air freight industry during 1965–1969 found that the major carriers (American and United) increased freighter capacity substantially, perhaps on the assumption that market share would outstrip capacity share. In fact, market share tended to follow capacity shares proportionately.

In addition, the carriers reduced prices in the hopes of stimulating substantial increases in traffic, as their new jet freighters supplanted the high operating cost piston aircraft.

The optimistic scenario would have been as follows: (a) purchase high capacity aircraft with low operating costs, (b) cut price, (c) stimulate substantial volumes of traffic, and (d) make sufficient profits from the increased traffic in order to purchase the next generation of aircraft with still lower operating costs.

What actually happened was the disastrous combination of high operating ratio (caused by low rates and low load factors) and low capital productivity, brought on by low rates and the increased costs of the capital equipment.

Should the industry continue to behave in the future as they have in the past, they will be tempted to invest in 747s and L-500s, reduce operating expenses per available ton-mile and, simultaneously, lower rates. Ironically, this policy could intensify the financial crisis of the airline industry. Capital productivity might decline, notwithstanding the investment in "high productivity" aircraft.

Table 4.8 demonstrates the dilemma. Ratios of annual revenue per plane to original cost of several types of flight equipment are calculated at freight rates of 20¢, 15¢, and 12¢ per ton-mile. Note that "capital productivity" in this example is different from the comparative capital productivity data for surface and air carriers cited earlier. In that instance, investment in net operating property was used, including aircraft and ground equipment as the denominator. For the purposes of this discussion, it was assumed that each type of plane was available for use in late 1969.

By excluding ground equipment, the data were biased in favor of the 747, for at least one study has estimated that ground equipment could amount to as much as 50% of the price of the 747 aircraft.[27] Historically, ground equipment investment as a percentage of freighter equipment has been 10%–12%.

If turbo-prop CL-44s had carried freight traffic at a yield of 20¢ per revenue ton-mile, the ratio of annual revenue to original cost would have been 1.52. In point

---

[27] IATA, *Economics of Air Cargo Carriage and Service*, p. 35. Warehousing and handling facilities could increase from 9% to 25% of total freight system investment.

of fact, Flying Tiger flew CL-44s at much lower yields, and its capital productivity suffered.

Fifteen cents was the second value chosen for parametric tests on the basis of the average prices charged by American and Flying Tiger, i.e., 13¢–16¢.

It is not unreasonable to assume that 747 freighter rates would have been reduced to perhaps the 12¢ revenue ton-mile level, because of the industry's desire to reduce the spread between air and surface costs, and its policy of passing on cost savings from new generations of aircraft to the customer.

As Table 4.8 indicates, the capital productivity (using original cost as the base) of a 707 at 15¢ rates would be 83% of a CL-44 at 20¢ rates. Pricing 747s at 12¢ would improve capital productivity over that of 707s at 15¢, yet the ratio of 747 revenue to original cost would be less than that experienced by CL-44s at 20¢.

If the load factor variable is now introduced, the capital productivity plummets, for 707 load factors were typically in the 40%–50% range. Clearly, 747s with low load factors (40%–50% range) and low rates would have much poorer capital productivity than CL-44s with high load factors (in actuality Flying Tiger's CL-44s had load factors in the 60%–70% range) and high rates.

Poor capital productivity would not be serious if operating ratios were low. Yet, the prospects for low operating ratios are poor, if the industry continues to favor low prices.

By 1975, if our estimates of air freighter transcontinental costs are accurate, line haul costs per available ton-mile will be about 6¢ for 707 freighters. At 50% load factor, the line haul cost per revenue ton-mile increases to 12¢. Traffic service expenses per revenue ton-mile will be as high as 3.1¢ per revenue ton-mile with other indirect operating costs adding an additional 3¢. Total operating expenses for transcontinental 707 service therefore might well exceed 18¢ per revenue ton-mile. Total operating expenses per revenue ton-mile for a carrier's total all-cargo service will be higher to the degree that average length of haul for the system is less than mileage moved by transcontinental shipments.

At a 50% load factor, a 707 will produce approximately 29 million revenue ton-miles per year. If 1975 transcontinental costs are 18¢ per revenue mile (50% load factor), cash costs excluding depreciation will be approximately 15.5¢ per revenue ton-mile. The time adjusted return for 707 freighter aircraft, spares, and ground equipment (assume $10 million with 12-year life) at yields of 18¢, 20¢, and 22¢ would be less than 1%, 8%, and 18%, respectively, before taxes. Therefore, an appropriate price policy would be to maintain yields of at least 20¢ per RTM in transcontinental service.

To the extent that load factors improve above 50%, lower rates could be charged with no change in the yield per plane mile. Indeed, one recent study calculated air freight costs for 747s using 70% load factors.[28]

There are several dangers with the assumption of higher load factors. The first is that with the exception of small capacity planes, QCs, and CL-44s, load factors on

[28] Westwood Research, *Commercial Air Freight Rate Analysis and Forecast*, p. 33.

TABLE 4.8
Capital Productivity of Freighter Aircraft
Compared to Original Cost
(*All Data Except Ratios are in Millions*)

Type of Aircraft	Original Cost	Year of Original Cost	ATM Per Year	REVENUE POTENTIAL 100% Load Factor at Yield per Revenue Ton-Mile			RATIO Revenue Potential to Original Cost— 100 Load Factor		
				20¢	15¢	12¢	20¢	15¢	12¢
DC-7F	$2.6	1956–59	8.2	$1.64	$1.23	$ .98	.54	.47	.38
L 1049 C	2.0	1955	4.5	.90	.68	.54	.45	.34	.27
CL-44 D	3.8	1960	28.8	5.76	4.32	3.46	1.52	1.14	.91
707-320 C	7.0	1963	58.1	11.62	8.72	6.97	1.66	1.25	1.00
DC-8F	6.5	1962	55.7	11.14	8.36	6.68	1.71	1.29	1.03
DC-8-63	8.8	1966	87.8	17.56	13.17	10.54	2.01	1.51	1.20
B 747F	19.0	1970	231.3	46.26	34.70	27.76	2.44	1.83	1.46
L-500	21.5	1970	234.7	46.94	35.20	28.16	2.18	1.64	1.31

NOTES: Aircraft original cost data from Lloyd's, *Aircraft Types and Prices* (1970). Costs do not include allowance for spares. Available Ton-Miles per Year based on average of data in Table 2.15 plus data in CAB, *Aircraft Operating Cost and Performance Reports.*

the average rarely have exceeded 56%. Because of seasonality of traffic, imbalanced flows, and peaking by day of week, it is extremely difficult to maintain consistently high load factors and meet the shipper's need for service.

Finally, load factors will depend upon the degree of competition. If the current pattern of three or more certificated carriers plus charters and private carriers continues to exist on major routes, it is doubtful that load factors will improve significantly.

As indicated in Table 4.9, westbound general commodity rates for transcontinental traffic in 1971 had climbed past the 20¢ per revenue ton-mile barrier, but eastbound general commodity rates were almost 20% less. The yields are overstated to the extent that shippers were able to reduce costs by utilizing containers.[29]

Specific commodity rates for similar weights were as low as 67% of the general commodity rates westbound and 59% of the general commodity rates eastbound.

If 707s are to be profitable in transcontinental freighter service, eastbound general commodity rates will have to be raised slightly. Both eastbound and westbound specific commodity rates will have to be increased by factors ranging from 30% to 100%. If the specific commodity rates have to be kept low to move the traffic, the general commodity rates would have to be increased still further. Or, if weight load factors stay below 50%, the break-even yields will have to be higher.

In short, profitable transcontinental 707 freighter operations will have to experience average yields of at least $25.00 per hundredweight during the mid-1970s. Even if 707 shipments were tendered in containers, the resulting savings of perhaps $45.00 per ton would warrant reductions of only $2.25 per hundredweight in the average yield. The direct operating costs alone will amount to over $15.00 per hundredweight for transcontinental shipments at 50% load factor during the 1970s.

Motor carriers, despite their high-cost wage settlements should still be able to make satisfactory profits with average yields of $15.00 per hundredweight.[30] The typical spreads between truck and profitable 707 air freight rates will be in the $10.00–$15.00 range during the decade, making it difficult for air freight to attract routine surface divertible traffic.[31]

Stretched DC-8s will improve the competitive position of the air freighters, for they will be able to operate profitably at yields of $21.00–$22.00 per hundredweight at 50% load factors. If the spread between truck and air freight rates were reduced to $6.00 per hundredweight on the average, prospects would be favorable, for the

[29] Robert H. Haskell, "The ABC's of Air Freight," *Transportation and Distribution Management* (September 1969), p. 43.

An analysis by the Air Transport Association of America revealed that shipments in containers moved at rates averaging 40% below general level rates. Container yields per ton-mile were 11.6¢ versus the general yield of 19.5¢ for all domestic air freight.

[30] Assume motor carrier yields of $15 per hundredweight (10.3¢ per revenue ton-mile). Line haul costs at even a 50% load factor will be 7.4¢ per revenue ton-mile, with terminal costs adding an additional 1.4¢. Total operating costs per revenue ton-mile including 10% for overhead should be approximately 9.6¢, thus the operating ratio at yields of $15 per hundredweight and a 50% load factor might well be 93.2.

[31] Compare text, Chapter 2, pp. 26–35.

TABLE 4.9
Pricing Transcontinental Air Freight Service

Nature of the Rate	Rate Per CWT	Rate Per Ton	Rate Per Ton-Mile
General Commodity Rates			
Westbound 100 lbs. (1968)	$26.45	$529	20.4¢
Westbound 1000 lbs. (1968)	24.95	499	19.3
Westbound 10,000 lbs. (1968)	22.45	449	17.3
Westbound 100 lbs. (1971)	31.25	625	24.1
Westbound 1000 lbs. (1971)	28.50	570	22.0
Eastbound 100 lbs. (1968)	20.45	409	15.8
Eastbound 1000 lbs. (1968)	18.95	379	14.6
Eastbound 10,000 lbs. (1968)	16.45	329	12.7
Eastbound 100 lbs. (1971)	25.30	506	19.5
1000 lbs. (1971)	23.55	471	18.2
10,000 lbs. (1971)	20.35	407	15.7
Specific Commodity Rates (Examples)			
Westbound Fish 1000 lbs. (1968)	16.80	336	13.0
1000 lbs. (1971)	19.10	382	14.7
Westbound Newspapers 3000 lbs. (1968)	16.00	320	12.3
3000 lbs. (1971)	18.20	364	14.0
Eastbound Vegetables NES 2000 lbs. (1968)	8.90	178	6.9
2000 lbs. (1971)	12.00	240	9.3

NOTE: Ton-Mile yields based on Los Angeles-Boston distance of 2,592 miles.

air freight industry could continue its rapid growth by diverting routine surface traffic.

This optimistic "stretched DC-8-63 scenario" must be qualified immediately on two grounds. As indicated previously, truck costs might be overstated to the extent that double bottom operations would reduce costs. And, if truck rates did increase to within $6.00 per hundredweight of stretched DC-8-63 rates, there would still be rail TOFC to contend with. Even including container stuffing costs, rail TOFC should be less than $6.00 per hundredweight throughout the mid 1970s.

Therefore, the industry will be under extreme pressure to invest in 747 or L-500 freighters in order to reduce operating costs and keep rates low. The financial state of the airline industry precludes massive investments in a new generation of freighter equipment at this time. But, should prosperity return by the mid-1970s, the investment in jumbo freighters could be attractive.

In 1975, for example, 747 line haul freighter costs per revenue ton-mile (100% load factor) will be approximately 4¢, or two-thirds that of a 707. Because of the heavy impact of depreciation charges, cash operating expenses per revenue ton-mile will be about 3.2¢. This estimate may be biased in favor of the 747, for other estimates in the literature claim that 747 freighters will reduce direct costs over

707s by only 20%.[32] At a 50% load factor, line haul cash costs would increase to 6.4¢. Indirect operating expenses will be between 3¢–5¢ per revenue ton-mile, of which terminal expenses will be 1.0¢–2.0¢. Thus, cash operating expenses per revenue ton-mile might be about 10.5¢ in 1975.

At yields of 10.5¢, 12.5¢, 14.5¢, and 16.5¢, cash operating profits would be $0.00, $2.3, $4.6, and $6.9 million, respectively. The approximate time adjusted return on the $22 million aircraft investment, including spares (12-year life), would be 0, 4%, 20%, and 35% before taxes, respectively. Thus, at yields of $19.00 per hundredweight (14.5¢ per revenue ton-mile), the return on investment would be very attractive even at 50% load factors. The keys are realistic pricing and attractive load factors. In this regard, it is not surprising that Boeing in its promotional literature during the late 1960s assumed freighter yields of 23¢ per revenue ton-mile, even though lower yields were being achieved in domestic freighter service using 707s and DC-8s.[33]

We can conclude that the introduction of 747s could enable the industry to hold rates at current levels, and perhaps reduce them somewhat, bringing average air freight rates within perhaps 20%–30% of truck rates. Even though the projections of 747 line haul plus terminal costs are within 10% of truck costs, the greater spread in rates will be necessary because of higher airline overhead charges and the need for a satisfactory return on investment.

If calculations such as the above show potentially high profits, why hasn't the industry invested in the 747 or L-500 to date? The risks are formidable as will be summarized below:

(1) It is not certain what the ultimate investment costs in jumbo freighters will be. If the ratio of ground investment to aircraft costs should climb as high as 50%, it would raise the 747 package of aircraft, spares, and ground equipment investment to over $30 million per unit. Return on investment would drop from 20% to 12% at average yields of 14.5¢ per RTM and costs of 10.5¢.

(2) The 747 requires a new generation of rectangular containers with lower tare to payload ratios than current surface containers. If intermodal operations are to be accomplished successfully, the container must have the strength to withstand over-the-road operations. Lufthansa has developed a lightweight 8 x 8 x 10-foot container, but it remains to be seen if it can withstand the rigors of intermodal service.

(3) 747 operations utilizing 20-foot and 40-foot rectangular containers (8 x 8-foot being the other dimensions) will require a complete change in the relationship between shipper and carrier. A relatively small percentage of domestic air freight moves in shipper packed containers.[34] Average weight of air freight shipments is far below the 12,000 pounds to 13,000 pounds that one would expect tendered

[32] IATA, *Economics of Air Cargo Carriage and Service*, p. 30.

[33] H. A. Carter, "The Boeing 747 and Its Impact on Future Airline Operations," paper presented at the Transportation Research Forum (September 1967). The exhibit is reproduced in the American Airlines case study included as Appendix A (Exhibit 7) in this study.

[34] See Footnote 47, Chapter 2.

in 20-foot rectangular containers. The implications of this observation will be elaborated more fully in the final chapter.

(4) The savings to be afforded by containerized operations may be overstated. The aforementioned IATA report commented:[35]

While there is evidence that economies can be achieved by containerization it would be misleading to hold out high hopes for large savings . . . total containerization might well produce savings of less than 10% of total costs—where containers are paid for by the shipper and all related costs are absorbed by him.

(5) Were jumbo freighters to be introduced into domestic service as substitutes for the 707s and DC-8s, their capacities would cause a substantial reduction in freighter flight frequencies in order to achieve reasonable load factors. On the other hand, if service frequencies were reduced, air freighter service would become more unattractive. For example, in 1970 scheduled air freight carried by the domestic trunks plus the all-cargo carriers crossed the 1.8 billion revenue ton-mile mark. If 60% were generated by freighters, it would be the equivalent of but five 747s at 100% load factor.

Even if domestic scheduled air freight traffic were to grow at 15% per annum during the next decade (an optimistic estimate), the resulting 7.3 billion revenue ton-miles in 1980 would support a fleet of nineteen 747s at 100% capacity, again with 60% of the traffic on freighters. Were larger planes substituted for the 747 by the carriers, the number of units would be reduced. With such concentrations of potential capacity in a few units, a serious question is raised as to the level of competition that could be sustained, not unlike the problems raised by the introduction of high capacity containerships in the North Atlantic trade.

(6) The above analysis assumes that more than 50% of freight traffic in the 1970s would move in jumbo freighters, with all existing freighters removed from service. A further problem stems from the fact that the introduction of the 747 DC-10, and L-1011 wide-body passenger aircraft adds additional air freight capacity to an industry suffering from low load factors. Cargo load factors in passenger aircraft have been historically lower than freighter load factors, almost by a factor of two. In 1968, for example, the belly cargo load factor for the domestic trunks was 22.3%.[36]

If the focus is solely upon the DC-10s and L-1011s coming into domestic service during the next four years, the result would be 1.4 billion available ton-miles of containerized capacity added to the domestic freight industry. In addition, 747s flying in domestic service might produce an additional 500 million to 1 billion ATMs.[37]

---

[35] IATA, *Economics of Air Cargo Carriage and Service*, p. 26.

[36] Irving Saginor, "Traffic and Revenue Trends in Scheduled Domestic Air Cargo, 1964–1968," p. 32.

[37] Aircraft-on-order data taken from Air Transport Association of America, *Air Transport Facts and Figures, 1971*, p. 22.

It is assumed that the 173 DC-10s and 1011s on order as of June 1, 1971, would almost exclusively be used in domestic service. Capacity factors of 8.6 tons for the 747 and 5.2 tons for DC-10s and 1011s were based on data contained in R. F. Otonicar, Free World Belly Cargo Forecast 1970–1985, CMRS 169 (Commercial Aircraft Marketing Research Department, Lockheed-Georgia, Marietta, 1969). Utilization factors were taken from the same source. The annual available ton-miles of belly capacity per plane were calculated as 747=15.1

Thus, even if no jumbo freighters were ordered, there will be 8-10 billion available ton-miles of capacity in the domestic combination plus freighter system during the 1970s. If growth rates in traffic should fall in the 5%–10% range, substantial overcapacity will continue. If the next generation of freighters were introduced into an environment of overcapacity, the probability of achieving load factors above 50% would be low.

(7) It will be difficult for both the combination and all-cargo carriers to keep air freighter rates at levels sufficient to produce satisfactory profits, for the combination carriers will most likely lower rates on containerized belly shipments on the assumption that only the incremental terminal costs need be covered to yield contribution to corporate overhead.

There is a great deal of uncertainty as to the true costs and profits of belly operations. The Director of the CAB's Bureau of Economics was quoted in 1970 as saying: "Nobody at the Board knows if cargo in the bellies is carried at a loss or not."[38]

The crucial question is whether belly cargo should be costed on a joint product or by-product cost basis. The former would require that a portion of the flight (or capacity) costs be allocated to cargo. The latter approach assumes that the plane flies anyway, therefore, belly cargo revenues equal costs for the purposes of determining which costs of combination aircraft operation should be borne by the passengers.

The Chief of the CAB's Cost Standards Section summarized the argument in a recent article. Depending on the joint product allocation scheme used, the operating loss from domestic belly cargo operations ranged from $43.7 million to $265.8 million in 1969.[39] Flying Tiger Lines strongly supported the joint product philosophy and alleged that the domestic trunks lost $232 million in 1969 by carrying belly freight.[40]

On the other hand, domestic belly cargo revenue was $335 million in 1969, and noncapacity expense directly identified with belly cargo was only $140 million.[41] Therefore, if no capacity costs were allocated to cargo, the carriers experienced a $195 million contribution to capacity expenses and corporate overhead!

The CAB in 1971 split over the issue of whether belly cargo rates should cover only noncapacity expenses or a portion of capacity expenses.[42] If the joint-product advocates are correct, the use of by-product costing will result in the passengers subsidizing the transportation of belly cargo. On the other hand, if belly cargo rates are kept too high in the name of covering "allocated" flight costs, traffic which could yield a contribution to capacity and overhead costs might be lost. The argument

million, and DC-10-1011=8.0 million. The 747-foot belly capacity of 1.5 billion available ton-miles will be used in both domestic and international service, therefore, a range of 500 million to 1 billion is assigned to domestic service.

[38] Harold D. Watkins, "Airlines, CAB Grapple with Cargo Tariffs," p. 43.

[39] Frank M. Lewis, "Is Belly Freight Profitable?", pp. 101–107.

[40] Harold D. Watkins, "Airlines, CAB Grapple with Cargo Tariffs," p. 41.

[41] Frank M. Lewis, "Is Belly Freight Profitable?", p. 103.

[42] *Ibid.*, pp. 105–106.

is quite familiar to the student of railroad pricing. What is different, however, is that traffic which would move on passenger schedules in combination aircraft might well be price inelastic, that is, falling into the emergency or routine perishable categories.

A second issue is the impact of low rates on the all-cargo carriers. Throughout the turbulent history of the industry an interesting game of oneupmanship has been played with devastating results to all parties: (1) the combination carriers lower rates for belly cargo, (2) the all-cargo carriers retaliate with a new generation of aircraft that enables rates to be lowered still further, (3) the combination carriers respond with even larger freighter aircraft and put rate pressure on the all-cargo carriers, (4) the all-cargo carriers inaugurate new lower cost freighters, and (5) the combination carriers put into service still larger passenger planes with the freight capacity of the smaller all-cargo aircraft. And the game goes on; as we have seen, freighter profits during the "game" are conspicuous by their absence.

It might be economically viable for the combination and all-cargo carriers to invest in the 747 or other jumbo-type freighters if prices are realistic and load factors are maintained at relatively high levels.

But, should the airlines (1) attempt to lower costs with too many "new generation freighters," (2) overcompete thereby reducing load factors, or (3) cut prices in order to stimulate belly cargo, disaster will result for the air freighter side of the business. The air freighters will indeed become "railroads with wings," carrying tremendous volume with little or no return on investment.

Chapter 5

Conclusions and Recommendations

RESEARCH FINDINGS

AT THE RISK OF REPETITION, the principal findings of this research project are listed below:

(1) The domestic air freight industry experienced dramatic growth in traffic during the past decade, and can look forward to above average growth by comparison with other industries in the future.

(2) Growth *per se* will not necessarily produce profits, particularly in the air freighter service segment of the industry. Indeed, the behavior of the carriers in terms of competition and pricing might well preclude satisfactory financial performance from freighter operations.

(3) Technology was not the major factor in unprofitable freight operations. Even though piston freighter service could not cover costs, the 707s, DC-8s, and particularly the stretched DC-8s had the capability of producing a satisfactory return on investment.

(4) Not only was the return on investment not satisfactory, but operating losses were often sustained in domestic freighter service. Even Flying Tiger operating DC-8-63s at 56% load factors was unable to show an operating profit.

(5) The problems were underpricing, and overcompetition. The industry felt that prices had to be kept as low as possible without considering whether it wanted to stimulate emergency, routine perishable, or routine surface divertible traffic.

(6) The domestic freighter carriers during the 1965–1969 period were divided into two camps, the optimists and conservatives. The optimists (American and United) poured on the capacity with little or no return. The conservatives (Trans World and Flying Tiger) lagged behind in additions to capacity, but usually suffered deficits, albeit on less investment.

(7) The excessive competition and low load factors may have stemmed from the hope that increased capacity shares would produce disproportionately high market shares and profits. In fact, market shares were proportionate to capacity, and profits were not correlated well with capacity shares.

(8) Economies of scale were somewhat evident in the traffic service (terminal) account, but overall freighter economies of scale were not readily apparent, given a generation of equipment.

(9) Pricing was important, but secondary to capacity in explaining levels of freighter traffic. United's routes and traffic mix resulted in high yields and high volumes of traffic, but Flying Tiger restricted capacity and saw its market share plummet, despite low yields per revenue ton-mile.

(10) Freighter load factors drifted downward with capacity increases intensifying the industry's economic problem.

(11) Increases in wages resulted in increasing freighter costs per available ton-mile by the end of the study period. Without a new generation of flight equipment, it would be impossible to pursue additional rate cuts in freighter service.

(12) The pricing and competitive problems were aggravated by the nature of the freight traffic. Low cargo densities caused aircraft to cube out rather than weight out, again increasing operating costs per revenue ton-mile.

(13) The scheduling policies of the carriers were analyzed with the assistance of a special computer program. Each of the four major domestic carriers operating air freighters had very distinctive scheduling strategies in terms of depth and breadth. In the absence of traffic data by segment, further research will be necessary to link performance with strategy.

(14) The results of the pricing and scheduling strategies of the airlines can be summarized in a single sentence which highlights the economic plight of air freighter service: During 1965–1969, the period of intensive growth of air freighter operations, freighter service exhibited the poor capital productivity of the railroads, and the high operating ratio of the motor carriers.

(15) Perhaps the financial malaise of the general airline industry prevented it from making a serious financial blunder during 1970–1971. If precedent had been followed, it might well have invested in jumbo freighters, cut prices, overcompeted, and generated even greater losses. Today, the industry has been granted a short reprieve; a time to take stock and plan more rational strategies for the future. Otherwise, once financial health is restored to the passenger sector, it will invest again in a new generation of freighter aircraft in the hope of lowering operating costs and prices.

In short, the air freight industry has left the infant stage and is in what might be called a turbulent adolescent period. There is still a great deal of fragmentation and confusion of responsibility as to the tasks of planning, aircraft operations, terminal services, billing and collection, promotion, etc. The major task of airline management and other interested parties will be to prepare and evaluate a series of alternative plans for their industry. The final section of this study is designed to aid in this effort.

THE NEED FOR FURTHER RESEARCH

Despite a rather extensive literature, there is still much to be learned about the character of air freight traffic, costs, management practices, and the perceptions of the industry by other interested parties. The answers to these questions will reduce the risks associated with air freight strategy in the 1970s and 1980s. The findings of this study suggest that the following kinds of research might be appropriate:

(1) What proportion of current air freight traffic is emergency, routine perishable, and routine surface divertible? If it is assumed that routine surface divertible traffic is more price elastic but less service elastic than the others, what are the actual elasticities? The findings suggest that at the current spreads between domestic surface and air rates, it would be difficult to convince firms to close field warehouses and give the airlines routine surface divertible traffic, although firms could partially reduce field warehousing, keep fast-moving items near the customer, and centralize slow movers in one location with air distribution. The economics of partial warehousing depends upon the values of stock-out, inventory, warehousing, and transportation costs.

(2) The surface-air competitive analysis relies on assumptions as to costs of the surface plus warehouse alternative. Yet, it is extremely difficult to obtain indices or absolute values of warehouse expenses. Studies of warehousing costs should be undertaken and publicized in order that the industry can plan rationally for the future. For example, are warehousing costs rising at a faster or slower rate than transportation costs for routine surface divertible traffic? Without a better understanding of warehousing costs, it is obviously impossible to project the growth of routine surface divertible traffic.

(3) If the domestic air freight industry chooses to try to attract substantial volumes of routine surface divertible traffic, what will the surface carriers do? My analysis suggests that the combination of truck feeder plus rail TOFC line haul service will continue to have a substantial cost advantage even over 747 type aircraft. If surface transportation is faced with substantial competition, will it be able to respond with the levels of service necessary to retain the traffic? A survey of attitudes of the surface carriers would be useful in determining how they view air competition.

(4) Although there is a great deal known about direct operating costs of freighter aircraft, there is a great deal of uncertainty as to the nature and level of air freight indirect costs, particularly those incurred in terminals. What proportion of terminal costs are fixed, once freighter schedules are established? At what point is extra labor expense incurred? How much revenue from improved load factors is carried through to profits?

(5) Will containerization reduce total system costs and charges or simply redistribute them? In other words, container stuffing must take place somewhere. What will be the costs, and what portion will be passed on to the shipper? Will organized labor allow air freight containers to be stuffed off airport land?

(6) How do the managers in the air freight industry and other interested parties view the prospects for domestic air freight for the 1970s and 1980s? To what extent are there significant differences in attitudes either within organizations or between them?

(7) In my opinion, there is a need for further studies of the policies of the individual carriers as perceived by management and shippers. For example, the statistical analysis spotlights the chronic weakness of TWA in terms of traffic and market share. Yet, TWA's scheduling tended to emphasize prime time departures and its marketing expenditures were relatively high. Is the explanation of TWA's performance one of simply poor service, weak marketing, inappropriate pricing, or a misperception of its service by the shippers?

Similarly, it would add significantly to the understanding of management behavior to pursue in greater depth the policies of United. Why did it choose to expand its air freighter service including Quick Change operations in the face of uncertain profits? Was management being rewarded on the basis of volume, market share, profitability, or return on investment? Although United's financial results improved dramatically during 1965–1968, it suffered the highest deficit of the study carriers during 1969. In 1971, it was announced that the Quick Change program would be cut back, yet United also stated that it intended to be the leader in air cargo.[1]

ALTERNATIVE STRATEGIES FOR THE U.S. DOMESTIC AIR FREIGHT INDUSTRY

The Importance of External Variables

There is little question that external variables will continue to have an important impact on the future of the domestic air freight industry. It is evident that traffic is quite responsive to changes in the Gross National Product. Should the GNP fail to grow at a satisfactory real rate of 4%–6%, air freight as well as the rest of the transportation industry will suffer.

Our trade policies will have direct effects on the volume of international air freight as well as that portion of international traffic moving in domestic service. Whether the current economic policies will reduce the growth of world trade remains to be seen.

Political strategy and regulatory policies will affect the air freight industry in several ways. Should the railroads be nationalized or at least supported by public subsidies, there may be direct efforts to route "routine surface divertible" traffic by rail.

The current move to promote more transportation deregulation may enhance the opportunities for private carriage using jumbo jets. It is somewhat surprising to find that the legal status of private carriage by air is very unclear, inasmuch as the issue has been plaguing the motor carrier industry for years. For example, a recent article concluded that "the prevailing opinion seems to be that [an operation jointly owned by two companies] would be considered private carriage."[2] In addition, the so-called

---

[1] As indicated in Footnote 16, Chapter 3, United's freighter losses increased to $19.8 million in 1970. United's change in strategy was discussed in Harold D. Watkins, "Sagging Cargo, Economy Cut Use of QC's," *Aviation Week & Space Technology* (August 2, 1971), p. 27. TWA discontinued its QC operations. United's ads proclaiming its cargo strategy appeared in several journals during the late summer of 1971.

[2] "Private Cargo Faces Tangled Legal Thicket," *Aviation Week & Space Technology* (October 26, 1970), p. 140.

commercial operators who do not hold a certificate of public convenience and necessity might be able to serve two or three clients in a specialized charter service. To the extent that tailored service raises load factors toward 100%, air transportation utilizing 747s or L–500s could easily compete with commercial trucking for transcontinental service, although rail container service would still be less expensive.

The aircraft manufacturers will continue to promote private carriage, particularly if they fail to crack the domestic certificated carrier market. The net result could be that the certificated scheduled carriers will be denied the guaranteed base of traffic on which to build the volume necessary to support the next generation of freighter aircraft.

The airline industry, as noted, will continue to be a major target of the ecologists and environmentalists concerned about noise and air pollution. It is highly probable, in the author's opinion, that jet flights at major airports within metropolitan areas will be restricted between the hours of 11 P.M. and 6 A.M., precisely the prime time for air freighter departures.

On the positive side is the trend toward the promotion of intermodalism. Air freight shipments by definition require in almost all cases prior and subsequent movement by surface transportation. Recent decisions enlarging the scope of authority of air freight forwarders should stimulate traffic through the provision of better service.[3] The new freedom for the forwarders will enable the industry to concentrate its terminal developments at relatively few hubs and use the interstate highway system for distribution. On the other hand, it probably means the demise of the Quick Change jet and the reduction of points served directly by freighters.

The aforementioned decision to move to private carriage by the Postal Service will be decided on political as well as economic grounds. The certificated carriers will resist the diversion strongly in the same way they fought the plans of the military to divert military traffic from the civilian carriers to an enlarged military air service using C-5As.

The Role of Management

Yet, the key decision variables which determine the profitability of air freight remain within the control of management. They involve corporate commitments on

For further articles on private and contract carriage see R. Stanley Chapman, "Air Cargo Markets Ponder Threat Posed by Shipper Interest in Private Jet Fleets," *Traffic World* (March 15, 1969), pp. 21 ff.

David A. Brown, "New Air Shipment Plan Evolving?" *Aviation Week & Space Technology* (December 22, 1969), p. 24.

David A. Brown, "Economic Value of Plan Stressed," *Aviation Week & Space Technology* (January 19, 1970), p. 30.

David A. Brown, "Suitable Aircraft for Plan Studied," *Aviation Week & Space Technology* (January 19, 1970), p. 32.

"Exploring Contract Carriage," *Distribution Worldwide* (January, 1971), p. 31.

Michael D. Dawson, "The Political Impact of International Air Freight Private Carriage vs. Common Carriage," presented at The Institute of Airline Marketing Seminar (March 6, 1969).

[3] Compare Footnotes 16 and 20, Chapter 2.

EXHIBIT 5.1

STRATEGIC ALTERNATIVES FACING THE U. S. DOMESTIC AIR FREIGHT INDUSTRY

Nature of Strategic Decision			Measurement
1. Carriers of loose packages	Versus	Carriers of containerized freight	1. Percent of shipments and tonnage that is containerized
2. Carriers handling a wide range of general commodities	Versus	Carriers specializing in particular kinds of traffic	2. The percentage distribution of tonnage and revenue by commodity
3. Carriers generating growth from air oriented commodities	Versus	Carriers diverting commodities from surface transportation	3. Percentage of shipments and revenue which is emergency, planned perishable and routine surface divertible
4. Carriers who view freight as a by-product of the passenger business	Versus	Carriers who view freight as a primary activity	4. Percentage of traffic carried on freighters and pricing policy based on freighter or combination service
5. Carriers offering scheduled service	Versus	Carriers specializing in non-scheduled service	5. Percentage of flights which are scheduled
6. Carriers with direct customer contact	Versus	Carriers dealing through intermediaries	6. Nature of marketing expenses
7. Carriers offering line haul service only	Versus	Carriers offering door-to-door service	7. Percentage of shipments handled door-to-door
8. Carriers only in the transportation business	Versus	Logistics companies both transporting and storing goods	8. Percentage of operating revenue generated from transportation
9. Carriers with the capability of intermodal operations using rectangular containers	Versus	Carriers utilizing a containerized technology unique to the airline industry	9. Investment in "jumbo" freighters plus percentage of shipments, tonnage and revenue associated with rectangular containers
10. Carriers experiencing high growth rates e.g. 15%–20% per year	Versus	Carriers experiencing growth rates more typical of the transportation industry e.g. 4%–8% per year	10. Growth rates of shipments, tonnage and revenue
11. Carriers willing to bear losses pending the development of a new generation of aircraft	Versus	Carriers that price realistically	11. The use of "profitability load factors," operating ratio and ROI data

major issues concerning the nature of traffic, growth targets, scope of service, and equipment. As indicated in Exhibit 5.1, the strategic alternatives can be arrayed and measured. For example, the statistic (percentage of operating revenue generated from transportation) would indicate the degree to which an airline thinks of itself being only in the transportation business versus a total logistics company concerned with transporting and storing goods. The measurement statistics are crucial for they enable top management to plan the strategies for their firm and evaluate officers and the workforce on the basis of these measures.

The fundamental strategic questions are: (1) the extent to which the domestic air freight carriers pursue vertical integration (that is, having full control over door-to-door service) or, even further, transform themselves into total logistics companies; (2) the industry's growth targets; and (3) whether the combination carriers view air freight as a by-product business, for to do so would have major implications with respect to pricing, equipment selection, and industry structure.

Vertical Integration and Transformation to a Logistics Service Industry

The question of vertical integration is not unlike the problem faced by the railroads in promoting trailer on flat car service. It involves not only the physical performance of pick up and delivery service but also direct contact with the customer. The railroads have tried to maintain customer contact and vertical integration wherever possible for fear that relying on motor carriers or forwarders to tender traffic would put them at the mercy of these large "shippers."

A strong case can be made for following a different course in the case of air freight characterized as we have seen by relatively low weight per shipment. If the airlines concentrate on line haul freighter service alone, it will free them from the responsibility of providing the expensive terminal services necessary to service air freighters. The substitution of a relatively few number of strong forwarders such as United Parcel Service or any of the major motor carriers for the large number of small truck lines providing pick up and delivery service might well bring about economies of terminal operation and route scheduling.

United Parcel's air freight operations are a classic example of successful implementation of intermodalism. UPS can spread its pick up and delivery plus terminal costs across surface and air shipments alike. It delivers locked containers to the airlines in specially designed vehicles and in effect performs almost all of the terminal functions. A transition to 747 or L–500 operation would be easy, and with the volume tendered by UPS, the problem of filling the larger rectangular containers of the jumbo jets would be reduced.

Admittedly, shifting the power from the line haul carriers to the pick up, delivery, and consolidation specialists—the forwarders—will mean that the individual line haul carriers would have to maintain excellent service at reasonable rates in order to obtain the traffic from the forwarders and large shippers. But, is this an unreasonable target in terms of national transportation policy? Shouldn't we encourage excellent service performance, but at the same time guard the industry against the dangers of excessive competition or predatory pricing practices? Minimum rate regulation could protect the line haul carriers from exploitation by the forwarders.

A step beyond simple vertical integration is to form total logistics companies which would provide integrated physical distribution services including warehousing, transportation management, and order processing service. In late 1971, Eastern Airlines announced that it had taken the initiative in forming National Distribution Services, a company which will build and operate a nationwide complex of distribution centers connected by a modern communications and computing network. Eastern owns 66% of the company with the Ralph M. Parsons Co. and TRW Inc., each providing 17%. Five centers will be established initially with an expansion program to 24 locations to come later.[4]

Although theoretically attractive, it should be recognized that movement to the total logistics service company requires a host of skills and techniques that the air freight industry does not currently possess. The airlines have not shown themselves to be masters in the air of designing, providing, and managing freight ground transportation and terminal operations. Airline management quite naturally has been rewarded primarily on the basis of aircraft design and performance, whereas surface carriers and warehousing firms have specialized in the physical handling of goods on the ground.

In addition, a total logistics company owned by an airline might well find itself in the role of promoting modes of transportation which compete with the primary owner. This could raise some interesting organizational problems, particularly if the outcome hinges on the pricing policies of the transportation carriers. For example, the air carrier might be willing to minimize transportation profits in the hope of convincing a customer to accept a total distribution system which requires air transportation, thereby gaining greater profits from the management of the shipper's air-oriented total logistics system. Although National Distribution Services has indicated that it would not necessarily be oriented toward air freight distribution,[5] the theoretical conflict still remains.

Growth Targets

The question of target growth must be reexamined. How high a growth rate can an industry subject to environmental and financial constraint sustain? If managers are rewarded on the basis of 15%–20% growth rates per annum while at the same time freighter profits are marginal or nonexistent and the organization is under traffic strain to keep up with the increased volume, who benefits? Certainly not the shippers who in the long run may be faced with a financially exhausted industry.

[4] "Eastern Airlines to Lead Three-Firm Group Forming Distribution Services Company," *Traffic World*, September 27, 1971, p. 33.

[5] Eastern Air, TRW and Parsons Co., "Plan Firm to Distribute Others' Goods in the U.S.," *The Wall Street Journal*, September 21, 1971, p. 6.

Air Freight: By-Product or Primary Business

If the combination carriers view freight as a by-product of the passenger business, it could well lead to a level of prices which would be insufficient to sustain profitable freighter operations. If those who believe that the demand for air freight service is extremely elastic are correct, the low prices might maximize belly freight contribution to overhead and fixed charges, though freighter service would remain unprofitable. The domestic all-cargo carriers, however, would be under extreme competitive pressure and would seek to have rates raised to a level to maintain profitable freighter service.

It is somewhat ironic that the combination carriers now tend to place emphasis on filling the bellies of the new passenger planes, for during the growth period of the 1960s, much of the publicity surrounding air freight hinged on the need for the next generation of freighters to handle the huge increases in projected volume. As emphasized throughout this study, the author believes that commitment to air freight is best measured by investment in freighter aircraft and ground facilities designed primarily to support freighter aircraft. The strategic decision by the combination carriers on whether to treat freight as a by-product is a crucial one, second only to the strategy of becoming a total logistics service company.

High-Risk Scenarios

One high-risk scenario is essentially to repeat the strategy of the past by: (1) cutting the prices on belly freight to stimulate increases in freight volume, (2) as volume increases investing in the next generation of freighter aircraft in the hopes of cutting unit costs without regard to restructuring the industry in order to reduce excessive competition, and (3) pursuing a policy of vertical integration without considering in depth the question of which institutions are best suited to perform individual functions within the air freight system.

For the combination carriers a high-risk strategy which does not involve the purchase of the next generation of freighters immediately is to simultaneously cut prices on belly cargo and continue to provide traditional freighter service, for as has been emphasized, the freighters will operate at a loss to the possible detriment of the morale of the freight organization.

Should the carriers then attempt to abandon freighter service at the end of the normal life of the 707–DC–8 equipment, they might face the wrath of shippers who depended on freighters, for example those utilizing the Type A igloos. Inasmuch as the substitution of jumbo freighters for 707s is attractive on an incremental basis,[6] the combination carriers would undoubtedly replace the 707s and DC-8s with the next generation of aircraft and again face the problem of an artificially low rate structure based on by-product pricing and excessive competition.

---

[6] Assuming that 747s replaced 707s on a capacity-for-capacity basis, it would require 3.4 707s at $10 million each for each 747 at $25 million. The 747s would also operate at lower costs. The critical question is whether freighters should be operated at all.

Low-Risk Scenarios

The keys to profitable domestic air freighter operation and domestic air freight service in general lie in the restructuring of competition and realistic pricing.

Inasmuch as the combination carriers have experienced little or no return on investment in freighter operations, and are uncertain as to the profitablity of belly service, a low-risk strategy would entail phasing out the traditional competitive air freighter service, spinning off terminal operations to the forwarders, motor carriers, or warehousemen, and promoting containerized belly cargo service.

Or, if they wanted to continue both belly and freighter service they could follow a policy of accepting cargo tendered only in containers for freighter flights, with the combination flights handling belly containers and loose packages. The extra handling expenses incurred in the processing of loose packages would be traded off against the fact that the line haul costs of combination aircraft would be borne primarily or even exclusively by the passengers. Belly cargo rates would not be permitted below those necessary for profitable containerized freighter service, for to do otherwise would raise anew the specter of predatory competition between the combination and all-cargo carriers.

A third low-risk strategy for the combination carriers would be to submit a proposal to the CAB to pool their freighter operations and create a strong all-cargo competitor to Flying Tiger for domestic traffic. Undoubtedly, this policy would hasten the demise of Airlift International,[7] therefore a reorganized and refinanced Airlift International could become the means for restructuring the industry. The objectives of this proposal would be to have two strong domestic all-cargo carriers with broad route authorities giving good service, yet operating at profitable load factors.

A further element in any low-risk strategy would be to phase out all Quick Change freighter operations and reduce the number of points served by freighters.

RECOMMENDATIONS

To the Combination Carriers

Strategic Planning. Now is the time for the combination carriers to decide the future of their involvement in domestic air cargo, before any general upturn in financial performance puts them back on the "promote freight volume at all costs" treadmill. A realistic assessment must be made of the growth prospects for profitable air cargo traffic, the likelihood of high load factors, the competitive posture of the surface carriers, the role of the all-cargo carriers, and the split between combination and freighter operations.

If the findings of this study are accurate, we can expect to see a reversal in the trend of percentage of freight carried on freighters. More likely, freighters will be

---

[7] Compare Footnote 5, Chapter 2, for references to the financial condition of Airlift International.

phased out with the wide-body jets taking the primary role in handling freight for the combination carriers.

Should the combination carriers reduce the relative importance of air cargo, the organizational implications are obvious. Freight will continue to be treated as a by-product, and air freight managers will learn how the managers of passenger service felt in the railroad industry. Yet, the shift may well be ncessary, at least for domestic service, if the economic factors cited in this book are correct.

The combination carriers should give serious consideration to the alternative plan, that is, pooling their resources and establishing a strong freighter competitor to Flying Tiger as suggested in the previous section. Two all-cargo carriers offering both scheduled and nonscheduled freighter service should be able to meet the requirements for large-scale air freight service during the next two decades.

A major strategic question will be relationships with the motor carriers and forwarders. Based on the analysis in this study, much greater reliance should be placed on the pick up and delivery terminal specialists. The fragmentation in the industry must be resolved through restructuring, and the carriers will have to take the initiative.

Planning for the new generation of freighter aircraft will have to be implemented on an industry-wide basis with the guidance of the CAB. The industry cannot run the risk of another round of "Russian Roulette" with its risks of overcapacity, poor load factors, unsatisfactory capital productivity, and nonexistent profits. If the next stage is to be true intermodalism with rectangular containers, joint planning is vital. Limiting intermodal air freight service to two line haul competitors should minimize the substantial risks.

Although domestic air freight is affected by developments in international trade, it is perhaps best to think of the domestic strategy separately. Otherwise, the temptation to subsidize domestic operations with international service arises. To the extent that the combination carriers do not have equal access to lucrative international routes raises problems of competitive disadvantage.

In short, the carriers should address themselves to each item in Exhibit 5.1 in developing a consistent scenario for the future.

Operational Planning. In addition to strategic decisions, the carriers might well institute new practices in their current operations to improve their financial position.

Clearly, the question of reassessment of pricing is primary. We already see a move to cut rates on freight moving in combination aircraft during daylight hours in the hopes of reducing the peaking problem and making better use of capacity.[8] The

---

[8] See "CAB Refuses to Suspend TWA 747 Container Rates Aimed at Heavy Shipments," *Traffic World* (August 30, 1971), p. 54.

TWA proposed LD-3 rates which would impose no additional charge if the container load exceeded 1,250 pounds. Up to a maximum of 2,600 pounds could be loaded. At 1,250 pounds, the density of the cargo would be approximately 8 pounds per cubic foot. If the cargo density were 12 pounds, the rate would represent a 30% discount over existing domestic containers. The maximum density based on 140 cubic feet would be 18 pounds per cubic foot. The rate applied only if the containers were tendered during daylight hours and loaded by the shipper.

results might well be a shift of traffic from motor carriers to the airlines, but the question of impact on cargo now moving by air must be raised. The airlines can ill afford any further reductions in rates of cargo carried on freighters, and the low rates in combination aircraft will prolong the general malaise of domestic air freight finances.

As an official at Flying Tiger exclaimed: "[Space available rates] will destroy the cargo business. Prices tend to find the lowest level and the whole price structure could come tumbling down."[9]

A second question concerns judging the performance of the operations. The most widely reported statistic is the weight basis load factor. This number, though used often in this report, is misleading for several reasons. It does not account for density. Although a carrier's load factor on the basis of weight may be below 50%, its density load factor could well be 60%–70%. Insofar as the airlines experience both directional and seasonal peaks, it may prove difficult to increase overall load factors on a weight basis. One policy would be to replace the concept of weight load factor with density load factor. Yet, this would not solve the problem, for a carrier could look "good" in terms of load factor, depending on the characteristics of the traffic tendered. Thus, a freighter might depart at 100% cubic load factor yet generate operating deficits.

An alternative is to report load factor in terms of actual and potential revenue per flight. Based on the stage length and type of aircraft, a revenue per flight bogey to cover operating costs would be established. The actual revenue could be compared with the target with the result being a "financial load factor." If revenue potential were below 50%–60% regardless of weight or density, it would be a signal for management to review policies.

An important operating decision that could have immediate impact on profits would be to review current scheduling decisions and attempt to reduce excess capacity either through voluntary reductions in flights, or set the stage with the CAB for the approval of pooling flights between the relatively few high density major origins and destinations. Pooling would be an interim policy pending the establishment of the strong all-cargo carrier mentioned above.

To the All-Cargo Carriers

The all-cargo carriers, particularly Flying Tiger, will have to take the initiative in making the case that the industry should restructure itself with relatively few (perhaps two) carriers providing freighter service. As noted, one of these carriers could well be a company formed by pooling the freighter operations of the combination carriers. Clearly there are dangers for Flying Tiger and Airlift International in that a new all-cargo competitor (or competitors) might prove to be stronger competition than several combination carriers offering both freighter and combination service.

The airline would perform no tracing for 36 hours, nor would it disclose to the shipper or consignee any information regarding the flight of the shipment or time of delivery.

[9] Harold D. Watkins, "Airlines, CAB Grapple with Cargo Tariffs," p. 51.

Yet, as cargo specialists, Flying Tiger and Airlift International obviously have the most to gain from any policies which enhance the financial attractiveness of air cargo.

The all-cargo carriers (including the freighter spin-off from the combination carriers) will provide both scheduled and nonscheduled service. Should the U.S. Postal Service seriously consider private operations, the all-cargo carriers (individually or as a group) should be prepared to procure and operate the line haul equipment. Likewise, they will have to seek contracts aggressively to operate other private fleets, should they prove to be an attractive investment. Thus, the all-cargo carriers will be the primary institutions for operating the next generation of freighter aircraft, either in scheduled or nonscheduled freighter service.

Before investing in jumbo freighters, however, the all-cargo carriers will have to make certain that the profit potential is realistic. An understanding will have to be reached within the air freight community that a viable air freight industry requires compensatory rates. In turn, the compensatory rates will have to be based on freighter service operations at realistic load factors and efficient operations, rather than the short-run costs of belly service incurred by the combination carriers.

The all-cargo carriers in planning their domestic strategy should also investigate a radical possibility which flies in the face of the trends to date, namely being the catalyst for the development of a high speed, efficient, transcontinental container train service. If the analysis of costs and the value of time saved are correct herein, much of what has been termed routine surface divertible traffic could well move transcontinental by surface if the origin-destination transit time were three to four days. This is particularly true for shipments sent Thursday and Friday which could easily be available for the customer on Monday or Tuesday of the following week.

If premium transcontinental shipments were pooled over one route by a consortium of motor carriers, forwarders, and air freight operators, it might well be feasible to operate one container train a day on a 60-hour schedule and permit third-morning delivery at exceptionally low rates. Obviously there are problems to be resolved. Can the railroads in fact operate transcontinental service at an average speed of 50 mph?

Will the railroads agree to the "one route" concept? There is probably not enough tonnage to support competition over more than one route. For example, A. T. Kearny in a study performed for the warehousing firm D. H. Overmeyer estimated that between New York and Los Angeles there were 669,000 tons westbound and 458,000 tons eastbound in 1969.[10] If we assumed the use of 50-car (100 van) trains of 1,800 payload tons each, this would be the equivalent of 371 westbound and 254 eastbound trains, sufficient to provide weekday service. Kearny's study goes one step further and envisions container trains linking major distribution container centers on a transcontinental route serving Cleveland, Detroit, Chicago, Dallas, Los Angeles, and San Francisco. Even with intermediate stops, Kearny estimates that containers could move from coast to coast in slightly over four days.

---

[10] Jack W. Farrell, "Domestic Containerization—A Possible Breakthrough?" *Traffic Management* (July 1971), pp. 55–57.

If such container trains operated, it would mean that air freight could well be restricted to emergency and routine perishable traffic by 1980. Clearly the all-cargo strategy should not include investment in the next generation of aircraft unless it is perfectly evident that high-speed, high-quality, low-cost surface transportation will not materialize.

Should the domestic all-cargo carriers find that the rail plan is feasible, they might try to inaugurate a freight version of Amtrak, whereby they would plan and market a total premium, high-speed transportation service and purchase transportation from the railroads, in effect substituting container trains for aircraft. Again, they would rely on the motor carriers, forwarders, and large shippers to tender loaded containers as in the low-risk air freighter scenario.

To the U.S. Civil Aeronautics Board and the U.S. Department of Transportation

Many of the issues discussed in this study involve the promotional and regulatory policies of the federal government. Industry structure (entry, merger, exit), routes, pricing, and scheduling in the passenger sector directly require action by the CAB. An additional function which is crucial to the future of domestic air cargo is suggested by the analysis and findings of this research, namely that a series of alternative scenarios for the industry must be developed in sufficient detail to guide the carriers, regulatory and promotional agencies, and other interested parties in their future activities. The CAB and the DOT must individually or jointly take the lead in providing the environment and support for long-range planning. If the industry continues to rely primarily on individual decisions by a host of competitors, goaded by the sales efforts of the aircraft manufacturers, the prospects for financial success seem poor.

Currently, the CAB has reactivated its study of the air freight industry.[11] The emphasis is to be on rates including commodity discounts, distance taper, weight breaks, density incentives, etc. Although pricing is obviously important, the findings of this study suggest that the investigation should be broadened to include the fundamental questions of industry structure, competition, and economics.

Rather than an exercise in legalistic maneuvering, one would hope that the investigation could provide the setting for the following kinds of activities:

(1) Development of alternative financial futures for domestic air cargo using simulation techniques including assumptions as to price, load factor, scheduling, equipment selection, costs and load factors of competitive modes, nature of traffic (emergency, routine perishable, routine surface divertible), industry structure, and environmental constraints.

The cost of this kind of analytical exercise might appear to be substantial, yet in comparison with the operating losses to date from freighter service, and the prospects of future losses, the true costs would be low.

---

[11] Richard Malkin, "Is A Rate Shakeup in Prospect?" *Cargo Airlift* (February 1971, p. 4) discusses the CAB investigation docketed as 22859. The investigation was delayed pending approval of the CAB total budget for 1972. See CAB, "Now Ready to Move on Long Delayed Cases Involving Cargo Matters," *Traffic World* (August 16, 1971), p. 73.

(2) Provide an open forum whereby the key assumptions underlying domestic air freight profitability could be aired in a manner conducive to specific actions which could resolve the problems. Too often, the various forums on air cargo have been either opportunities for the aircraft manufacturers to promote a new generation of aircraft sessions where the "have-nots" complain about unfair treatment from the "haves" (e.g., all-cargo versus the combination carriers), or sales efforts to woo new shippers.

Perhaps a series of workshops utilizing presentations, case studies, computer exercises, and the like, attended by representatives from the air carriers, surface carriers, suppliers, and government could bring the issues to the surface and contribute to the debate necessary for restructuring.

Obvious topics would include the future of Air Express, the existing air freight forwarders, the railroads and motor carriers acting as the "new" air freight forwarders, the role of the all-cargo carriers, strategies for the combination carriers, a timetable for the introduction of a new generation of freighter equipment, and perhaps most important, a better feel for the future mix of air freight traffic emergency, routine perishable, routine surface divertible.

One would hope that the Air Transport Association of America and the major carriers would take the lead in broadening and structuring the CAB investigation in this direction. Otherwise, the regulatory agencies will be left in their usual unenviable position of scrutinizing the short-term decisions, while the long-term strategic issues —primarily choice of equipment—go unquestioned. Yet, once the equipment choices are made, it is often too late to prevent competitive chaos.

It will not be easy for this kind of long-range participatory planning activity to take place. It is not unreasonable to assume that the individual airlines within the air freight industry are skeptical that joint planning could really succeed. It is almost a question of ideology. The pragmatic behavior of management to date almost assumes from the outset that cooperative planning with strong inputs from centralized government are doomed to failure.

The time for resolution of the problems of the air freight industry is running short. Already, off-peak price cutting has begun by the combination carriers. We can expect acrimonious debate in the regulatory halls as each of the carriers and interest groups tries to protect its position. One hopes that a new spirit of cooperation will emerge to challenge the assumptions of the past and recast the structure and practices of the industry for the future.

Otherwise the U.S. domestic common carrier air freight industry will remain frustrated and confused and, in the midst of technological progress and traffic growth, profits will be found wanting. The optimists will look to the future for salvation, but their hopes will not be realized.

Appendixes

Selected Bibliography

Appendix A

American Airlines (M)

Evaluation of an Air Freight Marketing Program

INTRODUCTION

In the summer of 1967, Mr. R. F. Lambert, Vice President—Freight, of American Airlines was reviewing a proposed air freight marketing program prior to making a presentation to the senior vice president-marketing. Inasmuch as the program would involve added expenditures of approximately $1,000,000 and change existing patterns of selling, he wondered if there should be any major modifications in the proposed program, or if the company should consider seriously other alternatives.

BACKGROUND OF THE PROPOSAL

American Airlines was one of the major airlines in the United States. On the basis of 1966 sales revenue, it ranked third behind United Airlines and Pan American World Airways. Exhibit 1 contains financial and operating data for the years 1960–1966. American's routes blanketed the Northeast and East North Central sections of the country and linked these regions with the West Coast and Southwest. Exhibit 2 contains a tabulation of some of the major market segments served by the company and its principal competitors over those segments.

American was the leading domestic air freight carrier in 1966. Exhibit 3 indicates share of the market data on the basis of freight ton-miles for 1965 and 1966. Exhibit 4 contains a tabulation of air freight revenue and freight ton-miles for American, the domestic trunk lines and the total industry for the years 1960–1966.

Although air freight ton-miles represented less than .2% of the nation's intercity

NOTE: This case was prepared by Asst. Prof. Lewis M. Schneider as a basis for class discussion rather than to illustrate either effective or ineffective handling of an administrative situation. (9-312-113, T 680.)

EXHIBIT 1
AMERICAN AIRLINES (M)
Selected Statistics 1960–1966, American Airlines

Year	Available Seat Miles (Billion)	Revenue Psgr Miles (Billion)	Revenue Psgrs (Million)	Total Revenue ($ Million)	Operating Expense ($ Million)	Net Income After Special Inc. ($ Million)
1960	9.78	6.37	8.19	428.5	404.4	11.8
1961	9.81	6.01	7.66	421.4	402.5	7.3
1962	11.36	6.48	8.11	460.9	439.6	9.5
1963	12.22	7.15	8.52	488.1	446.6	17.2
1964	13.60	8.11	9.55	544.0	479.5	33.5
1965	15.61	9.20	11.00	612.2	537.6	39.7
1966	18.72	11.80	13.99	724.7	629.8	52.1

SOURCE: Moody's *Transportation.*

EXHIBIT 2
AMERICAN AIRLINES (M)
Air Freight Competition in Major Markets—1967

Major Markets	Major Competitors of American Airlines
Boston-New York-Washington	Eastern, Northeast
New York-Chicago	TWA, United, Flying Tiger
New York-Los Angeles	TWA, United, Flying Tiger
New York-San Francisco	TWA, United, Flying Tiger
Chicago-Los Angeles	TWA, United, Flying Tiger
Chicago-San Francisco	TWA, United, Flying Tiger
Dallas-New York	Braniff, Delta

EXHIBIT 3
AMERICAN AIRLINES (M)
Share of the Domestic Air Freight Market
Scheduled Service
Selected Carriers—1965, 1966

Airline	Share of Total Air Freight Revenue Ton-Miles Scheduled Service		Share of Total Air Cargo Revenue Ton-Miles Scheduled Service Carried in All-Cargo Planes	
	1965	1966	1965	1966
American	24.4%	28.3%	31.0%	36.9%
United	20.4%	20.0%	19.3%	19.8%
TWA	14.2%	13.1%	13.4%	11.7%
Flying Tiger	12.1%	13.8%	24.5%	24.8%

NOTES: CAB reports revenue ton-miles for all-cargo scheduled service as the total of air freight, mail, and express. Air freight revenue accounted for approximately 88% of total revenue generated in all-cargo scheduled service.

In 1966 the International Association of Machinists struck Eastern, National, Northwest, Trans World, and United for 43 days.

SOURCE: CAB.

freight ton-miles, the growth of air freight traffic and revenue was highly significant. It was anticipated by all experts in the field that air freight would continue to grow at a rapid rate. For example, one authority predicted that 1980 domestic air freight ton-miles would be 13 times the 1966 volume, indicating a growth rate of approximately 20% per year.

Mr. Lambert was confident that air freight traffic would continue to grow in the aggregate. Yet he recognized that the growth would depend to a large degree on factors which were still uncertain. These included:

(1) The level of rates which would be made possible by the introduction of large cargo planes such as the Lockheed L-500 or Boeing 747. In 1966 the average revenue per freight ton-mile for domestic scheduled airlines was 20.21¢ but the range in yields was significant. For example, eastbound transcontinental freight traffic often moved at ton-mile yields of less than 10¢.

Exhibit 5 indicates the revenue and costs of the scheduled all-cargo operations of American, United, TWA, and Flying Tiger lines. Exhibit 6 shows various financial and operating data pertaining to American's all-cargo Boeing 707-300C operations for the 12 months ending September 30, 1966.

Boeing officials estimated that a fully loaded 747 operating on a range of 1,000–2,000 miles would experience direct operating costs of approximately 3.3¢ per revenue ton-mile (Exhibit 7). The 747 freighter could handle up to seven 8 × 8 × 40-foot containers or the equivalent in 10, 20, and 30-foot lengths on the main cargo deck.

In contrast, the average revenue per ton-mile for Class I and II trucks in 1966 was 6.5¢. An ICC study published in 1967 examined more closely the operating costs for transcontinental truck services. Its findings are summarized in Exhibit 8.

(2) Improvement in air-truck coordinated service. Many experts believed that air cargo traffic growth was unduly hampered by regulatory restrictions concerning the coordinated use of air and ground transportation. In 1967 the overwhelming majority of air freight traffic had origins and destinations within 25 miles of a given airport, the so-called exempt terminal zone. Shipments originating or terminating beyond the terminal zone sometimes moved on relatively high combination rates as compared to joint

EXHIBIT 4
AMERICAN AIRLINES (M)
Selected Statistics—Air Freight Operations
(All Data in Millions)

Year	American Airlines		Domestic Trunk Airlines		Consolidated Industry[a]	
	Revenue	Ton-Miles	Revenue	Ton-Miles	Revenue	Ton-Miles
1960	$24.9	115.1	$42.2	191.0	$108.8	451.0
1961	26.4	128.4	85.3	384.2	176.8	733.0
1962	31.0	156.4	102.4	474.0	203.8	898.2
1963	33.6	165.7	116.5	520.6	234.7	1,026.5
1964	37.5	190.1	141.0	650.7	285.7	1,301.5
1965	47.3	254.2	174.2	835.1	356.1	1,730.3
1966	$61.6	344.7	$201.3	988.5	$411.9	2,050.7

[a] Includes: Domestic Trunk, Local Service, Intra-Hawaiian, Helicopter, Intra-Alaskan, All Cargo, International.

SOURCE: Air Transport Association of America.

EXHIBIT 5
AMERICAN AIRLINES (M)
Comparative Revenue and Costs of Scheduled All-Cargo Operations
Specified Airlines, 1965–1966
(All Data in Thousands)

	American 1965	American 1966	Trans World 1965	Trans World 1966	United 1965	United 1966	Flying Tiger 1965	Flying Tiger 1966
Operating revenue								
Freight	26037	39351	11608	13586	16066	23072	16450	22650
Total	28828	44051	13597	16229	19849	29351	17282	23483
Total Operating Expenses	27416	39098	16264	18652	22553	29469	16930	20446
Flying Operations	7223	10844	4170	4293	5642	7159	4044	4808
Maintenance	5837	6709	2807	3326	5176	5761	4223	4844
Aircraft Servicing	2490	3442	1517	1678	1711	2189	775	881
Traffic Servicing	7073	10993	4014	4824	5814	8514	3080	3931
Reservations & Sales	537	889	749	1035	338	561	1307	1285
Advertising and Publicity	192	267	409	530	393	732	485	506
General and Administrative	1175	1508	766	1069	1000	1386	841	1137
Depreciation	2889	4446	1830	1897	2479	3167	2175	3054
Operating Profit or Loss after Taxes	732	2573	(1064)	(927)	(1406)	(61)	183	1837
Available Ton-Miles	278,900	461,100	165,300	173,400	193,400	246,400	173,600	226,700
Revenue Ton-Miles	161,718	253,424	69,649	80,191	100,634	136,216	127,611	169,811

NOTES: Direct operating expenses included all of Flying Operations, and portions of Maintenance and Depreciation. Indirect operating expenses included all of Aircraft Servicing, Traffic Servicing, Reservations and Sales, Advertising and Publicity, and General and Administrative. In 1965 American's maintenance and depreciation expenses were allocated between direct and indirect as follows:

	(Data in thousands)	
Direct: Flight equipment maintenance	$5,474	
Indirect: Ground property maintenance	363	
	Flight equipment depreciation	$2,685
	Ground property depreciation	205

Thus, American's direct operating expenses in 1965 were 56.1% of total expenses.

SOURCE: Civil Aeronautics Board, Form 242.

EXHIBIT 6

AMERICAN AIRLINES (M)
Operating Costs for Jet and Turbo-Prop Aircraft
12 Months Ending Sept. 30, 1966

Airline	B-707-300C		DC-8F	CL-44
	AA	TW	UA	FT
TRAFFIC AND SERVICE				
Rev. Acft. Miles (000)				
Scheduled	8091	2936	4782	6536
Hours Flown Rev.	17208	6332	9992	51122
TOTAL HOURS FLOWN	18400	7054	11321	52709
Percent Block to Airborne	117.7	118.6	115.0	107.1
Block Hours—Rev.	20254	7510	11491	54752
TOTAL BLOCK HOURS	21657	8366	13019	56451
Rev. Departures	9666	3759	4546	13368
Rev. Ton-Miles—Shd. (mil.)	203	63	96	149
Avail. Ton-Miles—Shd. (mil.)	361	134	185	196
Operating Indices				
Rev. Utilization—Flight	6:40	8:24	7:31	9:23
—Block	7:51	9:31	8:39	10:04
Avg. Flight Length	837	781	1063	1306
Avg. Speed—Airborne	470	464	484	342
—Block	400	391	420	319
Overall Load Factor (%)	56.30	47.22	51.73	76.26
Avg. Taxi Time	:12	:19	:19	:16
AIRCRAFT OPERATING EXPENSES **(DOLLARS PER TOTAL BLOCK HOURS)**				
Flying Operations				
Crew Salary/Exp.	$154.36	$147.14	$132.04	$109.62
Fuel, Oil & Taxes	182.99	165.79	182.81	96.14
Insurance	18.19	13.39	10.60	24.55
Other	.05	.84	.31	.04
TOTAL	355.59	327.16	325.76	230.35
Maintenance				
Airframe	50.98	44.70	46.55	39.26
Engine	44.47	(.12)	56.99	92.21
Other	2.49	9.56	13.67	36.58
Total Direct	97.94	54.14	117.21	168.05
Maint. Burden	79.93	84.75	94.09	45.37
TOTAL	177.87	138.89	211.30	213.42
Cash Acft. Oper. Ex.	533.46	466.05	537.06	443.77
Depr. & Rentals	182.94	176.43	159.30	126.83
TOTAL ACFT. OPER. EXP.	$716.40	$642.48	$696.36	$570.60
Cost Per Mile	191.75¢	183.08¢	187.63¢	184.49¢

All above statistics relate to all-cargo aircraft used in scheduled operations.

SOURCE: *Air Transport World*

EXHIBIT 7

AMERICAN AIRLINES (M)
Comparative Cost and Operating Data
Boeing 707-320C Versus Boeing 747

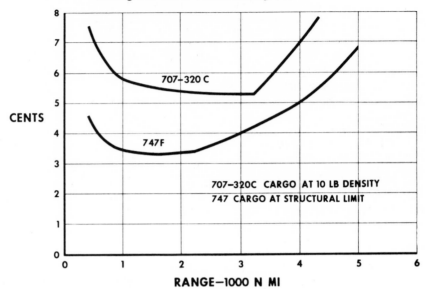

DIRECT OPERATING COST PER TON MILE

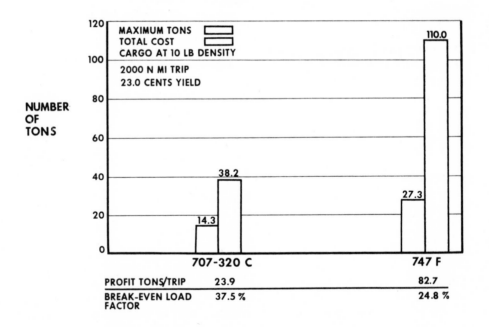

PROFIT TONS/TRIP	23.9	82.7
BREAK-EVEN LOAD FACTOR	37.5 %	24.8 %

CAPACITY VS BREAK-EVEN TONS 707 AND 747

SOURCE: H.A. Carter (The Boeing Company), "The Boeing 747 and Its Impact on Future Airline Operations," *Transportation Research Forum* (1967).

EXHIBIT 8

AMERICAN AIRLINES (M)

Comparison of Average Total Costs,[a] Eight Selected Transcontinental Motor
Carriers and All-Cargo Services of Three Air Carriers, 1965
(Cents Per Ton-Mile)

Elements of Expenses	Motor-Air Cost Comparison Without Adjustment for Density[b]		Motor-Air Cost Comparison after Adjustment for Density[b]	
	Motor Cost	Air Cost	Motor Cost	Air Cost
Equipment Maintenance	0.547	3.840	0.882	3.840
Transportation	1.262	4.480	2.035	4.480
Depreciation	0.151	1.847	0.243	1.847
All Other	0.532	7.558	0.858	7.558
Total Operating Expenses	2.491	17.727	4.018	17.727

[a] Costs reflect direct and indirect costs incurred in line-haul operations of the carriers specified in accompanying tables. Return on investment and income taxes are not included.

[b] The average density for the 8 motor carriers was computed at 12.9 pounds per cu. ft. On the assumption of 8 pounds per cu. ft. for the 3 airlines, the density of air-cargo is 62 per cent of that of the motor carriers. The line-haul motor unit costs were divided by a ratio of 0.62 to reflect the cost of traffic having the density of air cargo.

SOURCE: Interstate Commerce Commission, *Air-Truck Coordination and Competition* (1967).

air-truck rates for a through shipment. The quality of service beyond the 25-mile zone could vary widely. Carriers providing pickup and delivery service within the 25-mile zone were generally precluded by regulatory restrictions from serving more distant points. Carriers handling shipments beyond the 25-mile zone faced the prospect of empty return hauls unless they could combine their airline-oriented traffic with other business. Yet, there was resistance by many common carrier truckers to allowing pickup and delivery carriers to expand their operations beyond the 25-mile zone. American Airlines promoted vigorously the concept of joint air-truck rates for shipments beyond airport terminal zones ("Air-Truck/Truck-Air").

(3) The willingness of shippers to make fundamental changes in their distribution patterns. Many shippers used air freight only for emergency shipments or for perishable items. They believed that air freight was too costly for "normal" shipments. On the other hand, others were beginning to see transportation as but one part of an overall industrial logistics system. They found that they could "trade-off" high-cost air freight against the savings in inventory which might result from the use of premium high-speed transportation. The most dramatic trade-offs involved the substitution of air freight and a central warehouse for a system of regional or local warehouses supplied by surface transportation. Yet, many shippers were either unwilling or unable to undertake "total cost" studies. These companies believed that the future use of air freight for normal shipments would depend upon significantly reduced rates.

In 1967 the U.S. airlines had approximately 100 cargo jets in service with the capability of producing more than 4 billion ton-miles per year. The Air Transport Asso-

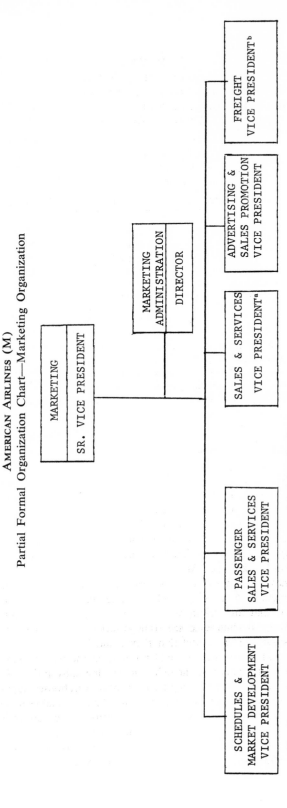

EXHIBIT 9
AMERICAN AIRLINES (M)
Partial Formal Organization Chart—Marketing Organization

MARKETING
SR. VICE PRESIDENT

MARKETING
ADMINISTRATION
DIRECTOR

SCHEDULES &
MARKET DEVELOPMENT
VICE PRESIDENT

PASSENGER
SALES & SERVICES
VICE PRESIDENT

SALES & SERVICES
VICE PRESIDENT[a]

ADVERTISING &
SALES PROMOTION
VICE PRESIDENT

FREIGHT
VICE PRESIDENT[b]

[a] Has line authority over the system passenger and freight sales forces.
[b] See Exhibit 11 for the organization reporting to the freight vice president.

EXHIBIT 10
AMERICAN AIRLINES (M)
Typical Freight Sales Representative's Profile

Years with Company: 11
Age: (25–59) weighted average 41
Education: 94% some college
39% college degree

(over 50% of the sales representatives
recommended for promotion have college degrees)
Compensation: Approximately $9,500 to $14,000 annually

ciation of America reported that the 160 freighter jets on order through 1970 would add another six billion or more ton-miles to the existing all-cargo capacity.[1]

As of May 1967, American owned one Boeing 707 convertible passenger freighter and eleven 707 jet freighters. The remainder of its equipment consisted of passenger aircraft. It had on order eighteen 707 convertible and seven 707 nonconvertible freighters, all to be delivered by 1970. The company had also ordered ten 747 passenger aircraft.[2] It had not at that time purchased a 747 in the freighter configuration. In 1966, approximately 60% of American's freight tonnage moved on all-cargo planes.

Mr. Lambert knew that several of his competitors currently carrying relatively small amounts of air freight were planning to expand their freight operations. He wondered if American's share of the market would decline significantly even within the context of a growing demand for freight service.

AMERICAN'S FREIGHT SALES EFFORT

Formal Organization

In 1967, the American Airlines freight sales program consisted of a national and local organization as shown on the formal organization chart in Exhibit 9. One hundred men called on customers at the local level. Exhibit 10 summarizes the backgrounds of the typical salesmen in the organization.

At the headquarters organization, Mr. Lambert had been with the company 27 years. His previous experience had been in all phases of American's Sales and Service Organization. He had assumed his current position in 1967. His staff is shown in Exhibit 11.

Mr. T. P. Gallagher, Director of Freight Sales, had come with American in February 1966. He had previously worked in the food and drug industries in various marketing capacities. He brought to American a completely new concept in the marketing of air freight.

Selling Strategy Prior to 1967

American's selling effort historically depended heavily on the local salesman. He was expected to make approximately 30 to 40 calls per week. About 15% of these calls

---

[1] These data included the so-called "quick-change" aircraft which could be operated in either an all-passenger or all-cargo configuration.

[2] It was anticipated that the passenger version of the B-747 would carry 40,000–50,000 pounds of freight in the "belly compartment" in addition to passenger baggage.

EXHIBIT 11. AMERICAN AIRLINES (M)
Partial Organization Chart—Freight Service and Sales Staff

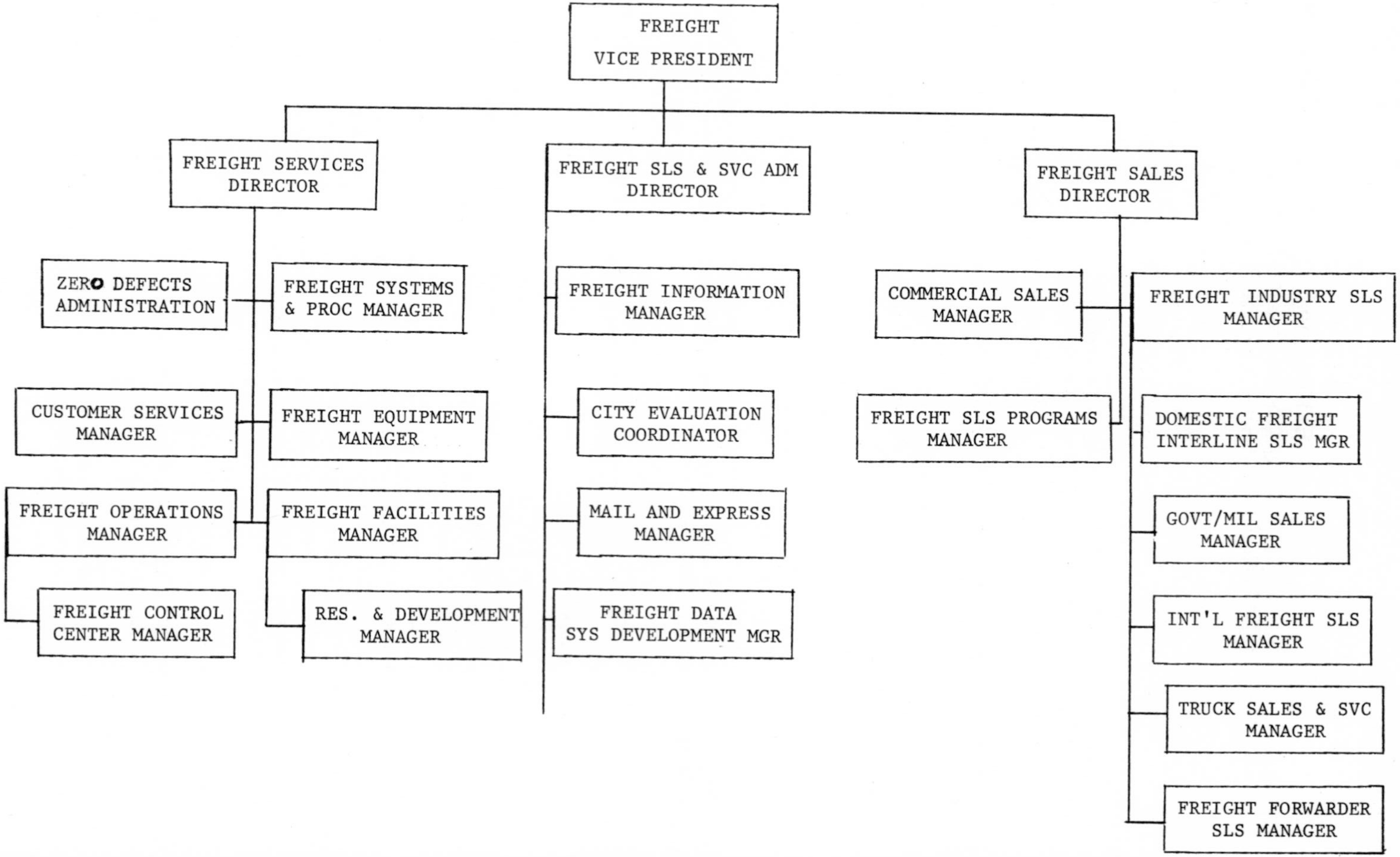

EXHIBIT 12
AMERICAN AIRLINES (M)
Excerpts From "This Is The American Way"

If you want to ship to customers practically anywhere in the U.S. including
all top 10 consumer markets
the 10 largest industrial areas
52 leading markets coast to coast
91% of all mail order firms
91% of all wearing apparel plants
91% of all TV and hi-fi plants
89% of all electrical machinery plants

were made on new accounts. The salesman obtained the names of possible new accounts either from the headquarters organization, the district office, or on the basis of his own efforts. Leads from the headquarters organization were often the by-product of personal contact between American's and industry's executives. Often firms would make inquiries directly to American's headquarters concerning the initiation of freight service. American tried to stimulate such inquiries through use of national advertising and promotional booklets. Exhibit 12 contains excerpts from a booklet which was distributed in response to customer inquiries generated by national advertising.

Salesmen calling on existing accounts tried to stimulate more business as well as handle routine problems (tracing, claims, packaging, etc.).

Small Group Marketing Campaign

In 1967 American began to strengthen its headquarters sales effort by sending out teams to make presentations to interested executives in companies wanting to learn more about air freight. Typically the presentation was made to less than six people, e.g., the firm's traffic manager, sales manager, production manager, comptroller, etc. A twelve-minute slide and audio presentation described the nature of American's freight system and the method by which the cost and service features of air freight could be analyzed as a part of the "total cost" concept. The American representative would then hand out promotional material and answer any questions concerning the particular problems faced by the firm. Approximately 30% of the presentations, in fact, were initiated by customer inquiries.

Mr. Gallagher felt that the small group marketing concept was quite valuable. However, he recognized that given the limitations on the size of the headquarters staff, relatively few companies could be approached in a given year.

THE SELECTIVE MARKETING PROPOSAL

In mid 1967, Mr. Gallagher and his staff began to develop a program for expanding the sales effort. The key features of the program involved the identification of a particular industry having significant air traffic potential, performing an extensive analysis of the distribution practices of the particular industry at American's headquarters, and supplying the local sales force with lead cards containing specific information for individual firms within the industry.

Appendix Table A-1 contains details of the selective marketing program.

Mr. Gallagher recognized that the new program would add additional costs to the sales effort. He believed that the budget would have to be increased by approximately 25% to cover the additional costs of research, training, and additional manpower necessary to make the sales calls. He summarized the advantages of the proposal as follows:[3]

(1) More profitable freight

(2) More efficient use of salesmen's time

(3) Qualified sales leads

On the other hand, he recognized that there were other alternatives available to him. One of his larger competitors was in the process of building up a regional sales engineering force to supplement the local sales people. The regional sales engineers would be equipped to assist potential customers in making extensive analyses of their logistics systems. These analyses involved determining the cost of transportation, warehouses, inventory control, order processing, and customer service. These requirements appeared to be the necessary prerequisites to any major shifts in a firm's shipping policies.

Another approach used by an international carrier was to invest in even greater headquarters staff support. This airline encouraged shippers to give the headquarters staff group the relevant costs and operational information necessary for a complete logistics analysis. The airline headquarters staff with the aid of a computer simulation recommended a distribution system to the potential customer. It was rumored that the cost of one such customer survey might run as high as $5,000 to $7,000.

Mr. Gallagher recognized that the selective marketing concept depended to a major extent on four factors: (a) the quality of the research effort at headquarters in identifying the crucial economic variables for a given industry, (b) locating potential customers, (c) determining what role the local salesmen should play, and (d) in providing for coordination between the local sales force and the headquarters staff support.

The market research would not be performed within the freight sales department but rather by a member of the schedules and marketing development staff (Exhibit 9). The potential customer list would be purchased from Dun & Bradstreet at a cost of approximately $115 per thousand.

If the proposed marketing program were approved, it was anticipated that it could be implemented in early 1968.

*   *   *

American Airlines Freight System

American Airlines Freight System is a combination of airplanes, trucks, freight terminals, ground handling equipment, freight specialists—all organized to move your freight to almost any part of the country within two days or less. It's a system designed to contribute to your profits by matching faster production paces and rapidly changing market conditions. It's a system designed for business today.

*   *   *

Door-to-Door Delivery

Whether your customer or supplier is located in a city, suburb, or in a rural area, American Airlines Freight System carries the speed of jet shipping off the runways and onto the streets and highways that go right to his door. By coordinating with leading

---

[3] See Appendix Table A-2 for Mr. Gallagher's complete summary of the selective marketing concept.

motor carriers we give you door-to-door pickup and delivery for hundreds of miles around any Freight System city. . . . And one bill covers everything—probably at lower combined rates than you have paid before.

*   *   *

Call the Nearest Freight Information Center and Talk to a Freight Specialist

Whether you ask about pickup, delivery, schedules, routes, or anything else, you'll get a straight answer from an American Airlines Freight Specialist who knows what he's talking about.

In fact, don't be surprised if he tells you more than you expected. For instance, say you're calling about rates. You'll get them. But if there's a way to ship at *lower* rates, he'll tell you about that too. He'll give you complete information and take care of all handling details.

That includes making sure that nothing slows down your shipment. Not even paperwork. At major terminals in the American Airlines Freight System, waybills are teletyped ahead to destination so your shipment is not held up while paperwork is being completed. And if you want to check on a shipment, an American Airlines Freight Specialist can give you the information faster because all Freight Information Centers are coordinated by the fastest communications network in the industry.

Only American Airlines has a 24-hour monitored open telephone line that puts all cities in instant contact with one another. That way, if you're in New York and want information on a shipment from Los Angeles, your request is relayed to Los Angeles within seconds after you call. No matter where you shipped or what you want to know, you find out faster because our Freight Specialists can get on the line to any city. Instantly. American Airlines Freight Information Centers, staffed by specialists, are the controlling nerve center of the system. They plan freight movement and space allocations far in advance of shipping schedules to make sure that your customers get on-time-delivery. At any time.

*   *   *

We're as Fast on the Ground as We Are in the Air

A fast terminal isn't an accident. It's a result of careful planning by the American Freight Planning Group which has supervised our terminal construction ever since we introduced commercial air shipping in 1944. . . .

On the loading side, special crews are assigned to load up "igloos." An American Airlines innovation, igloos are protective containers shaped to conform to the contours and dimensions of the Jetfreighters. The igloos make it possible to load or unload Jetfreighters in a matter of minutes.

*   *   *

The Most Advanced Equipment for Loading and Flying Your Freight

In October of 1944 American Airlines carried the first commercial air shipment. And because we were first with air shipping, we've had more time to develop advanced handling techniques and equipment. More time to find out what kind of service shippers need—and when and where they need it. . . .

Today American Airlines Freight System serves shippers with the biggest fleet of Jetfreighters now flying. In addition, there are over two thousand other freight hauls made every week by other American Airlines jet flights.

*   *   *

Quality Control Makes Sure You Get the Best Service Every Time

Quality control is not just a gesture at American Airlines Freight System. We take it seriously. Because we do, we've developed the industry's most comprehensive Quality

Control Program. Used everywhere throughout the system, on the ground and in the air, Quality Control tests performance and measures it against predetermined standards. Of course, those standards don't stand for very long because they're constantly being upgraded. For instance, in 1964 all phone calls to the Freight Information Centers had to be answered within 90 seconds. By 1965, answering time had been pared to 40 seconds.

Truck docking is another good example of constantly improving performance standards. In '64 all trucks had to be docked within 15 minutes after they arrived at a terminal. Now, it's 10 minutes or less—and most trucks get docked the minute they arrive.

The Quality Control staff is made up of specially trained engineers who do nothing but travel from city to city checking on telephone service, freight dispatch, intraline and interline transfer, freight availability, truck-docking service, delivery, everything.

To make sure their recommendations get prompt attention, Quality Control is organized as a separate department that answers directly to top management. And what if they find that somebody goofed? Relax. Heads don't roll. Instead, a detailed Delay Analysis Report examines the reasons why performance isn't up to snuff and indicates where improvements can be made. Then we make them. That way, we keep your shipment moving as efficiently as possible every step of the way to your customer's door.

*   *   *

Use the American Way to Jet to Market and Cut the Total Cost of Distributing Your Products

The cost of distribution is not only what your company spends to ship its products, but also what it spends to handle them, inventory them, warehouse them—even package them. Add it all up and you find that the *total* cost of distribution accounts for 21¢ out of every operating dollar the average company spends.

One of the prime reasons it costs so much is that distribution is frequently geared exclusively to surface transportation. Jet shipping is generally ignored because it is assumed to be too expensive. Yet for many companies, regular jet shipping offers tremendous cost-cutting opportunities!

First of all, the difference between surface and jet rates is generally less than assumed. But remember that shipping rates are just part of total distribution cost. If inventory possession is being forced back on your company, jet shipping can help solve the problem by combining equal or better service to customers with a stock reduction and stock streamlining program. The savings in taxes, interest, handling, and distant-warehousing-costs can more than offset the differential between surface and jet rates.

But perhaps even more important than the money jet shipping can save is the new money it can bring in by providing your company with new marketing techniques.

Since American Airlines Freight System delivers almost anywhere in the U.S. inside of two days, it makes it possible to compete in new markets no matter how distant. With jet speed, you can test in new markets without the expense of remote inventories, you can restock and meet increased demand almost immediately. Jet shipping enables your company to offer service that's as fast as that given by local competition.

Now, exactly how can jet shipping be used by your company to cut costs and bring in money? There are not cut-and-dried answers. Instead, it takes a special evaluation that matches the way you do business with one of the many ways American Airlines Freight System jet ships to your markets. Our specialists have already evaluated jet shipping for hundreds of companies of every type and size. They would be glad to advise you. To reach them, call the Information Center of your nearest American Airlines Freight System Office.

*   *   *

APPENDIX TABLE A-1
American Airlines (M)
Outline of American Airlines "Selective Marketing" Program

Nature of Task	*Status as of the Summer of 1967*
1. Analyze total cargo movements in United States to determine potential airline share	1. Completed by headquarters staff
2. Using the 1963 Census of Transportation identify industry group with high air potential	2. Out of the 24 broad industry groups, one industry group was spotlighted for further action.
3. Convert the industry codes used in the Census of Transportation to the equivalent Standard Industrial Classification codes (SIC)	3. Completed
4. Using the SIC codes as guides produce a list of potential accounts from Dun & Bradstreet's master files	4. Dun & Bradstreet cards would be purchased containing the following information for a given SIC: a. Name and address of each plant b. Number of employees of total company and at each plant c. Sales volume and net worth of firm d. Telephone number e. Name of chief executive f. Line of business (corresponding to primary SIC) g. Year firm began
5. Break down the lead cards by American Airlines sales office 6. Supply the salesman with background information on the particular industry (See discussion below) 7. Determine which firms should be visited 8. Implement program and monitor performance	5.–8. Depends upon acceptance of program

Discussion

The first broad industry group chosen had over 10,000 firms in the favorable SIC categories.

The "Selective Marketing" concept required that the following background information be obtained if available and analyzed at American's headquarters.

Source and Nature of Information	*Information Detail*
1. Annual reports of individual firms For information on individual firms	1. Annual sales 2. Geographical areas covered 3. Locations of warehouses and sales offices 4. Distribution channels 5. Inventory value 6. Estimate of sales/distribution cost 7. Principal officers 8. New products 9. Major investments in facilities
2. Trade press For information on the industry and individual firms	1. Promotional practices 2. Jargon and buzz words 3. Current topics of interest to industry 4. Distribution and sales channels 5. Seasonal patterns 6. New products
3. Trade associations For information on the industry	1. Ranking of manufacturers 2. Sales by geographic area 3. Economic indices 4. Identity and location of major wholesalers 5. Distribution practices and trends 6. Discount schedules 7. Inventory policies 8. Promotional practices 9. Order size at all distribution levels 10. Jargon and buzz words 11. Seasonal patterns 12. Relative profitability of product line 13. Existing use of air freight 14. Private brand competition 15. Manufacturer/Dealer attitudes
4. Research surveys For information on the industry and individual firms	1. Manufacturer/Dealer attitudes 2. Retail store attitudes particularly concerning delivery time 3. Lost sales because of stockout 4. Retail order lead time 5. Brand preferences 6. Seasonal preferences 7. Promotional effectiveness 8. Order sizes, stocking problems 9. Turnover rates 10. Awareness of distribution problems, opportunities, and costs

The objective of the backup information was to answer the basic questions: (1) How does the industry work, and (2) How can air freight help?

The "Selective Marketing" campaign was designed to persuade selected firms to ship "desirable freight." "Desirable" was defined as:
1. Density above system average
2. High weight per shipment
3. Good packaging and unit loads
4. Not perishable with time
5. Able to withstand normal range of climatic conditions
6. Predictable loads
7. Off peak pickup and delivery. (80% of cargo arrives at American's terminals within two hours of flight time.)

The "Selective Marketing" campaign would include: media advertising, direct mail, sales promotion brochures, special giveaways, telephone campaigns, sales training, sales incentives but, most important, direct selling supported by the background information generated at headquarters.

If at all possible the customer would be encouraged to make a "total cost" analysis with American's representative supplying input data as needed.

APPENDIX TABLE A-2
Mr. Gallagher's Summary of the Selective Marketing Concept

Selective Marketing is a synchronized sales effort directed toward specific industries, and specific companies within those industries—and even specific products within those companies during a selected period. The criteria are predetermined for the Sales Representative and maximize the use of his valuable sales time and efforts.

There are three major points which briefly describe our objective through Selective Marketing:
1. PROFIT . . . by targeting our efforts to those accounts who ship what we call "desirable freight" we end up with a higher return per ton-mile.
2. MORE EFFICIENT USE OF SALESMAN'S TIME
   Our Sales Representatives in the field can get a much greater return on their own time if their leads are selected and qualified for them . . . professionally . . . and ahead of time—with one central source rather than requiring each salesman to do it himself . . . so multiply that tremendous economy across the entire system.
3. AN INTEGRATED EFFORT
   Instead of operating in assorted vacuums, every function of marketing will be aiming its guns at the same target. Research, direct sales, advertising, sales promotion, and public relations will all be leveling their guns at the same industry with specified companies and products as the sales objectives.

As the leader in our industry, it is mandatory to embark on a long-range marketing strategy that is designed to expand the base with profitable air freight.

Appendix B

Aeolus Airlines (A)

Replacing a Distribution Warehouse with Air Freight

INTRODUCTION

In the summer of 1968, Mr. Bruce Smith, air freight marketing manager of Aeolus Airlines, was reviewing an analysis made by his staff prior to meeting with the top management of the Carter Clothing Company. The report had recommended that Carter proceed with a series of actual test shipments to determine if it would be feasible to close its Indianapolis regional warehouse and substitute direct shipments by air from Carter's home plant in Houston, Texas.

EXISTING DISTRIBUTION SYSTEM

Carter Clothing Company produced work and sports clothing at its Houston plant for distribution to department stores and men's specialty clothing shops throughout the United States. Its Indianapolis warehouse was one of four regional facilities. Exhibit 1 shows Carter's volume broken down by warehouse service area.

The Indianapolis warehouse stock was replenished from Houston by motor truck in weekly truckload lots. On the average, Carter's slacks weighed one pound, were worth $3.00 per pound, and had a density of 16.6 pounds per cubic foot.

AEOLUS COST ANALYSIS

Inasmuch as the value and density of Carter's product was quite suitable for air freight, Aeolus' Houston freight sales manager was eager to demonstrate that air freight could give Carter better service at lower costs than its existing distribution system. He

NOTE: This case was prepared for the Harvard Business School by Associate Professor Lewis M. Schneider as a basis for class discussion rather than to illustrate either effective or ineffective handling of an administrative situation. (9-370-109, T 702.)

EXHIBIT 1
AEOLUS AIRLINES (A)
Carter Clothing Company
Annual Volume of Freight
by Market Area
(*Data in pounds*)

Indianapolis	1,500,000
San Francisco	800,000
Philadelphia	2,000,000
Atlanta	400,000

EXHIBIT 2
AEOLUS AIRLINES (A)
Carter Clothing Company
Major Operating Costs at
Indianapolis Warehouse

Inventory
  2 months = $718,896

Operating Cost Data

Warehouse rent	$ 23,000
Warehouse labor (includes fringe)	51,000
Taxes (warehouse and inventory)	14,000
Insurance (warehouse and inventory)	2,000
Utilities	5,000
Other costs[a]	38,000
Total	$133,000
Inventory replenishment transportation cost— truck	$ 45,000
Total	$178,000

[a] Other costs include packaging, warehouse pallets, and warehouse equipment, etc.

EXHIBIT 3
AEOLUS AIRLINES (A)
Carter Clothing Company
Warehouse Inventory Costs

2 months inventory =	$718,896
Cost of money =	6.5%
Return on investment =	13.5%
Total =	20.0%

20% of $718,896 = $143,779

$143,779 = Value of capital tied
          up in inventory

EXHIBIT 4
AEOLUS AIRLINES (A)
Carter Clothing Company
Transit or Pipeline Inventory Costs

Truckload shipment = 30,000 lbs.

Product = $3.00 per lb. $\times$ 30,000
        = $90,000 per load

$90,000 @ 20% = 18,000 $\div$ 365 days
             = $50 daily cost

Multiply $50 $\times$ 7 (no. of days in
  transit) = $350

$350 $\times$ 40 (no. of truckloads per
  year) = $14,000

$14,000 = Transit or pipeline inventory
  cost

EXHIBIT 5
AEOLUS AIRLINES (A)
Carter Clothing Company
Cost of Stockouts

Inventory value = $720,000
Product value = $3.00 per item
Net profit   = $1.50 per item

Number of items in inventory =

$\dfrac{\$720,000}{\$3}$ = 240,000 items

10% = Number of stockouts
  per year
10% $\times$ 240,000 = 24,000

24,000 $\times$ $1.50 profit =
  $36,000 = Cost of stockouts

EXHIBIT 6
AEOLUS AIRLINES (A)
Carter Clothing Company
Total Costs of Distribution
via Warehouse

Warehouse operating costs (including inbound transportation)	$178,000
Warehouse inventory costs	143,779
Transit or pipeline inventory costs	14,000
Cost of stockouts	36,000
Total	$371,779

convinced Carter's top management that a "total cost" analysis performed by Aeolus' staff should be undertaken to see if the increased transportation costs of air freight might be offset by savings in inventory and warehouse operating costs.

Exhibits 2 through 6 contain excerpts from the airline's analysis including existing warehouse operating costs at Indianapolis, a detailed analysis of warehouse inventory costs, a calculation of transit or pipeline inventory costs, the cost of stockouts, and the total surface system costs.

Unfortunately the airline was unable to obtain data on the costs of order processing, materials handling, safety stocks, or production setups. Mr. Smith believed that these costs would tend to increase the total surface distribution expenses compared to an air-oriented distribution system.

Mr. Smith's staff then computed the service and cost elements of air distribution by analyzing the following: air freight rates; air freight schedules; order assembly procedures at Houston; consolidation of shipments in a large container; preparation of manifest of total shipment on one airbill; loading of container and movement to the destination airport; and movement of production from the destination airport via motor truck, United Parcel, and Parcel Post. The total cost of air distribution was $170,000—composed of air transportation $150,000 and additional labor at Houston $20,000. Thus, it appeared that Carter could save almost $202,000 annually by utilizing direct air distribution.

Appendix C

APPENDIX TABLE C.1

Data Base

U.S. Domestic Air Freighter Service 1965–1969

(Data in Millions Except Where Percentages are Indicated)

Airline and Date	Load Factor	Available Ton-Mile (Capacity)	Cargo RTM (Freighters)	Combination RTM (Belly)	Total Schedule RTM (Carriers with Freighters)	Percent Cargo RTM	Operating Ratio (Operating Expense ÷ Operating Revenue)
American							
1965	58%	278.9	161.7	143.2	304.9	53	95.1
1966	55	461.1	253.4	162.9	416.4	60.9	88.8
1967	49.2	539.7	265.7	171.7	437.3	60.7	96.8
1968	47.7	698.1	333.0	198.2	531.2	62.7	99.4
1969	44.4	724.0	321.0	196.0	517.0	62.1	109.5
United							
1965	52	193.4	100.6	196.3	296.9	33.9	113.6
1966	55.3	246.4	136.2	200.5	336.7	40.5	100.4
1967	54.7	405.8	222.2	235.3	457.5	48.6	97.0
1968	50.1	605.0	303.4	276.0	579.4	52.4	98.6
1969	45.3	829.9	375.5	291.6	667.1	56.3	108.9
TWA							
1965	42.1	165.3	69.6	123.4	193.0	36.1	119.6
1966	46.5	172.4	80.2	130.2	210.4	38.1	114.9
1967	40.1	295.2	118.2	156.6	274.8	43.0	119.0
1968	39.9	364.1	145.3	176.4	321.7	45.2	112.7
1969	40.5	406.3	164.5	178.7	343.2	47.9	117.9

182

APPENDIX TABLE C.1 (continued)

Flying Tiger

Year							
1965	73.9	172.6	127.6	0	127.6	100	98.0
1966	74.9	226.7	169.8	0	169.8	100	87.1
1967	66.2	246.3	163.3	0	163.3	100	108.3
1968	63.1	263.3	166.0	0	166.0	100	116.0
1969	56.3	309.7	174.4	0	174.4	100	112.6

Other Carriers

Year							
1965	57.6	107.4	61.8	172.6	234.5	26.4	135.1
1966	56.9	82.5	47.0	199.2	245.7	19.1	112.9
1967	46.5	235.0	109.2	294.9	404.0	27.0	105.6
1968	47.5	360.5	171.3	348.1	519.7	33.0	113.2
1969	47.7	471.1	224.7	426.6	651.3	34.5	114.7

Data Base Source: CAB Forms 242 and 41.

APPENDIX TABLE C.2
Data Base
U.S. Domestic Air Freighter Service 1965–1969
Share of Market

Airline and Date	Freighter Traffic	Combination Traffic	Total Sched. Air Freight Traffic	Freighter Revenue	Freighter Capacity (ATM)
American					
1965	31.0%	22.5%	26.4%	31.6%	30.4%
1966	36.9	23.5	30.2	35.4	38.8
1967	30.2	20.0	25.2	26.7	31.3
1968	29.8	19.8	25.1	27.1	30.5
1969	25.5	17.9	22.0	23.0	26.4
United					
1965	19.3	30.9	25.7	21.8	21.1
1966	19.8	28.9	24.4	23.6	20.7
1967	25.3	27.4	26.3	28.5	23.6
1968	27.1	27.6	27.4	28.2	26.4
1969	29.8	26.7	28.4	30.5	30.3
TWA					
1965	13.4	19.4	16.7	14.9	18.0
1966	11.7	18.8	15.3	13.1	14.5
1967	13.5	18.2	15.8	14.2	17.1
1968	13.0	17.7	15.2	13.7	15.9
1969	13.1	16.4	14.6	13.9	14.8

APPENDIX TABLE C.2 (*continued*)

Flying Tiger					
1965	24.5	0	11.0	18.9	18.8
1966	24.7	0	12.3	18.9	19.1
1967	18.6	0	9.4	13.8	14.3
1968	14.8	0	7.8	10.7	11.5
1969	13.8	0	7.4	9.7	11.3
Other Carriers					
1965	11.9	27.2	20.3	12.8	11.7
1966	6.8	28.7	17.8	9.0	6.9
1967	12.4	34.3	23.3	16.9	13.6
1968	15.3	34.9	24.5	20.4	15.7
1969	17.8	39.0	27.7	22.9	17.2

APPENDIX TABLE C.3

Data Base

U.S. Domestic Air Freighter Service 1965–1969

(Data in Millions of Dollars)

Airline and Date	Operating Revenue	Operating Expense	Flying Operations	Maintenance Expense	Aircraft Service	Traffic Service	Reservations and Sales
American							
1965	28.8	27.4	7.2	5.8	2.5	7.1	.5
1966	44.1	39.1	10.8	6.7	3.4	11.0	.9
1967	42.1	40.7	11.7	5.1	3.3	12.5	1.0
1968	54.2	53.8	16.0	8.4	4.4	13.2	1.1
1969	53.1	58.1	17.0	9.0	4.2	14.9	1.3
United							
1965	19.8	22.6	5.6	5.2	1.7	5.8	.3
1966	29.4	29.5	7.2	5.8	2.2	8.5	.6
1967	44.9	43.5	11.3	7.9	3.3	12.1	.9
1968	56.3	55.5	17.7	9.9	4.8	11.2	1.0
1969	70.3	76.6	24.6	13.3	6.8	13.9	2.9
TWA							
1965	13.6	16.3	4.2	2.8	1.5	4.0	.7
1966	16.2	18.7	4.3	3.3	1.7	4.8	1.0
1967	22.3	26.6	7.2	3.3	2.3	6.9	1.3
1968	27.4	30.8	8.6	3.5	2.6	8.0	1.9
1969	32.0	37.7	10.1	5.0	2.7	10.4	2.1

APPENDIX TABLE C.3 (*continued*)

Flying Tiger

Year						
1965	17.3	16.9	4.0	4.2	.8	3.1	1.3
1966	23.5	20.4	4.8	4.8	.9	3.9	1.3
1967	21.7	23.5	5.8	6.2	1.1	3.8	1.3
1968	21.4	24.9	6.5	6.0	1.2	4.2	1.4
1969	22.5	25.3	8.3	4.4	1.5	4.7	1.1

Other Carriers

Year						
1965	11.7	15.8	5.4	4.0	.8	2.5	.9
1966	11.2	12.7	4.6	3.2	.6	2.5	.5
1967	26.6	28.1	9.3	4.9	2.1	4.6	1.7
1968	40.8	46.2	14.4	8.4	3.3	6.8	1.6
1969	52.9	60.7	19.9	12.5	4.7	10.8	2.1

NOTE: The computerized data base which was used for calculations rounded off the data to the nearest thousands of dollars. The above data have been rounded to the nearest $100 thousand.

APPENDIX TABLE C.4
Data Base
U.S. Domestic Air Freighter Service 1965–1969
(*Data in Thousands Except Where Indicated*)

Airline and Date	Advertising and Publicity	General Administrative	Depreciation	Profit Before Tax	Profit After Tax	Yield Revenue (Cents) Per Revenue Ton-Mile	Operating Expense (Cents) Per RTM
American							
1965	$ 192	$1175	$ 2889	$1412	$ 732	17.83¢	16.95¢
1966	267	1508	4446	4953	2573	17.38	15.43
1967	291	1622	5107	1354	704	15.83	15.32
1968	484	2192	7974	339	164	16.26	16.16
1969	534	2431	8722	-5036	-2358	16.54	18.11
United							
1965	393	1000	2479	-2704	-1406	19.72	22.41
1966	732	1386	3167	-118	-61	21.55	21.63
1967	1096	2079	4851	1333	693	20.2	19.6
1968	816	3137	7089	782	407	18.56	18.31
1969	903	4136	10080	-6274	-3200	18.73	20.4
TWA							
1965	409	766	1830	-2667	-1064	19.52	23.35
1966	530	1069	1897	-2423	-927	20.24	23.26
1967	618	1271	3646	-4237	-1391	18.89	22.47
1968	754	1584	3822	-3484	-1209	18.83	21.23
1969	834	1796	4758	-5719	-1756	19.47	22.95

APPENDIX TABLE C.4 (*continued*)

Flying Tiger

1965	485	841	2175	352	183	13.54	13.27
1966	506	1137	3054	3037	1837	13.83	12.04
1967	739	1309	3246	−1808	−1190	13.29	14.39
1968	690	1328	3544	−3424	−3010	12.91	14.97
1969	313	1456	3627	−2836	−2068	12.9	14.53

Other Carriers

1965	225	708	1234	−4093	−3871	18.86	25.42
1966	160	426	685	−1449	−991	23.87	26.97
1967	607	1086	3764	−1490	−1245	24.35	25.66
1968	1140	1602	9029	−5405	−3011	23.82	26.96
1969	1416	2119	7245	−7760	−3963	23.57	26.88

APPENDIX TABLE C.5
Data Base
U.S. Domestic Air Freighter Service 1965–1969
(Data in Cents Per Available Ton-Mile)

Airline and Date	Operating Revenue	Operating Expense	Flying Operations	Maintenance Expense	Aircraft Service Expense	Traffic Service Expense	Research and Sales Expense
American							
1965	10.0	9.8	2.6	2.1	.9	2.5	.2
1966	9.6	8.5	2.4	1.5	.7	2.4	.2
1967	7.8	7.5	2.2	.9	.6	2.3	.2
1968	7.8	7.7	2.3	1.2	.6	1.9	.2
1969	7.3	8.0	2.3	1.2	.6	2.1	.2
United							
1965	10.3	11.7	2.9	2.7	.9	3.0	.2
1966	11.9	12.0	2.9	2.3	.9	3.5	.2
1967	11.1	10.7	2.8	1.9	.8	3.0	.2
1968	9.3	9.2	2.9	1.6	.8	1.8	.2
1969	8.5	9.2	3.0	1.6	.8	1.7	.3
TWA							
1965	8.2	9.8	2.5	1.7	.9	2.4	.4
1966	9.4	10.8	2.5	1.9	1.0	2.8	.6
1967	7.6	9.0	2.4	1.1	.8	2.4	.5
1968	7.5	8.5	2.4	1.0	.7	2.2	.5
1969	7.8	9.3	2.5	1.2	.7	2.6	.5

APPENDIX TABLE C.5 (*continued*)

Flying Tiger							
1965	10.0	9.8	2.3	2.4	.4	1.8	.8
1966	10.4	9.0	2.1	2.1	.4	1.7	.6
1967	8.8	9.5	2.4	2.5	.5	1.5	.5
1968	8.1	9.5	2.5	2.3	.4	1.6	.5
1969	7.2	8.2	2.7	1.4	.5	1.5	.3
Other Carriers							
1965	10.8	14.7	5.0	4.7	.7	2.3	.9
1966	13.6	15.3	5.6	3.9	.7	3.0	.6
1967	11.3	11.9	3.9	2.1	.9	1.9	.7
1968	11.3	12.8	4.0	2.3	.9	1.9	.4
1969	11.2	12.9	4.2	2.7	1.0	2.3	.4

APPENDIX TABLE C.6
Data Base
U.S. Domestic Air Freighter Service 1965–1969
(Data in Cents Per Available Ton-Mile)

Airline and Date	Advertising and Publicity Expense	General and Administrative Expense	Depreciation Expense	Profit Before Taxes	Profit After Taxes
American					
1965	.07	.42	1.04	.51	.26
1966	.06	.33	.96	1.07	.56
1967	.05	.30	.95	.25	.13
1968	.07	.31	1.14	.05	.02
1969	.07	.34	1.20	−.70	−.33
United					
1965	.20	.52	1.28	−1.40	−.73
1966	.30	.56	1.29	−.05	−.02
1967	.27	.51	1.20	.33	.17
1968	.13	.52	1.17	.13	.07
1969	.11	.50	1.21	−.76	−.39
TWA					
1965	.25	.46	1.11	−1.61	−.64
1966	.31	.62	1.10	−1.41	−.54
1967	.21	.43	1.24	−1.44	−.47
1968	.21	.44	1.05	−.96	−.33
1969	.21	.44	1.17	−1.41	−.43

APPENDIX TABLE C.6 (*continued*)

Flying Tiger					
1965	.28	.49	1.26	.20	.11
1966	.22	.50	1.35	1.34	.81
1967	.30	.53	1.32	−.73	−.48
1968	.26	.50	1.35	−1.30	−1.14
1969	.10	.47	1.17	−.92	−.67
Other Carriers					
1965	.21	.66	1.15	−3.81	−3.60
1966	.19	.52	.83	−1.76	−1.20
1967	.26	.46	1.60	−.63	−.53
1968	.32	.44	2.50	−1.50	−.84
1969	.30	.45	1.54	−1.65	−.84

APPENDIX TABLE C.7
Data Base
U.S. Domestic Air Freighter Service 1965–1969
(Data in Index Numbers 1965 = 100.0)

Airline and Date	Operating Revenue	Operating Expense	Flying Operations	Maintenance	Aircraft Service	Traffic Service
American						
1965	100.0	100.0	100.0	100.0	100.0	100.0
1966	152.8	142.6	150.1	114.9	138.2	155.4
1967	145.9	148.4	161.9	87.5	133.3	177.1
1968	187.9	196.3	221.5	144.3	176.5	187.0
1969	184.2	212.1	235.5	154.9	169.5	210.6
United						
1965	100.0	100.0	100.0	100.0	100.0	100.0
1966	147.9	130.7	126.9	111.3	127.9	146.4
1967	226.1	193.1	200.7	153.1	191.9	208.8
1968	283.7	246.3	313.0	191.2	278.0	192.0
1969	354.3	339.6	436.5	257.0	398.8	238.7
TWA						
1965	100.0	100.0	100.0	100.0	100.0	100.0
1966	119.4	114.7	103.0	118.4	110.6	120.2
1967	164.2	163.3	173.0	116.6	148.5	173.0
1968	201.2	189.6	205.8	126.2	174.0	200.3
1969	235.5	232.1	242.8	177.8	181.2	259.5

APPENDIX TABLE C.7 (*continued*)

Flying Tiger						
1965	100.0	100.0	100.0	100.0	100.0	100.0
1966	135.9	120.8	118.9	114.7	113.7	127.6
1967	125.5	138.8	143.2	147.1	147.1	121.9
1968	124.0	146.8	161.4	142.0	149.4	137.0
1969	130.2	149.6	206.0	103.2	188.8	152.8
Other Carriers						
1965	100.0	100.0	100.0	100.0	100.0	100.0
1966	96.1	80.3	84.5	81.8	72.6	98.2
1967	228.0	178.2	171.5	125.0	265.7	183.3
1968	349.8	293.2	265.0	213.2	412.0	271.4
1969	453.9	385.2	367.6	315.3	588.5	431.2

APPENDIX TABLE C.8
Data Base
U.S. Domestic Air Freighter Service 1965–1969
(Data in Index Numbers 1965 = 100.0)

Airline and Date	Reservations and Sales	Advertising and Publicity	General and Administrative	Depreciation	Profit Before Taxes	Profit After Taxes	Yield Cents Per RTM
American							
1965	100.0	100.0	100.0	100.0	100.0	100.0	100.0
1966	165.5	139.1	128.3	153.9	350.8	351.5	97.5
1967	191.6	151.6	138.0	176.8	95.9	96.1	88.8
1968	211.4	252.1	186.6	276.0	24.0	22.4	91.2
1969	239.5	278.1	206.9	301.9	NM	NM	92.8
United							
1965	100.0	100.0	100.0	100.0	NM	NM	100.0
1966	166.0	186.3	138.6	127.8	NM	NM	109.3
1967	252.1	278.9	207.9	195.7	NM	NM	102.4
1968	301.5	207.6	313.7	286.0	NM	NM	94.1
1969	843.5	229.8	413.6	406.6	NM	NM	95.0
TWA							
1965	100.0	100.0	100.0	100.0	NM	NM	100.0
1966	138.2	129.6	139.6	103.7	NM	NM	103.7
1967	179.2	151.1	165.9	199.2	NM	NM	96.8
1968	249.8	184.4	206.8	208.9	NM	NM	96.5
1969	276.6	203.9	234.5	260.0	NM	NM	99.7

APPENDIX TABLE C.8 (*continued*)

Flying Tiger

Year							
1965	100.0	100.0	100.0	100.0	100.0	100.0	100.0
1966	98.3	104.3	135.2	140.4	862.8	1003.8	102.1
1967	99.9	152.4	155.6	149.2	NM	NM	98.2
1968	105.9	142.3	157.9	162.9	NM	NM	95.3
1969	82.2	64.5	173.1	166.8	NM	NM	95.3

Other Carriers

Year							
1965	100.0	100.0	100.0	100.0	NM	NM	100.0
1966	58.5	71.1	60.2	5.6	NM	NM	126.6
1967	184.1	269.8	153.4	305.0	NM	NM	129.1
1968	171.7	506.7	226.3	731.7	NM	NM	126.3
1969	224.9	629.3	299.3	587.1	NM	NM	124.9

NOTE: NM = Not meaningful.

APPENDIX TABLE C.9
Data Base
U.S. Domestic Air Freighter Service 1965–1969
(Data in Constant 1958 Dollars)

Airline and Date	Operating Expense (Dollars in Millions)	Traffic Service (Dollars in Millions)	Operating Expense/ ATM	Traffic Service Expense/ ATM	Profit Before Tax (Dollars in Millions)
American					
1965	24.1	6.2	8.6¢	2.2¢	1.2
1966	33.5	9.4	7.3	2.0	4.2
1967	34.2	10.5	6.3	2.0	1.1
1968	42.2	10.4	6.0	1.5	.3
1969	42.9	11.0	5.9	1.5	−3.7
United					
1965	19.8	5.1	10.2	2.6	−2.4
1966	25.2	7.3	10.2	3.0	−.1
1967	36.6	10.2	9.0	2.5	1.1
1968	43.5	8.7	7.2	1.4	.6
1969	56.6	10.2	6.8	1.2	−4.6
TWA					
1965	14.3	3.5	8.6	2.1	−2.3
1966	16.0	4.1	9.3	2.4	−2.1
1967	22.3	5.8	7.6	2.0	−3.6
1968	24.2	6.3	6.6	1.7	−2.7
1969	27.9	7.7	6.9	1.9	−4.2

APPENDIX TABLE C.9 (*continued*)

Flying Tiger					
1965	14.9	2.7	8.6	1.6	.3
1966	17.5	3.4	7.7	1.5	2.6
1967	19.7	3.2	8.0	1.3	−1.5
1968	19.5	3.3	7.4	1.3	−2.7
1969	18.7	3.5	6.0	1.1	−2.1
Other Carriers					
1965	13.8	2.2	12.9	2.0	−3.6
1966	10.8	2.1	13.1	2.5	−1.2
1967	23.6	3.8	10.0	1.6	−1.3
1968	36.2	5.3	10.0	1.5	−4.2
1969	44.8	8.0	9.5	1.7	−5.7

APPENDIX TABLE C.10
Data Base
U.S. Domestic Air Freighter Service 1965–1969
Percentage Analysis of Freighter Operating Expenses

Airline and Date	Flying Operations	Mainte- nance	Aircraft Service	Traffic Service	Reservations and Sales	Advertising and Publicity	General and Administrative	Depre- ciation
American								
1965	26.3	21.3	9.1	25.8	2.0	.7	4.3	10.5
1966	27.7	17.2	8.8	28.1	2.3	.7	3.9	11.4
1967	28.7	12.6	8.2	30.8	2.5	.7	4.0	12.5
1968	29.7	15.6	8.2	24.6	2.1	.9	4.1	14.8
1969	29.3	15.6	7.3	25.6	2.2	.9	4.2	15.0
United								
1965	25.0	23.0	7.6	25.8	1.5	1.7	4.4	11.0
1966	24.3	19.5	7.4	28.9	1.9	2.5	4.7	10.7
1967	26.0	18.2	7.5	27.9	2.0	2.5	4.8	11.1
1968	31.8	17.8	8.6	20.1	1.8	1.5	5.6	12.8
1969	32.2	17.4	8.9	18.1	3.7	1.2	5.4	13.2
TWA								
1965	25.6	17.3	9.3	24.7	4.6	2.5	4.7	11.3
1966	23.0	17.8	9.0	25.9	5.5	2.8	5.7	10.2
1967	27.2	12.3	8.5	26.1	5.1	2.3	4.8	13.7
1968	27.8	11.5	8.6	26.1	6.1	2.4	5.1	12.4
1969	26.8	13.2	7.3	27.6	5.5	2.2	4.8	12.6

APPENDIX TABLE C.10 (*continued*)

Flying Tiger								
1965	23.9	24.9	4.6	18.2	7.7	2.9	5.0	12.8
1966	23.5	23.7	4.3	19.2	6.3	2.5	5.6	14.9
1967	24.6	26.4	4.9	16.0	5.6	3.1	5.6	13.8
1968	26.3	24.1	4.7	17.0	5.6	2.8	5.3	14.3
1969	32.9	17.2	5.8	18.6	4.2	1.2	5.7	14.3
Other Carriers								
1965	34.4	25.1	5.0	15.9	5.8	1.4	4.5	7.8
1966	36.2	25.6	4.5	19.4	4.2	1.3	3.4	5.4
1967	33.1	17.6	7.5	16.3	6.0	2.2	3.9	13.4
1968	31.1	18.3	7.1	14.7	3.4	2.5	3.5	19.5
1969	32.8	20.6	7.7	17.8	3.4	2.3	3.5	11.9

Appendix D

A Description of A Program for Analyzing Air Freighter Schedules

Lewis M. Schneider and John W. Drake

Introduction

The basic purpose of this program is to enable managers and researchers to analyze efficiently the scheduling policies of the airlines offering domestic air freight service. (It should be noted that the program can be modified to handle combination as well as freighter flights.)

The output can be used to answer important questions including:

(1) Are the strategies of the major competitors similar or different?
(2) Is market share in a given market correlated with time of departures, type of equipment, or quality of service (nonstop, multistop, connecting)?
(3) Are certain carriers dominant in individual markets even though they appear to have a competitive disadvantage? If so, why?

Inputs

The program uses punched card input and is run on IBM 360-65 equipment. It can be modified to accept tape input. The input consists of:

(1) Origin and destination city.
(2) Time of freighter departure.
(3) Nonstop, multistop, or connecting status, and if connecting same information on connecting flights.
(4) Type of equipment.
(5) Number of departures per week of a given scheduled flight.
(6) Name of airline.

Outputs

A.   For each *individual city-pair* in each direction and "both ways":

(1) Flights per week by carrier by equipment type.

(2) Available ton-miles by carrier and by equipment type. (Calculated by linking equipment type and mileage with a payload-range curve for each type stored in memory.)

(3) "Weighted capacity" by carrier and by equipment. The actual capacity is weighted in a similar manner to the calculation of the Quality Service Index in passenger operations. Weights include number of stops, frequency per week, type of aircraft, and time of departure.

(4) All of above by time of day. Three periods of the day identified: Prime (1900–0300 hrs.), Fair (0300–0700) and (1700–1900), and Worst (0700–1700). The exact time divisions may be changed as desired. Totals are then computed for the full 24 hours.

(5) Percentage calculations for all of the above. For example, within a given market, one can determine each carrier's share of flights (by type of equipment), available ton-miles, and weighted ton-miles by time of day.

B.   *Industry totals.* Again, the display includes for each carrier the actual number of flights (by type of equipment), available ton-miles, and weighted ton-miles by time of day. Percentages are calculated on an industry total basis as well.

C.   *City-Pair "Counter."* The program calculates the total number of city-pairs in "each direction" and "both ways" and tabulates the number and percentages of city-pairs served by each carrier by time of day. Thus, it is easy to determine "breadth strategies" (number of city-pairs served) and "depth strategies."

D.   *Three basic reports* containing all of the above information are prepared:

(1) Nonstop service.

(2) Nonstop and multistop one-plane service.

(3) Nonstop, multistop, and connecting service utilizing the same airline.

Further Research

Currently the program contains no traffic data; however, it is hoped to include origin-destination traffic data when these become available. It is important, therefore, that current efforts to improve data collection insist at a minimum that freighter traffic be separated from combination traffic.

EXAMPLES OF PRINTOUTS

Percentage Data—Nonstops Only

JOHN W. DRAKE'S ALL-CARGO-FLIGHT SCHEDULE ANALYSIS: ALL THRU FLIGHTS, DEC 1968

Absolute Data—Nonstops Only

JOHN W. DRAKE'S ALL-CARGO-FLIGHT SCHEDULE ANALYSIS: ALL THRU FLIGHTS, DEC 1968

CHI-BOS ONE WAY (846 STAT. MI.)

	PRIME HOURS (1900–300)			FAIR HOURS (300– 700 AND 1700–1900)			WORST HOURS (700–1700)			TOTAL 24 HOURS		
AIR AIR	FLIGHTS PER WK.	AVAILABLE TON-MILES	AVAIL. T-M (TIME WTD)	FLIGHTS PER WK.	AVAILABLE TON-MILES	AVAIL. T-M (TIME WTD)	FLIGHTS PER WK.	AVAILABLE TON-MILES	AVAIL. T-M (TIME WTD)	FLIGHTS PER WK.	AVAILABLE TON-MILES	AVAIL. T-M (TIME WTD)
L C	NO. %DR	(000) %DR	(000) %DR	NO. %DR	(000) %DR	(000) %DR	NO. %DR	(000) %DR	(000) %DR	NO. %DR	(000) %DR	(000) %DR WTD QSI
UA 4JT	5 100	180 100	719 100	0 0	0 0	0 0	0 0	0 0	0 0	5 100	180 100	719 100 168
UA 3JT	5 100	85 100	340 100	0 0	0 0	0 0	0 0	0 0	0 0	5 100	85 100	340 100 168
UA TOT	10 100	265 100	1059 100	0 0	0 0	0 0	0 0	0 0	0 0	10 100	265 100	1059 100 336
TW 4JT	5 0	181 0	722 0	0 0	0 0	0 0	0 0	0 0	0 0	5 0	181 0	722 0 112
TW TOT	5 0	181 0	722 0	0 0	0 0	0 0	0 0	0 0	0 0	5 0	181 0	722 0 112
AA 4JT	0 0	0 0	0 0	6 0	217 0	433 0	6 0	216 0	649 0	12 0	432 0	649 0 63
AA TOT	0 0	0 0	0 0	6 0	217 0	433 0	6 0	216 0	649 0	12 0	432 0	649 0 63
FT OBS	1 100	45 100	178 100	0 0	0 0	0 0	1 100	45 100	178 100	1 100	45 100	178 100 0
FT TOT	1 100	45 100	178 100	0 0	0 0	0 0	0 0	216 0	0 0	1 100	178 100	0 0
TOTAL	16 69	490 63	1960 63	6 0	217 0	433 0	6 0	216 0	649 0	28 39	922 34	2609 47 511

BOS-CHI ONE WAY (846 STAT. MI.)

	PRIME HOURS (1900–300)			FAIR HOURS (300– 700 AND 1700–1900)			WORST HOURS (700–1700)			TOTAL 24 HOURS		
UA 3JT	5 100	85 100	338 100	0 0	0 0	0 0	0 0	0 0	0 0	5 100	85 100	338 100 168
UA TOT	5 100	85 100	338 100	0 0	0 0	0 0	0 0	0 0	0 0	5 100	85 100	338 100 168
TW 4JT	0 0	0 0	0 0	5 0	180 0	360 0	0 0	0 0	0 0	5 0	180 0	360 0 56
TW TOT	0 0	0 0	0 0	5 0	180 0	360 0	0 0	0 0	0 0	5 0	180 0	360 0 56
AA 4JT	1 0	36 0	144 0	0 0	0 0	0 0	0 0	0 0	0 0	1 0	36 0	144 0 0
AA TOT	1 0	36 0	144 0	0 0	0 0	0 0	0 0	0 0	0 0	1 0	36 0	144 0 0
FT OBS	5 100	223 100	892 100	0 0	0 0	0 0	0 0	216 0	0 0	5 100	223 100	892 100 168
FT TOT	5 100	223 100	892 100	0 0	0 0	0 0	0 0	216 0	0 0	5 100	223 100	892 100 168
TOTAL	11 91	344 90	1374 90	5 0	180 0	360 0	0 0	216 0	0 0	16 63	523 59	1734 71 392

CHI-BOS BOTH WAYS (846 STAT. MI.)

	PRIME HOURS (1900–300)			FAIR HOURS (300– 700 AND 1700–1900)			WORST HOURS (700–1700)			TOTAL 24 HOURS		
UA 4JT	5 100	180 100	719 100	0 0	0 0	0 0	0 0	0 0	0 0	5 100	180 100	719 100 168
UA 3JT	10 100	170 100	679 100	0 0	0 0	0 0	0 0	0 0	0 0	10 100	170 100	679 100 336
UA TOT	15 100	349 100	1398 100	0 0	0 0	0 0	0 0	0 0	0 0	15 100	349 100	1398 100 504
TW 4JT	5 0	181 0	722 0	5 0	180 0	360 0	0 0	0 0	0 0	10 0	360 0	1082 0 168
TW TOT	5 0	181 0	722 0	5 0	180 0	360 0	0 0	0 0	0 0	10 0	360 0	1082 0 168
AA 4JT	1 0	36 0	144 0	6 0	217 0	433 0	6 0	216 0	468 0	13 0	468 0	793 0 63
AA TOT	1 0	36 0	144 0	6 0	217 0	433 0	6 0	216 0	468 0	13 0	468 0	793 0 63
FT OBS	6 100	268 100	1071 100	0 0	0 0	0 0	0 0	216 0	0 0	6 100	268 100	1071 100 168
FT TOT	6 100	268 100	1071 100	0 0	0 0	0 0	0 0	216 0	0 0	6 100	268 100	1071 100 168
TOTAL	27 78	834 74	3335 74	11 0	396 0	793 0	6 0	216 0	0 0	44 48	1446 43	4343 57 903

Appendix E

Regression Equations—Data Base—Study Carriers 1965–1969

Equation Number	Dependent Variable	Constant & Standard Error	Independent Variable and Standard Error	Number of Observations	Standard Error of Estimate	R^2
1	SOM Traffic (Percent)	−.01 (.015)	+.9497(SOM Capacity) (.0702)	25	.027	88.34
2	SOM Traffic (Percent)	−.0084 (.0103)	+1.0497(SOM Capacity)−.0153(AAL)−.0052(UAL)−.0313(TWA) (.0684) (.0145) (.0106) (.0075) +.0439(FTL) (.0073)	25	.0113	97.94
3	SOM Revenue (Percent)	.0217 (.0154)	+.8917(SOM Capacity) (.0721)	25	.0277	86.36
4	SOM Revenue (Percent)	.0285 (.0152)	+1.0385(SOM Capacity)−.0679(AAL)−.0171(UAL) (.1015) (.0215) (.0157) −.0561(TWA)−.0401(FTL) (.0111) (.0168)	25	.0618	94.96
5	Oper. Expense 1958 Dollars (Millions)	7.218 (1.779)	+.0567(Capacity) (.0044)	25	4.277	87.3
6	Oper. Expense 1958 Dollars (Millions)	11.415 (1.668)	+.0575(Capacity)−7.1(AAL)−1.3(UAL) (.0039) (2.2) (2.1) −6.6(TWA)−7.4(FTL) (1.9) (1.9)	25	3.0	93.75
7	Flying Operations Expense 1958 Dollars (Millions)	1.3811 (706.755)	+.018(Capacity) (.0017)	25	1.699	81.97
8	Flying Operations Expense 1958 Dollars (Millions)	3.443 (443.997)	+.020(Capacity)−4.202(AAL)−2.092(UAL) (.001) (.589) (.549) −3.567(TWA)−3.584(FTL) (.506) (.505)	25	.799	96.02
9	Traffic Service Expense 1958 Dollars (Millions)	1.487 (599.4)	+.0132(Capacity) (.0015)	25	1.441	76.49

Appendix E (*continued*)

Equation Number	Dependent Variable	Constant & Standard Error	Independent Variable and Standard Error	Number of Observations	Standard Error of Estimate	R^2
10	Traffic Service Expense 1958 Dollars (Millions)	1.937 (554.0)	+.0093(Capacity)+2.519(AAL)+2.121(UAL)+939.0(TWA) (.0013)(735.2)(684.9)(631.4) −1.011(FTL) (630.3)	25	.996	88.76
11	Profit Before Tax 1958 Dollars (Millions)	−16.689 (3.610)	+263.068(Load Factor)+3.942(AAL)+2.071(UAL)+2.701(TWA) (68.958)(1.051)(1.051)(1.235) −1.582(FTL) (1.506)	25	1.661	54.4
12	Profit Before Tax 1958 Dollars (Millions)	−1.514 (1.038)	−.0068(Capacity)+5.796(AAL)+3.519(UAL)+.423(TWA) (.0025)(1.377)(1.183) +2.482(FTL) (1.181)	25	1.867	42.4
13	Operating Expense Per ATM (Cents) (Deflated)	10.72 (.621)	−.000 0065(Capacity) (.000 0015)	25	1.49	41.6
14	Operating Expense Per ATM (Cents) (Deflated)	12.93¢	−.000 0072(Capacity)−2.2(AAL)−.947(UAL) (.000 0008)(.436)(.406) −3.1(TWA)−3.6(FTL) (.374)(.374)	25	.591	90.9
15	Traffic Service Expense Per ATM (Cents) (Deflated)	2.46	−.000 0023(Capacity)+.637(AAL)+.755(UAL)+.215(TWA) (.000 0003)(.150)(.140)(.129) −.554(FTL) (.129)	25	.204	82.89
16	Log Freighter Traffic	15.217 (1.291)	−1.207(Log Price) (.478)	25	.487	18.32
17	Log Freighter Traffic	2.764 (.849)	+.830(Log Capacity)−.475(Log Price) (.051)(.143)	25	.138	93.44
18	Freighter Traffic	25544.4 (9891.65)	+.4319(Capacity) (.0245)	25	23784.2	92.83
19	Freighter Traffic	19060.6 (6407.1)	+.4128(Capacity)+24852.8(AAL)+20259.3(UAL) (.0152)(8502.5)(7920.9) −19333.0(TWA)+40560.6(FTL) (7301.3)(7288.7)	25	11523.0	98.32

NOTE: Units of Capacity are Available Ton-Miles.

Selected Bibliography

A. U.S. Government Publications and Legal Documents

American Airlines Freight System, Memorandum Tariff No. 63, Boston, April 1971.
Before the Civil Aeronautics Board. Docket 21866–7, Washington, D.C., August 1970.
> *Costing Methodology—Domestic Fare Structure* (Version 6).
> *Domestic Passenger Fare Investigation, 1970,* American Airlines Testimony.
> *Domestic Passenger Fare Investigation,* Direct Exhibits of the Bureau of Economics.
> *Domestic Passenger Fare Investigation,* Testimony and Exhibits, Department of Transportation.
> *Domestic Passenger Fare Investigation,* Brief of the Flying Tiger Line, Inc., to the Board.
> *Three-Level Freight Rates,* Proposed by American Airlines, Inc., Complaint of Trans World Airlines, Inc.
Brief of United Airlines, Inc., to the Civil Aeronautics Board. The Board Should Adhere to the Revenue-Offset Method for Determining the Cost of Scheduled Passenger Service, May 24, 1971.
Interstate Commerce Commission, Bureau of Accounts, *Railroad Carload Cost Scales by Territories* (selected years), Washington, D.C.
Interstate Commerce Commission, Bureau of Accounts, *Costs of Transporting Freight by Class I and Class II Motor Common Carriers of General Commodities by Regions or Territories* (selected years), Washington, D.C.
Interstate Commerce Commission, Bureau of Economics, *Air-Truck Coordination and Competition.* Prepared by Wm. N. W. Kendall, Jack S. Ventura, under supervision of Joel W. Harper, Section of Research. U.S. Government Printing Office Statement No. 67–1, Washington, D.C., February 1967.
Letter from American Airlines to Civil Aeronautics Board (i.e., New Tariffs). Exhibit B—"Freight Handling Costs—250 Pound Shipment, 1968," December 18, 1969.
U.S. Congress, House Subcommittee on Military Airlift, *Military Airlift,* 91st Con-

gress, Jan.–Feb. 1970, U.S. Government Printing Office 37–066, Washington, D.C., 1970.

U.S. Department of Labor, Bureau of Labor Statistics, *Patterns of U.S. Economic Growth,* Bulletin 1672, Washington, D.C., 1970.

B. Books, Reports, and Pamphlets

"Air Cargo," *Civil Aviation Research and Development Policy Study,* Department of Transportation and National Aeronautics and Space Administration, Washington, D.C., March 1971.

Air Transport Association of America, Economics and Finance Department, *Major U.S. Airlines Current Economic Review and Financial Outlook,* 1969–1973, Washington, D.C.

Airline Industry Planning Committee, *Airline Inflation/Productivity,* 1960–1980, Proceedings of a Technical Seminar by the Association (November 1971), published February 1972.

Industry Report: A.T.A. Airline Airport Demand Forecasts, Washington, D.C., July 1969.

American's Sound Transportation Review Organization, *The American Railroad Industry, A Prospectus,* Washington, D.C., 1970.

American Trucking Associations, Inc., Department of Research and Transport Economics, *American Trucking and The Future of Air Freight,* Washington, D.C., February 1968.

Blanding, Warren. *Profit Opportunities in Physical Distribution,* United Air Lines, 1965.

The Boeing Company. *Airborne/Intermodal Pallets and Containers,* Air Freight Development Commercial Airplane Group, D6–58502–R2, Renton, Washington, November 2, 1970.

Air Parcel Post Demand Analysis, Prepared for Air Freight Development by Operations Research/Management Sciences, Commercial Airplane Group, D6–55059, Renton, Washington, Vol. II, May 1970.

Boeing 747C Convertibility, Commercial Airplane Division, D6–13929, Renton, Washington, May 1969.

Post Office Parcel Post System. Renton, Washington, 1968.

747F. A2–5254, Renton, Washington, January 1971.

Boeing 747F Freighter, Commercial Airplane Division, D6–13920–R1, Renton, Washington, June 1969.

747F Freighter. Commercial Airplane Group, D6–13920–R2, Renton, Washington, January 1971.

Boeing Air Cargo Market Analysis Activities. Air Cargo Analysis Unit, Commercial Airplane Group, A9–4710, Renton, Washington, May 1970.

Brewer, Stanley H. *Air Cargo Comes of Age,* Graduate School of Business Administration, University of Washington, Seattle, 1966.

The Complexities of Air Cargo Pricing, Graduate School of Business Administration, University of Washington, Seattle, 1967.

The Environment of International Air Carriers in the Development of Freight Markets, Graduate School of Business Administration, University of Washington, Seattle, 1967.

The Impact of Mail Programs and Policies on United States Air Carriers, Graduate School of Business Administration, University of Washington, Seattle, 1967.

Brewer, Stanley H., and James E. Rosenzweig. *Military Airlift and Its Relationship to the Commercial Air Cargo Industry,* Graduate School of Business Administration, University of Washington, Seattle, 1967.

The Domestic Environment of the Air Cargo Industry, Graduate School of Business Administration, University of Washington, Seattle, 1967.

Brewer, Stanley H., and Don T. DeCoster. *The Nature of Air Cargo Costs,* Graduate School of Business Administration, University of Washington, Seattle, 1967.

Brown, J. B. *Major Appliances—A Brief Total Cost of Distribution Analysis,* Lockheed-Georgia Co., ER10520, Marietta, Georgia, March 1970.

Calkins, P. F. *The Density Story,* Analysis by T. H. Baker and E. J. Joiner, Programming by J. R. Crawford. Lockheed-Georgia Company, CMRS 163, Marietta, Georgia, November 1969.

Currier, Clifford D. *The New Role of Air Freight Forwarding,* Prepared for the Air Freight Forwarders Association of America. Cargo Economics, Inc., Washington, D.C., March 1970.

Dawson, Michael D. *The Outlook for Air Cargo,* Arthur D. Little, Inc., Cambridge, Mass., March 1968.

Eckard, E. W. *Air Cargo Profitability Study 1957–1966,* Lockheed-Georgia Co., CMRS, Marietta, Georgia, February 1968.

Free World Scheduled All-Cargo Capacity, Lockheed-Georgia Co., CMRS 77, Marietta, Georgia, June 1967.

Marketing Planning Report—Air Cargo Growth Study, Lockheed-Georgia Co., MRS-49, Marietta, Georgia, December 1965 (reprint September 1967).

Marketing Planning Report—Free World Air Cargo, 1965–1980, Rate Elasticity Forecast, Lockheed-Georgia Co., CMRS 59, Marietta, Georgia, August 1966.

Emery, Ronald B., Bonnie Johnson, Roger B. Ulverstad (consultant). *Analysis of Air Freight Rate Structure,* Prepared for Department of Transportation (Contract No. DOT OS–00051). Resource Management Corporation, RMC Report UR-142, December 15, 1970.

Fruhan, William E., Jr. *The Fight for Competitive Advantage: A Study of the United States Domestic Trunk Air Carriers,* Division of Research, Graduate School of Business Administration, Harvard University, Boston, 1972.

Gorham, James E. *How to Identify Potential Uses of Air Freight,* Prepared for Emery Air Freight Corp., Southern California Laboratories of Stanford Research Institute, South Pasadena, SRI Project No. IS-4104, April 1963.

Harker, J. S. *Freight Transportation Demand, U.S. Domestic 1975,* The Boeing

Company, Commercial Airplane Group, Orgn. 6–1354, Renton, Washington, May 1970.

Howe, Charles W., and Patrick J. Lynch. *The Air Cargo Industry: Its Growth, Problems and Future* (Institute for Quantitative Research in Economics and Management), Purdue University, Institute Paper No. 31, Lafayette, Indiana, September 1962.

Institut du Transport Aerien, *Forecasting for Air Transport—Methods and Results* (G. Besse and G. Desmas), Paris 1966.

International Air Transport Association. *Economics of Air Cargo Carriage and Service,* Study by IATA Financial and Economic Studies Subcommittee, Montreal, Canada, October 1969.

Jackson, Paul, and William Brackenridge. *Air Cargo Distribution,* Gower Press, London, England, 1971.

Lemieux, P. M., L. A. Wickstrom, and L. L. Pressler. *All Air Freight Distribution U.S. To Europe,* Honeywell International, Minnesota, 1966.

Lewis, Howard T., James W. Culliton, and Jack D. Steele. *The Role of Air Freight in Physical Distribution,* Division of Research, Graduate School of Business Administration, Harvard University, Boston, 1956.

Lloyd's Aviation Department, *Aircraft Types and Prices,* London 1970.

Lockheed-Georgia Company, Marietta, Georgia.

Commercial Aircraft Marketing Engineering, *Lockheed L-500—Operational & Economic Summary,* CMER 491, Marietta, Georgia, May 1969.

Commercial Operations Analysis Department, Advanced Studies Division, *California Lettuce—A Brief Total Cost of Distribution Analysis,* ER 10518, Marietta, Georgia, June 1969.

Commercial Operations Analysis Department, Advanced Studies Division, *Electronic Equipment—A Brief Total Cost of Distribution Analysis,* ER 10517, Marietta, Georgia, June 1969.

Commercial Operations Analysis Department, Advanced Studies Division, *Imported Cars—A Brief Total Cost of Distribution Analysis,* ER 10519, June 1969. *Lockheed L-500 and the Automobile,* Marietta, Georgia.

McDaniel, William R. Commercial Operations Analysis Department, Advanced Studies Division, *Heavy Construction Machinery Equipment—A Brief Total Cost of Distribution Analysis,* Lockheed-Georgia Co., ER 10521, Marietta, Georgia, March 1970.

McDonnell Douglas Corporation. *A Guide to Commercial Air Cargo Development and the MDC Air Cargo Forecast,* Advanced Cargo Systems, Report No. C1-801–1610–1, Long Beach, California, September 1969.

Merrill, J. Roberts & Associates. *Intermodal Freight Transportation Coordination, Problems and Potential,* December 1966.

Nickerson, A. W. Commercial Marketing Research Department, *Marketing Planning Report,* Lockheed-Georgia Co., CMRS 62, Marietta, Georgia, October 1966.

Otonicar, R. F. Commercial Aircraft Marketing Research Department, *Free World*

Belly Cargo Forecast 1970–1985, CMRS 169, Marietta, Georgia, November 1969.

Planning Research Corporation, Trans Oceanic Cargo Study. *Forecasting Model and Data Base,* Vol. I., Prepared for the U.S. Department of Transportation, March 1971.

The Port of New York Authority, Aviation Dept., *Air Cargo in the N.J./N.Y. Metropolitan Region* (Staff Study Report), 1969.

Proceedings International Forum for Air Cargo, 5th, Frankfurt, 1970 (New York, Society of Mechanical Engineers, 1970).

Proceedings International Forum for Air Cargo, Chicago (New York, American Institute of Aeronautics and Astronautics, 1966).

Proceedings International Forum for Air Cargo, Montreal, 1964 (New York, Society of Automotive Engineers, 1964).

Reeher, D. H. *The Domestic Air Freight Industry and Introduction of Large Subsonic Transports,* Independent Research Program, Falls Church, Virginia, AD 658 397, August 1967. (Processed for Defense Documentation Center, Defense Supply Agency.)

Saginor, Irving. *Traffic and Revenue Trends in Scheduled Domestic Air Cargo, 1964–1968,* Civil Aeronautics Board, Economic Research Section and Planning, Programming and Research Division, Bureau of Economics, June 1969.

Saginor, Irving, and David B. Richards. *Forecast of Scheduled Domestic Air Cargo for the 50 States, 1971–1975,* Civil Aeronautics Board, Economic Research Section and Planning, Programming and Research Division, Bureau of Economics, February 1971.

Schriever, Bernard A., and William W. Seifert. *Air Transportation 1975 and Beyond —A Systems Approach,* Report of the Transportation Workshop, 1967. The M.I.T. Press, Cambridge, Mass., 1968.

Simat, Helliesen & Eichner, Inc. and Trans Plan, Inc. *Study of Air Cargo and Air Passenger Terminal Facilitation,* Prepared for Office of Facilitation, Department of Transportation, Washington, D.C., March 1969.

Stanford Research Institute. *How To Identify Potential Uses of Air Freight.* A Report prepared for Emery Air Freight Corporation, by James E. Gorham, South Pasadena, 1963.

Systems Analysis and Research Corporation. *Air Cargo Cost Study—Phase I: Review of Existing Studies,* Prepared for the Western Railroad Traffic Association, CC-617–68, Cambridge, Mass., October 1967.

Taneja, N. N. *Airline Competition Analysis,* M.I.T. Flight Technology Laboratory, FTL Report R-68-2, Cambridge, Mass., September 1968.

The Traffic World/Transportation & Distribution Management 1968 Air Cargo Study, Conducted for The Traffic Service Corp., Croton-on-Hudson, N.Y.

United Air Lines, *Air Freight Profit Analyzer,* 2841-5M-2/61, 1961.

United States Civil Aeronautics Board, *Handbook of Airline Statistics,* 1969 Edition, Washington, D.C., 1970.

Aircraft Operating Cost and Performance Report For Calendar Years 1965–1966, Bureau of Accounts and Statistics, Washington, D.C., September 1967.

An Economic Study of Air Freight Forwarding, Bureau of Operating Rights, Washington, D.C., May 1968.

An Introduction to Air Freight Rates, Washington, D.C., November 1968 (revised).

Summary of CAB-NITL Regional Air Cargo Workshops, National Industrial Traffic League, September–November 1966, Washington, D.C., 1967.

Trends in All-Cargo Service, Costs and Statistics Division, Bureau of Accounts and Statistics, Washington, D.C., June 1970.

United States Department of Transportation, Federal Aviation Administration. *Aviation Forecasts Fiscal Years 1971–1982.* Office of Aviation Economics, Aviation Forecast Division, January 1971.

Wein, Harold H. *Domestic Air Cargo: Its Prospects,* Occasional Paper 7, Michigan State, East Lansing, 1962.

Westwood Research, Inc. *Commercial Air Freight Rate Analysis and Forecast,* Prepared for Douglas Aircraft Company, Long Beach, California, project no. WR 155, Los Angeles, California, November 1970.

C. GENERAL REFERENCES

Air Cargo Magazine, Annual Survey of Shippers.

Air Transport Association of America, *Air Transport Facts and Figures,* The Annual Report of the U.S. Scheduled Airline Industry, Washington, D.C., 1971.

Air Transport World.

Airline Management and Marketing.

American Aviation.

American Trucking Associations, *American Trucking Trends,* Washington, D.C.

Aviation Week & Space Technology.

Civil Aeronautics Board, *Quarterly Airline Industry Economic Reports,* March 1971.

Air Carrier Analytical Charts and Supplemental Carrier Statistics, U.S. Government Printing Office, Washington, D.C.

Air Carrier Financial Statistics, U.S. Government Printing Office, Washington, D.C.

Handbook of Airline Statistics, U.S. Government Printing Office, Washington, D.C.

Commercial Car Journal.

Council of Economic Advisors, *Economic Indicators.*

Distribution Worldwide.

Handling and Shipping.

Moody's Transportation Manual, 1970.

Traffic World.
Transportation Association of America, *Transportation Facts and Trends.*
Transportation and Distribution Management.
The Wall Street Journal.
World Air Transport Statistics, International Air Transport Association, Montreal, Canada.

D.   ARTICLES AND PAPERS

Adams, A. T. "Ground Handling Problems and Their Costs," *Airline Management and Marketing,* June 1968.
"The Air Cargo Airplane," *Handling and Shipping,* July 1968, pp. 47–54.
"Air Freight Problems in New York Gall Shippers, Importers," *The Wall Street Journal,* May 1, 1969.
"Airlift Plans Strong Air Freight Emphasis," *Aviation Week & Space Technology,* August 31, 1970, pp. 34–36.
"Airline Economist Gloomy on Cargo Traffic Growth: Sees Passenger Upturn," *Traffic World,* June 21, 1971, p. 16.
"Airlines, Shippers Battle Break-in Problems," *Aviation Week & Space Technology,* April 15, 1968.
"Airlines Switch Orders for Jumbo Freighters to Passenger Versions," *The Wall Street Journal,* October 28, 1968, p. 26.
Allen, W. Bruce and Leon Moses. "Choice of Mode in U.S. Overseas Trade—A Study of Air Cargo Demand," Papers, *Ninth Annual Transportation Research Forum,* 1968 (Oxford, Richard Cross, 1968) pp. 235–248.
Barrett, Colin. "The Box Sprouts Wings," *Traffic World,* June 29, 1968, pp. 39–41.
"Boeing Revives Convertible 747, Prepares for USAF Tanker Tests," *Aviation Week & Space Technology,* Feb. 21, 1972, p. 29.
Burnham, Frank. "An Airfreighter from Start to Finish," *American Aviation,* September 30, 1968, pp. 12–22.
"CAB Bars Rate Discussion in Approving Airline Talks on Cargo Container Pact," *Traffic World,* May 3, 1971.
"CAB to Examine Need for Air Express: New REA Rate Structure is Suspended," *Traffic World,* August 3, 1970, p. 56.
"CAB Now Ready to Move on Long-Delayed Cases Involving Cargo Matters," *Traffic World,* August 16, 1971, p. 73.
"CAB Refuses to Suspend TWA 747 Container Rates Aimed at Heavy Shipments," *Traffic World,* August 30, 1971, pp. 54–55.
Carter, H. A. "The Boeing 747 and Its Impact on Future Airline Operations," Paper presented at the *Transportation Research Forum,* Eighth Annual Meeting, September 1967.
Chapman, R. Stanley. "Moment of Truth for Jumbo Jet Era," *Traffic World,* December 13, 1969, pp. 40–48.

Coburn, Richard F. "Four Carriers Drop Plans to Buy 747F's and 747C's," *Aviation Week & Space Technology,* March 11, 1968, pp. 29–30.

Coburn, Richard F. "New York Seeks Tighter Airport Security," *Aviation Week & Space Technology,* January 1, 1968.

"Contract Container Rates for Wide-Bodied Jet Flights Filed by American Airlines," *Traffic World,* October 18, 1971, pp. 31–32.

Erb, Norman H. "Truckers as Air Forwarders: Economic Implications for Shippers," *Transportation Journal,* Vol. 9, No. 3, Spring 1970, pp. 51–56.

Farrell, Jack W. "Domestic Containerization—A Possible Breakthrough?" *Traffic Management,* July 1971, pp. 55–57.

"Four Carriers Drop Plans to Buy 747F and 747C's," *Aviation Week & Space Technology,* March 11, 1968.

Gellman, Aaron J. "Surface Transportation," *Technological Change in Regulated Industries* (Edited by William M. Capron), Brookings, Washington, D.C., 1971.

Glines, Carl. "Trucking's Stake in Air Freight," *Commercial Car Journal,* March 1968, pp. 69–80.

Haskell, Robert H. "The ABC's of Air Freight," *Transportation and Distribution Management,* September 1969, pp. 42–44.

de Hayes, Daniel W., Jr. "Industrial Transportation Planning Estimating Transit Time for Rail Carload Shipments," *Transportation Research Forum,* papers, Tenth Annual Meeting, 1969.

Herron, David P. "Buying Time and Saving Money with Air Freight," *Transportation and Distribution Management,* December 1968, pp. 25–29.

Hersey, Irwin. "L-500 Air Freighter of Tomorrow," *Airline Management and Marketing,* February 1969, pp. 50–53.

"High Flying Fashions," *Transportation and Distribution Management,* February 1969, pp. 29–30.

Himmel, Nieson. "Freight Handling Evolving Slowly Toward Giant Jet Age," *Aviation Week & Space Technology,* October 26, 1970.

"Inside And Either Side of the L-500," *Transportation and Distribution Management,* April 1969, pp. 52–55.

Jamison, Paul E. "Starting Next Month—The Age of the QC Jet," *Transportation and Distribution Management,* July 1966, pp. 31–34.

Lambert, Richard. "Air Transportation," *Proceedings of the NASA Symposium,* Boston, February 10, 1969.

Lewis, Frank M. "Is Belly Freight Profitable?" *Transportation Research Forum,* Proceedings, Twelfth Annual Meeting, Oxford, Richard Cross, 1971.

Lockheed Aircraft Corporation, "Economics of Air Cargo Ground Handling and Control," *International Forum for Air Cargo,* International Forum for Air Cargo, Montreal, 1964.

Longstreth, Wallace I. "Airports and Terminals are Air Freight's Villains," *Air Cargo,* April 1970.

Longstreth, Wallace I. "Special Report: Air Cargo," *Distribution Worldwide,* January 1971, pp. 19–34.

"Losses Cited as Civil Aeronautics Board Initiates Domestic Freight Rate Inquiry," *Traffic World,* December 1970, p. 60.

Malkin, Richard. "Is A Rate Shakeup in Prospect?" *Cargo Airlift,* February 1971.

Marshall, Kenneth. "The 747—Vast Promise, Some Problems," *Transportation & Distribution Management,* September 1969, pp. 34–38.

Martin, Britt. "The Coming Effect of Jumbo Jets on Warehousing," *Jet Cargo News,* April 28, 1969.

McKinnell, Henry A. "How to Identify Potential Air Freight Users," *Transportation Journal,* Summer 1968, pp. 5–10.

O'Lone, Richard G. "Cargo Slump Laid to Chaos on Ground," *Aviation Week & Space Technology,* June 17, 1968.

Reeher, David H. "Air Freight Has Problems on the Ground," *Business Horizons,* February 1968.

"Reorganized Air Cargo Inc. Takes on a Marketing Role; Denies Financial Problems," *Traffic World,* October 4, 1971.

Romberg, Lars G. "Airfreight: The Billion Dollar Confusion," *Airline Management,* September 1971, pp. 24–31.

Ryan, William F. "Air Freight on the Road," *Air Cargo,* March 1970.

Schutz, Peter W., and Max J. Reinhart. "Economic Analysis of Power Options for Line Haul Vehicles," Proceedings *National West Coast Meeting Society for Automotive Engineers,* 1970.

Stephan, Glenn E. "How Big is Air Cargo Containerization?" *Traffic World,* December 14, 1970, pp. 58–60.

"Three 747's for the Price of One," *Airline Management and Marketing,* April 1969, pp. 40–41.

"TWA Aims at Truck Rates with Per-Container Filing; Eastern Plans Discounts," *Traffic World,* August 1972, p. 62.

Watkins, Harold D. "Airlines, CAB Grapple with Cargo Tariffs," *Aviation Week & Space Technology,* October 26, 1970, pp. 39–51.

Watkins, Harold D. "Sagging Cargo, Economy Cut Use of QC's," *Aviation Week & Space Technology,* August 2, 1971, pp. 27–30.

"What's Happening in Transportation," *Transportation Association of America,* September 28, 1971.

Woolsey, James P. "Airlines Push Containers, but Purchase Program Lags," *Aviation Week & Space Technology,* October 26, 1970, pp. 80–87.

E.   Unpublished Material

Dahir, Victor W. "A Comparative Study of Three Ground Handling Systems for Air Freight." Unpublished Master's dissertation, Harvard Business School, 1969.

Narodick, Kit G. "The Domestic Air Cargo Industry." Unpublished dissertation, Columbia University, 1967.

Orion, Henry. "Domestic Air Cargo, 1945–1965: A Study of Competition in a Regulated Industry." Unpublished dissertation, Columbia University, 1967.

Schary, Philip Braudt. "Competition in the Domestic Air Cargo Industry." Unpublished dissertation, University of California at Los Angeles.